# INTELLIGENT LEARNING PARADIGMS AND STUDENT EMPOWERMENT

*Digital Integration and Transformation*

# INTELLIGENT LEARNING PARADIGMS AND STUDENT EMPOWERMENT

*Digital Integration and Transformation*

*Edited by*

**Souvik Pal, PhD**

**Ton Quang Cuong, PhD**

**R. S. S. Nehru, PhD**

APPLE ACADEMIC PRESS

First edition published 2025

**Apple Academic Press Inc.**
1265 Goldenrod Circle, NE,
Palm Bay, FL 32905 USA

760 Laurentian Drive, Unit 19,
Burlington, ON L7N 0A4, CANADA

**CRC Press**
2385 NW Executive Center Drive,
Suite 320, Boca Raton FL 33431

4 Park Square, Milton Park,
Abingdon, Oxon, OX14 4RN UK



**Library and Archives Canada Cataloguing in Publication**

Title: Intelligent learning paradigms and student empowerment : digital integration and transformation / edited by Souvik Pal, PhD, Ton Quang Cuong, PhD, R.S.S. Nehru, PhD.
Names: Pal, Souvik, editor | Ton, Quang Cuong, 1970- editor | Nehru, R. S. S., 1974- editor
Description: First edition. | Includes bibliographical references and index.
Identifiers: Canadiana (print) 20240444086 | Canadiana (ebook) 20240444116 | ISBN 9781774915967 (hardcover) | ISBN 9781774915974 (softcover) | ISBN 9781032721699 (ebook)
Subjects: LCSH: Educational innovations.
Classification: LCC LB1027 .I58 2025 | DDC 370—dc23

**Library of Congress Cataloging-in-Publication Data**

Names: Pal, Souvik, editor. | Cuong, Ton Quang, 1970- editor. | Nehru, R. S. S., 1974- editor.

Title: Intelligent learning paradigms and student empowerment : digital integration and transformation / Edited by Souvik Pal, PhD, Ton Quang Cuong, PhD, R. S. S. Nehru, PhD.

Description: Palm Bay : Apple Academic Press, [2025] | Summary: "The Covid-19 pandemic brought about dramatic change in the education sector, deeply affecting schools as they were forced to shut down and as online learning became common. Post-Covid, it is clear that many of the practices brought about by the pandemic are actually beneficial in education in the long run. This new volume, Intelligent Learning Paradigms and Student Empowerment: Digital Integration and Transformation, explores the development and evolution of smart learning, learning analytics, intelligent learning, and the Internet of Things as they pertain to student empowerment in the classroom. The book covers a wide range of topics on digital pedagogy, including educational robotics, immersive technology-based education systems, interactive e-books, using virtual reality and augmented reality (XR) technology, online proctoring, digital transformation of teaching method modules, and much more. Key features: Incorporates and transforms digital pedagogy across the board of functional processes Explores state-of-the-art smart tools in education Offers ideas for the successful transformation to digital teaching methods Discusses how digital education can foster student agency and promote cross-disciplinary collaboration"-- Provided by publisher.

Identifiers: LCCN 2024036225 (print) | LCCN 2024036226 (ebook) | ISBN 9781774915967 (hardback) | ISBN 9781774915974 (paperback) | ISBN 9781032721699 (ebook)

Subjects: LCSH: Education--Effect of technological innovations on. | COVID-19 Pandemic, 2020---Influence. | Internet of things. | Student-centered learning. | Educational technology. | Web-based instruction.

Classification: LCC LB1028.3 .I56548 2025 (print) | LCC LB1028.3 (ebook) | DDC 371.33--dc23/eng/20240808

LC record available at https://lccn.loc.gov/2024036225

LC ebook record available at https://lccn.loc.gov/2024036226

ISBN: 978-1-77491-596-7 (hbk)
ISBN: 978-1-77491-597-4 (pbk)
ISBN: 978-1-03272-169-9 (ebk)

# About the Editors

**Souvik Pal, PhD**
*Associate Professor, Department of Computer Science and Engineering, Sister Nivedita University, Kolkata, West Bengal, India*

Souvik Pal, PhD, is an Associate Professor in the Department of Computer Science and Engineering at Sister Nivedita University (Techno India Group), Kolkata, India. He has more than a decade of academic experience and is an author or co-editor of more than 18 books from reputed publishers, including Elsevier, Springer, CRC Press, and Wiley. He also holds three patents. He published more than 65 publications in indexed journals and conferences. He is serving as a series editor for the book series *Advances in Learning Analytics for Intelligent Cloud-IoT Systems; Internet of Things: Data-Centric Intelligent Computing, Informatics, and Communication;* and *Conference Proceedings Series on Intelligent Systems, Data Engineering, and Optimization*. He has been the organizing chair, keynote speaker, and proceedings editor of various conferences, including RICE, ICICCT, ICMMCS, and ICWSNUCA. His professional activities include roles such as associate editor, guest editor, and editorial board member for more than 100 international journals and conferences. His research area includes cloud computing, big data, Internet of Things, wireless sensor networks, and data analytics. He is a member of many professional organizations in his field. Dr. Pal received his MTech and PhD degrees in the field of Computer Science and Engineering from Kalinga Institute of Industrial Technology (KIIT University), Bhubaneswar, India.

**Ton Quang Cuong, PhD**
*Dean, VNU University of Education, Vietnam National University, Hanoi, Vietnam*

Ton Quang Cuong, PhD, is a prominent figure in the field of education technology, renowned for his groundbreaking research and unwavering enthusiasm for leveraging technology to enhance learning experiences. He has received a PhD degree in Philology from Voronhez State Pedagogical

University, Russia Federation, served as an editor and author of a series of influential research publications, was a keynote speaker and chair panel of numerous conferences that have shaped the discourse around technology-enhanced learning, and also provided practical insights for educators and policymakers seeking to harness the power of technology in education. As the Dean of the Faculty of Education Technology at the University of Education, VNU-UEd, he established himself as a trailblazer in the realm of educational innovation. Dr. Cuong's visionary leadership has led to the development of cutting-edge programs and initiatives that have transformed the educational landscape in Vietnam. In addition to his academic pursuits, Dr. Cuong has played a pivotal role as a consultant for the Ministry of Education and Training (MOET) as well as for EdTech research organizations and enterprises, as co-founder of Vietnam Australia EduTech Alliance, Vietnam TechFest Association, advising on policies and best practices for the effective implementation of education technology initiatives at a national level. His expertise and guidance have been instrumental in driving forward key projects aimed at modernizing the education system and ensuring that students have access to high-quality, technology-enabled learning opportunities.

**R. S. S. Nehru, PhD**
*Assistant Professor, Department of Education, Sikkim University (Central University), Sikkim, India*

R. S. S. Nehru, PhD, is an Assistant Professor in the Department of Education at Sikkim University, Gangtok, Sikkim, India. He has been an invited lecturer at the University of Education, Hanoi, Vietnam. Dr. Nehru has published 14 books as main and co-author and more than 30 edited book chapters related to education and educational technologies as well as several research papers in Scopus-indexed national and international journals and conferences. He is an editorial board member for two international multidisciplinary journals and was invited to many conferences as chair, keynote speaker, co-chair, and resource person for national workshops on multidisciplinary research. Under his research guidance, several MPhil students have received their degrees in Education from Periyar University and Alagappa University, Tamil Nadu, and six scholars have received their PhDs in Education from Bharathiar University, Coimbatore, Tamil Nadu, India. He is an approved faculty member of the Indira Gandhi National Open University (IGNOU), Kuvempu University, and other online and distance education mode programs on education and teacher education. Dr. Nehru is a member in many professional organizations, such as the International Comparative

Education Society (ICES), USA; Comparative Education Society of Asia (CESA), Japan; WWF-India; Dolphin Nature Conservation Society (DNCS); Institute of Advanced Education and Research (IAER); Indian Association of Teacher Educators (IATE); and Indian Psychiatry Society (IPS). His research area includes information and communications technology in education, comparative education, teacher education with a multidisciplinary focus. Dr. Nehru received his MEd degree in Education from Osmania University, Hyderabad, and MPhil from Madurai Kamaraj University, Madurai, Tamil Nadu, India. He earned his PhD in Education from Andhra University, Visakhapatnam, India. He also acquired a MSc in Zoology, MSc (Psychology), MSW, PGDHR, PGDSE&IP, Honors Diploma in Computer Science (HDCS), and certificates for programs in Internet of Things, virtual reality, interconnected reality, and Rabbits.

# Contents

# Contributors

**Tran Nguyen Thanh Binh**
University of Education, Vietnam National University, VNU-UED, Hanoi, Vietnam

**Ranita Chakrabortty**
Faculty of Education, Salesian College Siliguri Campus, Siliguri, West Bengal, India

**Robert J. Cloutier**
Systems Engineering, The University of South Alabama, Mobile, USA

**Ton Quang Cuong**
University of Education, Vietnam National University, VNU-UED, Hanoi, Vietnam

**Minh Tuan Dang**
University of Education, VNU, Hanoi, Vietnam

**Hoang Anh Duc**
EdLab Asia Educational Research and Development Center, Hanoi, Vietnam

**Dau Thuy Ha**
The Online Management Training Company (OMT), Hanoi, Vietnam

**Nguyen Hoa Huy**
VNU-Center for Education Accreditation, Vietnam National University, Hanoi, Vietnam

**Mohammad Nasfikur R. Khan**
Systems Engineering, The University of South Alabama, Mobile, USA

**Linh Bui Khanh**
Information Technology Faculty, Electric Power University, Hanoi, Vietnam

**Nguyen Tung Lam**
University of Education, Vietnam National University, VNU-UED, Hanoi, Vietnam

**R. Lenin**
Department of Management Studies, Guru Shree Shantivijai Jain Arts and Science College, Chennai, Tamil Nadu, India

**Kari J. Lippert**
Systems Engineering, The University of South Alabama, Mobile, USA

**R. S. S. Nehru**
Assistant Professor, Department of Education, Sikkim University, Gangtok, Sikkim, India;
Post-Doctoral Scholer (DLit, in Education), Sambalpur University, Sambalpur, Odisha, Inda

**Nguyen Thi Viet Nga**
Hanoi Pedagogical University 2, Vinh Phuc, Vietnam

**Sandra Paredes**
Assistant Professor, School of Humanities and Education, Tecnologico de Monterrey, Mexico

**Hai Yen Pham**
Foreign Language Specialized School–VNU University of Languages and International Studies, Hanoi, Vietnam

**Kim Chung Pham**
University of Education, VNU, Hanoi, Vietnam

**Nguyen Ngoc Minh Phuong**
University of Education, Vietnam National University, VNU-UED, Hanoi, Vietnam

**Anh Nguyen Quynh**
Information Technology Faculty, Electric Power University, Hanoi, Vietnam

**V. Rachel**
Avinashilingam Institute for Home Science and Higher Education for Women, Coimbatore, Tamil Nadu, India

**P. Subburaj**
Agurchand Manmull Jain College, Chennai, Tamil Nadu, India

**Tran Khai Thien**
Ho Chi Minh City University of Foreign Languages–Information Technology, Vietnam

**Ha Nguyen Thi Thu**
Department of E-Commerce, Electric Power University, Hanoi, Vietnam

**An Bien Thuy**
Hanoi Pedagogical University 2, Vinh Phuc, Vietnam

**Vu Minh Trang**
University of Education, Vietnam National University, VNU-UED, Hanoi, Vietnam

**Nguyen Thi Linh Yen**
University of Languages and International Studies, Vietnam National University (VNU-ULIS), Hanoi, Vietnam

# Abbreviations

| | |
|---|---|
| AE | adventure education |
| AI | artificial intelligence |
| AIPS | AI-based proctoring systems |
| AP | academic program |
| AR | augmented reality |
| BIOE | bachelor of biological education |
| CAI | computer-assisted instruction |
| CML | computer managed learning |
| CoE | cone of experience |
| COLLES | constructivist on-line learning environment survey |
| CPE | college with potential for excellence |
| CRC | collaborative research center |
| DC | digital competence |
| DLGF | digital literacy global framework |
| ER | educational robotics |
| FCIT | Florida Center for Instructional Technology |
| FFNN | feed-forward neural network |
| GPS | global positioning system |
| HE | higher education |
| HEIs | higher education institutions |
| HHDs | handheld or mobile devices |
| HMDs | head-mounted displays |
| HUST | Hong Kong University of Science and Technology |
| ICT | information and communication technology |
| IISB | Indian Institute of Science Bangalore |
| INTERACT | integrated interactive multimedia model |
| LAN | local area network |
| LMS | learning management system |
| MCoA | multimedia cone of abstraction |
| MHRD | Ministry of Human Resource Development |
| MOET | Ministry of Education and Training |
| MOOCs | massive open online courses |
| NAD | National Academic Depository |

| | |
|---|---|
| NCERT | National Council for Education Research and Training |
| NKN | national knowledge network |
| NOFN | national optical fiber network |
| NPTEL | National Project on Technology-Enhanced Learning |
| ODK | open data kit |
| OE | online examination |
| OER | open education resource |
| OP | online proctoring |
| QRC | quick response code |
| SDGs | sustainable development goals |
| STEAM | science, technology, engineering, arts, and mathematics |
| STEM | science, technology, engineering, or mathematics |
| SWAYAM | study webs of active learning for young aspiring minds |
| TAM | technology acceptance model |
| TIM | technology integration matrix |
| UNICEF | United Nations Children's Fund |
| VNU-UED | Vietnam National University, Hanoi |
| VR | virtual reality |

# Preface

The purpose of the book, titled *Intelligent Learning Paradigms and Student Empowerment: Digital Integration and Transformation,* is to explore the development of smart learning, learning analytics, intelligent learning, and the Internet of Things as they pertain to student empowerment in the classroom. The primary objective of this volume is to consolidate the technologies associated with the digital teaching learning process into a single platform, making it accessible to postgraduate students, researchers, and, most importantly, academicians and teaching staffs.

This edited collection features leading academic policymakers, researchers, educators, and scholars in discussing and sharing their insights on various dimensions of digital pedagogies in the education of things. Digital pedagogies, educational design, and student empowerment provide a world-class multidisciplinary venue for scholars, practitioners, and educators to communicate and debate the latest breakthroughs, concerns, trends, as well as real-world issues experienced, and solutions adopted.

In the context of teacher and teaching education, IoT-based education, flipped learning, the evaluation process, and new findings from the researchers, the purpose of this book is to explain the fundamentals of relevant IoT-based digital technologies. This book also includes new findings from researchers. The primary members of the audience that this work is intended for are individuals with specialized knowledge, including academic and administrative decision-makers, researchers, educationalists, and specialists in topics related to educational research.

This book hopes to be an interdisciplinary resource for learning about the latest research and advancements in the disciplines of digital pedagogies for education and intelligent learning approaches, with a focus on student agency and the intelligent learning paradigm. Creating academically relevant, flexible, and scalable digital teaching-learning systems is becoming increasingly important. Topics include digital pedagogy and integration of IoT in teaching-learning process, flipped learning and blended learning in education of things, technology-based digital learning and its challenges, IoT semantics and knowledge extraction in education of things, and the future of digital learning.

This book covers a wide range of topics that are pertinent to the field of digital pedagogy. Some examples of these topics include intelligent object identification in SMS, protocols for educational and administrative policies, and digital pedagogy: collaboration. This book is a valuable resource for educators as well as students who are interested in learning anything from the fundamentals to the more sophisticated ideas of online teaching and learning. This book was written for researchers, academics, educationalists, and professionals working in the field of educational research. Those who formulate and implement educational policy at the collegiate and institutional levels are also the target audience for this book. This book serves two purposes: first, as an accessible resource for professionals working in the field of digital education; second, as an introduction to the industry's foundational advancements for anyone interested in learning more about them.

## BENEFITS TO READERS:

- Incorporates and transforms digital pedagogy across the board of functional processes.
- Covers both introductory and advanced topics, serving as a manual for seasoned educators and a primer for those just entering the field interested in IoT-based pedagogy.
- Discusses state-of-the-art tools, addressing key issues, concerns, and innovations in blended and flipped education.
- Discusses the potential for collaborative efforts between non-academic institutions and digital pedagogy.
- Outlines the basic ideas behind and challenges to the field of networked learning and education of things.
- Discusses how digital education can foster student agency and promote cross-disciplinary collaboration.
- Explores how to evaluate students and teachers through testing and other forms of assessment

# CHAPTER 1

# Integrating Educational Robotics into the Training Program for Developing Students' ICT Competence in Teaching

KIM CHUNG PHAM,[1] MINH TUAN DANG,[1] and HAI YEN PHAM[2]

[1]*University of Education, VNU, Hanoi, Vietnam*

[2]*Foreign Language Specialized School, VNU University of Languages and International Studies, Hanoi, Vietnam*

## ABSTRACT

This chapter focuses on the integration of educational robots into the training curriculum at the University of Education, Vietnam National University in Hanoi with the goal of improving the ICT competency of future natural science teachers. It also explains the conceptual framework for the design of educational programs based around the use of sensors and mobile devices in robot construction. The course is built around a series of illustrative scientific experiments that aim to improve students' ICT teaching skills while also exposing them to the potential benefits of incorporating educational robotics (ER) and constructivist methods into their future classroom instruction at the secondary and tertiary levels.

## 1.1 INTRODUCTION

In the 2018 general education program of Vietnam, STEM education is a teaching model that is encouraged to be implemented in both basic

Intelligent Learning Paradigms and Student Empowerment: Digital Integration and Transformation.
Souvik Pal, Ton Quang Cuong, & R. S. S. Nehru (Eds.)

education and career-oriented education (Ministry of Education and Training, 2018). To prepare for the implementation of STEM education in the 2018 program, many references on STEM topics have been designed and taught on the basis of current program content.

In the era of the Internet of Things and the Fourth Industrial Revolution, connecting and operating devices by connecting to the Internet or setting up automatic control is one of the directions that is being cared for and developed. This research direction is related to the field of robotics, and this is also one of the practical issues of interest in the field of STEM education. As defined by NASA, educational robotics (ER) is the study of robotics, in which programmable machines can typically perform a series of actions automatically or semi-automatically (Robotiq, 2017). A complete robot on the market today usually includes complete parts and assemblies. In STEM education, students will have to learn and assemble the robot components themselves, then come up with appropriate design options and practice experiments to solve a specific problem. Through that process, students will learn and develop the teaching competencies relevant to STEM education.

Currently, the teaching of robotics in Vietnam also has obstacles in terms of facilities as well as the content, implementation method, and appropriate assessment form. Some products of many research and business units have been marketed or supplied to schools to carry out robotics activities. Especially, Lego with different product lines depending on the appropriate level of students (HS). That is also the premise for students to participate in some creative competitions with domestic and international robots. However, besides competitions and playgrounds on robotics, science education has not been specifically mentioned or implemented into teaching. Besides, some studies have mentioned that middle school age is the best time to attract students' interest in STEM field (Christensen & Knezek, 2017; Mohr-Schroeder et al., 2014). Thus, the design of a STEM teaching topics of extracurricular robotics for middle school students in order to develop the teaching competence is a matter of concern.

The theme of STEM, such as a simple automatic water supply system, creates opportunities for students to explore, learn, and apply knowledge of electricity, combining modern technology application equipment into the design of water supply systems. The simple automatic system is for a small potted plant that properly meets the moisture needs of the plant. The topic of the automatic water supply system is simply related to the content of some subjects such as Physics, Technology, Biology, and Informatics in the current national curriculum program. This content of knowledge in the new national curriculum program of Natural Science, Technology, and Informatics 2018 still has an appropriate level of responsiveness. Therefore, this is a topic that is practical and can be applied in both the national curriculum and extracurricular experiences. The topic is designed according to students' ability to discover knowledge and design thinking techniques.

## 1.2 ROLE OF ROBOTICS IN K-12 EDUCATION

In recent years, robots have appeared more and more in everyday life. From robots that can vacuum the house to robots that assist in medical surgery, even during the COVID pandemic, mobile devices can be controlled to remotely communicate with patients, customers are becoming more common.

Robots are a K-12 learning technology that tackles robotics and automation. It combines STEM knowledge into K12 classroom learning after school.

Foundations of ER and STEM are based on Piaget's constructivist learning theory. According to this theory, knowledge is gained through experience of interacting with the environment. When real-world content is used in learning, it makes learning more effective. Some other studies also show that the use of Robotics in teaching and learning STEM can help students understand more about related topics in depth and engage them in complex problem solving.

Over the past few years, Robotics and STEM activities have been introduced into many schools around the world. The fact shows that Robotics helps increase students' interest and motivation, promoting effective learning (Sokratis & Theodosios, 2022).

To be more precise, robotics is a subfield of engineering concerned with all aspects of robot creation and management. In the classroom, ER helps students to develop the basic programming and design skills. In addition, we can combine natural science and mathematics understanding, helping them to develop expertise skills such as planning and teamwork, and qualities such as perseverance and honesty. At the same time, robotics helps students understand the applications of technology in agriculture such as robots to improve farmland, harvest crops, and take care of crops in difficult conditions for humans. Artificial intelligence (AI) is being used to help persons with disabilities in the healthcare industry. In the automotive sector, robots with mechanical arms install high-precision parts.

To implement robotics topics, students need to be familiar with technology, understand key concepts and programming, specific requirements such as:

i. **Know the Hardware:** Identify and classify the main components of the robot such as structure, motion, electronics, and other tools.
ii. **Learn the Function of Devices:** Such as gears, motors, sensors, and other components.
iii. **Make Robots (If Any):** There are several skills to make robots.
iv. **Know How to Program:** Using intuitive programming blocks to control the devices integrated tasks that make the robot to move.

In addition, students also need to understand the knowledge of the field of science in which robots are applied. So that, building a complete robot can be difficult for students and even for teachers.

## 1.3 ICT APPLICATION IN EDUCATIONAL ROBOTICS (ER)

In automation and robotics, design thinking plays an important role. Design thinking requires the mobilization of knowledge and imagination to create products with what is technologically possible that meet customer needs. Design thinking consists of the following five steps: empathize, define, ideate, prototype, and build, and experiment (Owen, 2007).

Automating processes through robotics requires understanding every detail, understanding processes and knowledge that help solve problems, form possible solutions to problems. Discuss many possible solution alternatives for further exploration. Next, is the prototype building phase, a product built to solve the identified problems. Analysis, observations, possible alternatives, and end-to-end solutions provide robot designers with the information needed to create a robot. Prototypes are designed and created, taking into account ideal conditions with minimal exception handling. Build and test to validate the solution is the last step in the design thinking process. The phases of design, construction, and testing are repeated until a stable, working prototype is achieved.

A five-step process can be used to organize robotics education. First, they should become acquainted with the kit and conduct independent study to learn about robotics' requirements. They collaborate throughout the process, from coming up with initial concepts to building a prototype to presenting their finished product to the rest of the class.

A robot's function requires calculation, and it executes control commands in order to determine the characteristics. Students should begin by learning about the capabilities of mechanical and electronic devices, as they form the backbone technology for this endeavor. Technology is used so that students may become accustomed to the kit and figure out for themselves how to do tests on things like lights, servos, motors, and sensors. For example, designing an automatic fire alarm system, how the sensors work, arranging them in the kitchen, for example, software such as Crocodile Technology capable of 2D or 3D simulation will help students form ideas for that system (Figure 1.1).

Once familiar with automated systems, it is necessary to brainstorm solutions and finally select a solution to move to the prototype stage. Before beginning prototyping with physical materials, students need to draw up a design. The design must specify the materials to be used and explain how the problem will be fixed so that the system functions flawlessly. However, students don't have much time, so they should make sure to test their ideas as quickly as possible. The use of simulation software makes it possible to quickly design and test solutions. For example, to design an electronic system to control traffic lights, Crocodile Technology software can be used to design electrical circuits and control devices (Figure 1.2).

After the students have developed a design strategy, the next step is to begin prototyping, testing their prototype, and receiving usability feedback on their overall design. Students can evaluate the functionality of the robots they create in terms of electronic circuits and mechanical systems using software if they do not have the time or the resources to swiftly build the gadget they have designed. This is because students may not have both of these resources. For example, check the operation of the reversible motor (Figure 1.3).

Students are required to give final presentations of their work before the project on robotics can be considered complete. Students may or may not be required to produce a prototype that is operational; nonetheless, they must be able to discuss their accomplishments, as well as their setbacks, and what they would do differently if they were given additional time. It will be easier to determine whether or not this idea is feasible if we employ software that simulates automated systems or robots.

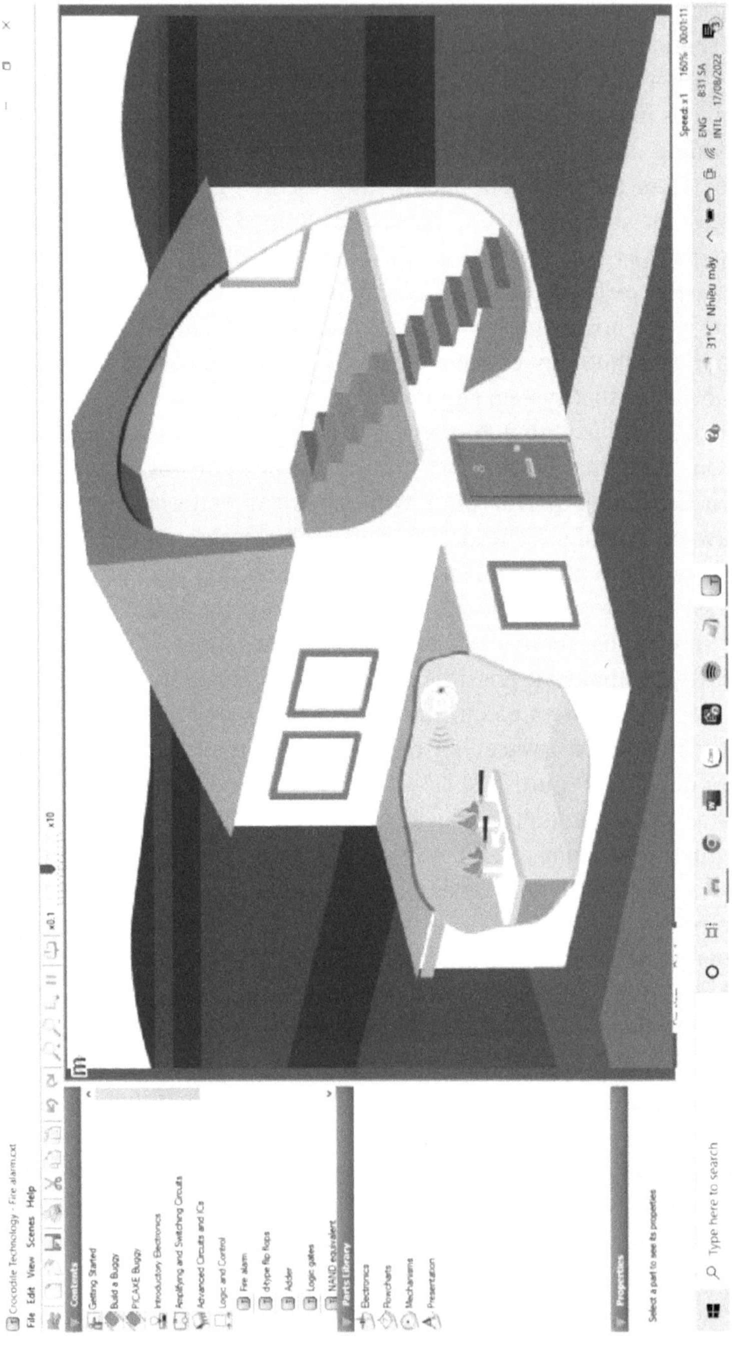


**FIGURE 1.1** Simulation fire alarm system by Crocodile Technology.

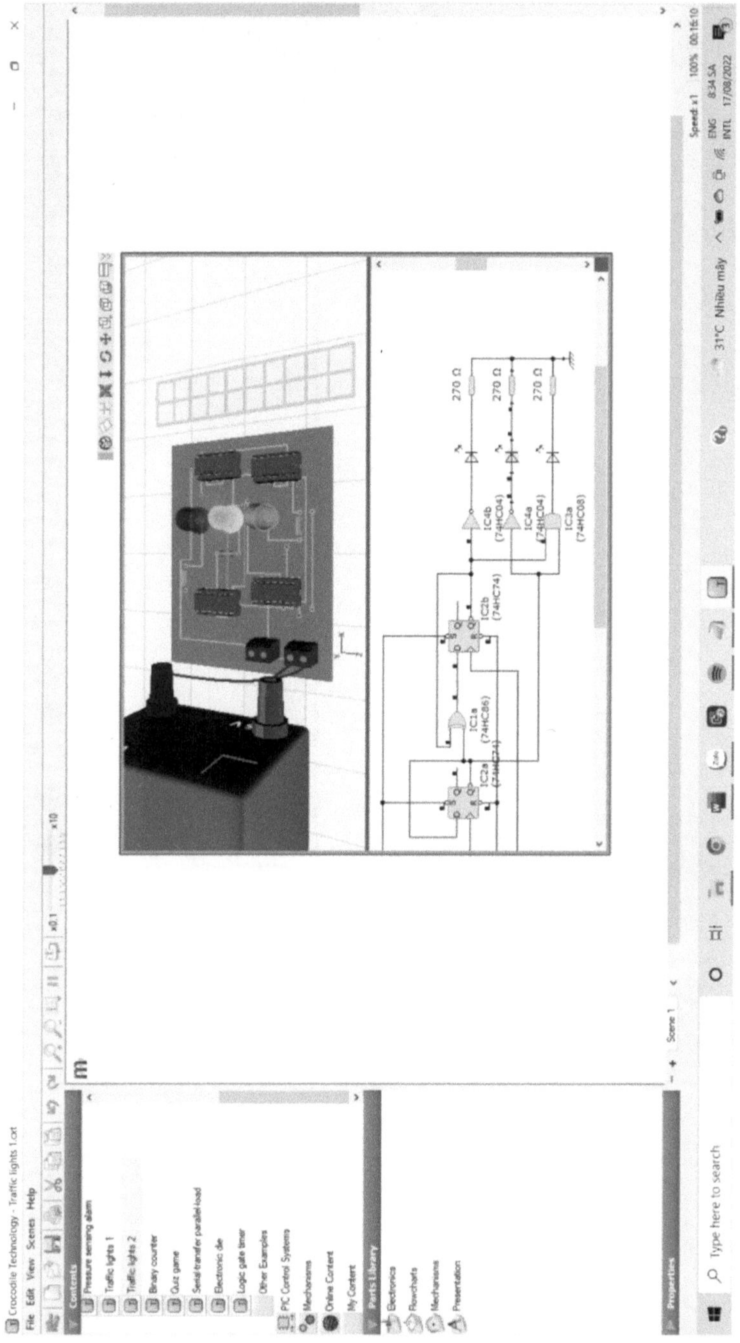

**FIGURE 1.2** Design an electronic system to control traffic lights by Crocodile Technology software.

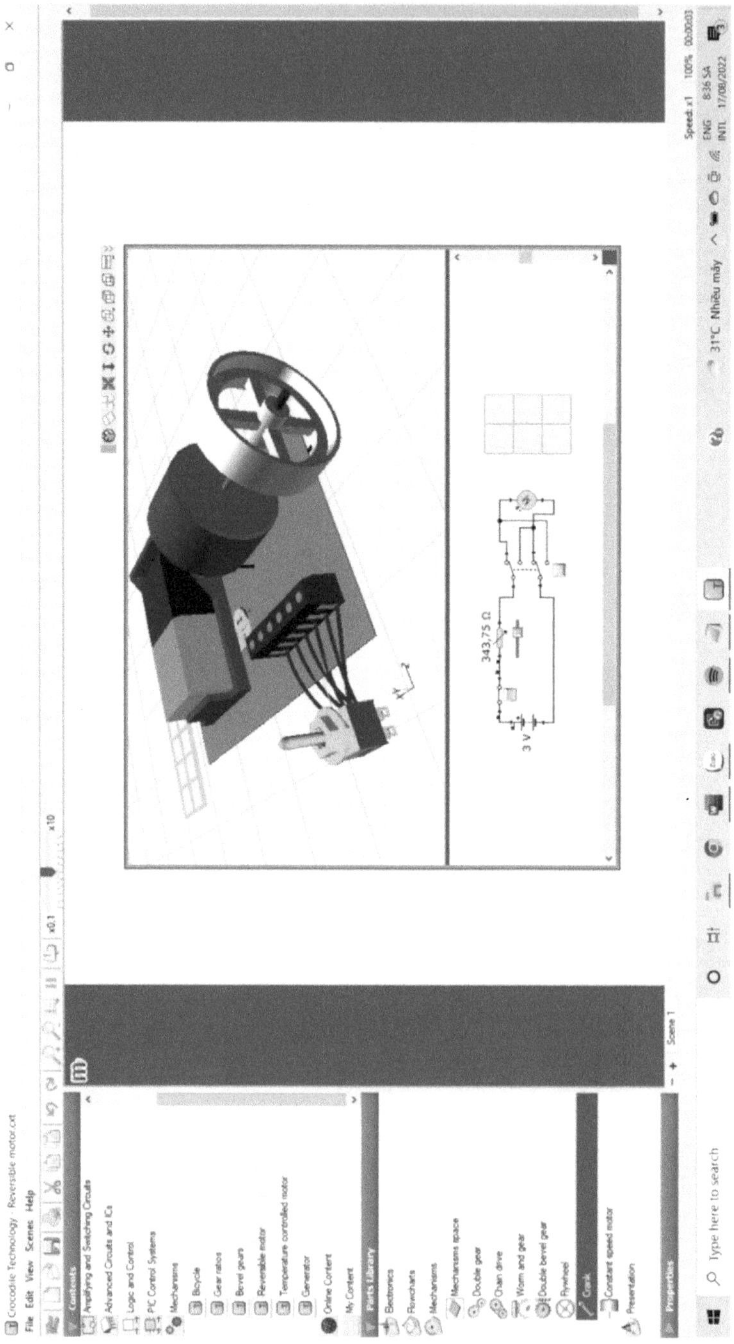

**FIGURE 1.3** Testing reversible motor action.

To build a robot, it is necessary to select materials and check the conditions of the environment. This work requires measuring tools and equipment in laboratories or workshops. However, students are not always able to work at school. Students can conduct test experiments at home using mobile phones.

With sensors integrated in phone and smartphone applications to measure physical quantities. Much software allows the use of smart phone sensors to replace measuring devices in the laboratory and in everyday activities, allowing students to take measurements of physical phenomena outside of laboratories. Measurements can be performed as mechanical, electro-acoustic or optical. For example, the Phyphox software (Figure 1.4) allows the use of sensors in the phone to perform experiments such as measuring the frequency of a pendulum with an accelerometer or measuring the velocity of a moving object using the doppler effect using a microphone of smartphones.

As another example, students might investigate the magnetic field around a current-carrying coil such as an electrical transformer. Figure 1.5 is an experiment to investigate the magnetic field around an electric transformer, with a 1 m ruler and a mobile phone with Gauss Meter software installed.

Mobile phones with many functions integrated with sensors, wireless connection via Bluetooth, Wi-Fi... become tools for students to conduct their research.

Applying ICT in teaching science subjects, especially using mobile learning in teaching physics, brings high efficiency in teaching and learning in the fourth industrial revolution era. In order to expand the use of mobile learning in teaching, schools and teachers should pay more attention to apply ICT in teaching and study.

## 1.4 TEACHERS' COMPETENCE REQUIREMENTS IN EDUCATIONAL ROBOTICS (ER)

The use of digital technologies facilitates the cognitive activities of learners. In ER, ICT has a role to support learners in designing and testing designs with high accuracy. The improvement of the ability to think and solve scientific and technical problems. Using technology as a cognitive tool requires understanding as well as expert systems, computer programming, databases, spreadsheets, multimedia, integrating mobile technology, embedded computing devices, virtual and augmented reality (AR). Applying

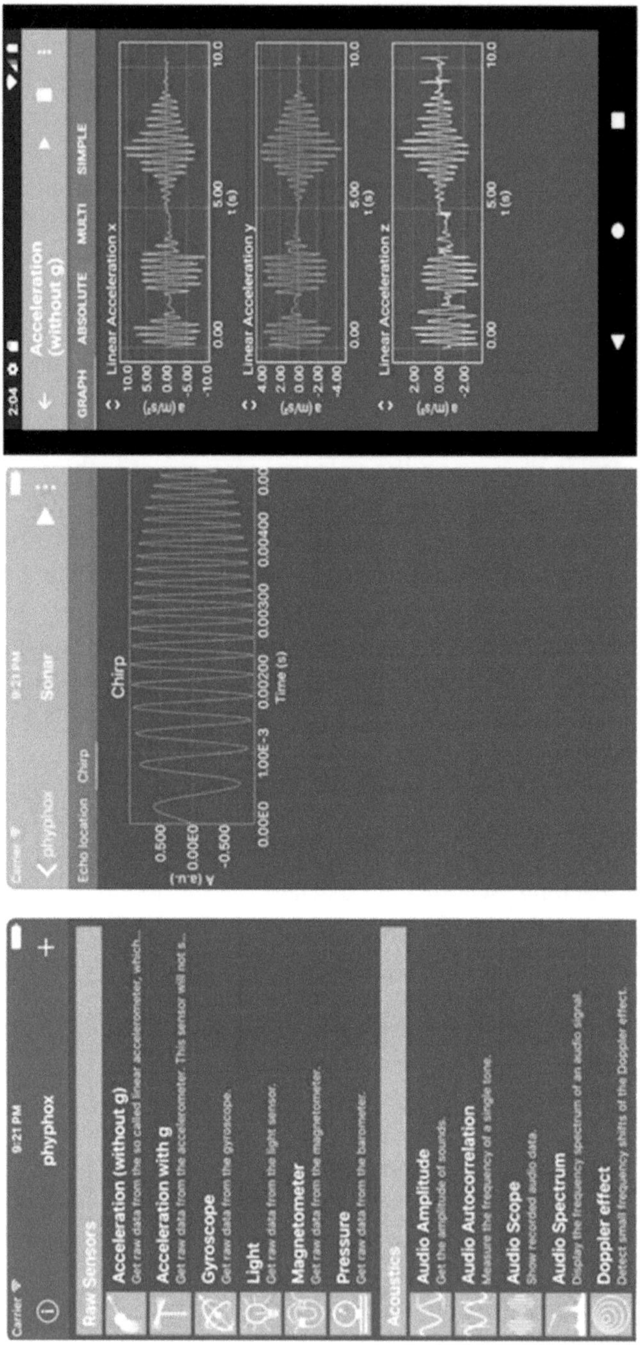


**FIGURE 1.4** Phyphox software screen on smartphone.

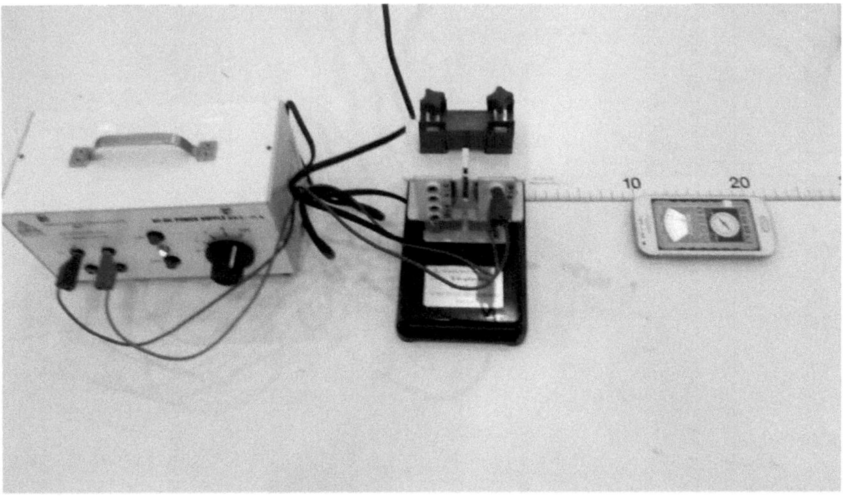


**FIGURE 1.5** Experiment to investigate the magnetic field around an electric transformer with Gauss Meter software on a mobile phone.

ICT in ER is a way to develop students' digital skills (Despoina, Esteve-González, & Mireia, 2021). However, it is unclear whether educators are up to the task of incorporating ICT into robotics education in order to engage in pedagogical practices that encourage the growth of students' digital skills, such as the ability to connect mechanical and electronic devices and write code to control robots in various life and technical contexts (Adem, 2020).

Studies by Agatolio et al. (2017); Scaradozzi et al. (2019); Zhou et al. (2015); Kucuk & Sisman (2018); Hynes & Dos Santos (2007) suggest activities to help teachers teach ER topics effectively as shown in Table 1.1.

## 1.5 DEVELOPING STUDENTS-TEACHERS' ICT COMPETENCE IN EDUCATIONAL ROBOTICS (ER)

In STEM and ER education, the technology component must play a more central role. Teachers need to be able to use technology in a variety of ways for successful teaching and learning. Technological competence and trust in teachers are a preparation for implementing STEM and ER in the classroom. UNESCO's ICT Competency Standard for Teachers (2015) indicates that teachers need to use ICTs to be technologically savvy, create knowledge, and deepen knowledge, all of which support classrooms to

**TABLE 1.1** Best Practices of Teachers in Education Robotics (Despoina, Esteve-González, & Mireia, 2021)

| Categories | Best Practices |
|---|---|
| Collaboration | • To create a robotics project through group effort among educators. |
| | • To share lessons learned through utilizing ER activities with students. |
| | • To discuss how you've used robots in the classroom with success. |
| | • To discuss problems and possible solutions for ER projects involving many disciplines. |
| Practice | • To gain experience with robotics and computer programs, and to put into practice technical expertise in areas such as assembly and programming. |
| | • Why To give people a chance to learn about the tools, try their hands at programming and assembly, and practice with progressively more difficult tasks. |
| | • To engage in robotics outreach events or bring ER projects into their classrooms. |
| Materials | • Assemble classroom-ready robotics kits with tools that teachers can put to use immediately in their own lessons. |
| | • To give lecturers something to work with. |
| | • To provide educators sufficient time throughout their training to create ER lesson plans and eventually use them in their own classrooms. |
| | • Objective: To compile a record of ER-related actions. |
| Pedagogy | • Utilize a pedagogical approach to introducing ER initiatives and incorporating ER into new contexts. |
| | • To instruct attendees on classroom management skills applicable to ER settings. |
| Feedback and support | • Response time for training programs. |
| | • Attending classes and assisting with activities alongside the participants. |

study in STEM education. These standards are designed to move teachers along a continuum of skills and competencies in the use of new technology (Vimala et al., 2017).

The UNESCO ICT Competency Framework for Teachers (2018) provides an essential guide to developing teachers' ICT competencies. At three ascending competency levels: tech-savvy, creative knowledge, and knowledge deepening, all of which support the STEM and ER classroom. A tech-savvy approach, including digital literacy fundamentals. Higher levels of competence allow teachers to select and use pre-existing applications that are appropriate for Robot projects and activities in laboratories or with limited classroom facilities to complement other tasks-curriculum standards, assessment approaches, planned units, and didactic teaching methods. At the highest level of UNESCO ICT. (https://www.open.edu/openlearncreate/pluginfile.php/306820/mod_resource/content/2/UNESCO%20ICT%20Competency%20Framework%20V3.pdf).

Competency framework, teachers and students create works of learning using selected technologies, teachers act as coaches in the classroom. For student teachers to progress from one competency level to another, it requires effective ICT professional development.

While most of the time and content of training natural science pedagogical students, students need to learn basic science content such as Physics, chemistry, biology. Content for ER-related electronics and information technology is very limited. The biggest challenge for students is to understand the variables of ICT devices and device control programming techniques. In addition, deep scientific understanding and practical application also require the ability to combine multidisciplinary knowledge and ICT to solve ER problems.

Analysis of the training program for teachers of natural sciences shows that the curricula at universities are still limited in providing teachers with the necessary skills to teach STEM and ER subjects. Therefore, it is necessary to develop a training program to help teachers acquire basic scientific knowledge, and at the same time have the ability to integrate teaching, especially with STEM and ER, as well as apply ICT for effective teaching strategies.

Here are some solutions to develop ICT competencies in ER for students of natural science pedagogy.

1. **Develop Training Program in Stages: Intensive-Integrative-Applied.** Developing ICT capacity in ER for students of natural

science pedagogy requires not only information technology knowledge and skills, but also requires students to have knowledge in many fields and practices. With the length of the training program usually about four years, it is difficult to fully equip students. However, basic scientific knowledge such as Mathematics, physics, chemistry, biology is always the foundation knowledge to develop applications in Robotics. Therefore, the program can be organized in stages as shown in Table 1.2.

**TABLE 1.2** Integrated Curriculum in Student Teacher of Natural Science Pedagogy

| Intensive | Integrative | Applied |
|---|---|---|
| Mathematics, physics, chemistry, biology, foundation of ICT, basics of electronics. | Integrated themes: Energy and transformation, earth and sky, STEM, ER, and professions. | Vocational subjects: Physics, chemistry, biology in professions, control, and automation. |

2. **Organize Course Content by Topics and Projects.** In order to gain a deep knowledge of the subjects, and at the same time develop the ability to apply knowledge and practice in general and ER in particular, it is possible to restructure the course content according to topics and follow projects to enhance students' self-study ability, and at the same time apply ICT to support students to carry out learning projects. Through these activities, students search for software, design project products, and conduct experiments on computers. Thereby students develop ICT competencies in the ER.
3. **Organize Teaching in the Form of Blended Learning.** Blended learning combines face-to-face and online training. One of the limitations of online learning is that learners will not get the same interaction with other students and instructors as in regular classes. In "face-to-face" learning, issues are discussed and considered from multiple perspectives. All students can state their point of view, can listen, and think based on the opinions of others, and classroom discussions can move from the topic being studied to life. It can be seen that the classroom environment has a positive impact on learners, which is something that a full online school cannot guarantee.

   Blended learning should be seen as a pedagogical approach that integrates effectiveness and social opportunities in the classroom with the possibilities of promoting active, technology-assisted learning in the classroom, online environment, not just a way of teaching! In other words, blended teaching is not a new teaching design today but a way to restructure the teaching model (Huang, Zhou, & Wang, 2006).

The general education renovation program requires student teacher training to meet innovative education requirements. Blended learning's great capabilities and efficiency will save time, money, and improve teacher training courses.

## 1.6 A CASE STUDY INTEGRATING EDUCATIONAL ROBOTICS (ER) INTO THE TRAINING PROGRAM FOR DEVELOPING STUDENTS-TEACHERS' ICT COMPETENCE IN TEACHING AT UNIVERSITY OF EDUCATION, HANOI, VNU.

The natural science pedagogical student training program at University of Education - Hanoi VNU equips learners with basic and core knowledge of the natural sciences such as Physics, Chemistry, Biology including the educational sciences and pedagogical competence and skills. Their careers meet the requirements of the current educational and training program innovation in Vietnam.

The program with 140 credits includes general knowledge sections, basic knowledge sections, general outlines in groups of natural sciences such as Mathematics, Physics, Chemistry, Biology, integrated knowledge sections such as: Energy and changing form, Environmental Ecology, Biosphere, and climate change, Chemistry, and life, Environmental Chemistry, Introduction to Biotechnology, Microbiology, Petrochemistry, Cosmology, Introduction to Nanotechnology (http://education.vnu.edu.vn/files/ngày%20đầu%20tiên%20đi%20học%202.3.2020/DHGD%20KHTN-2019.pdf).

Currently, the University of Education VNU has been training three courses, during the training process, the program is regularly adjusted to suit reality.

Form of training organization according to blended learning, courses are organized on learning management system (LMS), providing students with the digital University of education–Hanoi VNU learning materials, software applications in teaching.

The system contains courses that are flexibly designed in a topic or week-by-week format. Learning activities are flexibly organized to meet the individual needs of learners, including:

1. **Search for Learning Materials:** The learning materials are digitized as PDF files or e-lectures packaged according to SCORM standards, software put into the course's resources section and linked to icons on the main screen. Students can click on the icons to read on the computer or download to read on the computer when there is no Internet connection.
2. **Exchange, Discuss:** By forums or Chat room, students can submit questions, answers, or attach files for discussion, group work.
3. **Take the Test:** The text can be in the form of multiple choice or essays in the file upload format (upload file). Students can do self-study exercises on Word, PDF files... and upload files to the LMS.

## 1.7 RESULTS AND DISCUSSION

With the training program for pedagogical students of natural sciences at the University of Education - Vietnam National University, Hanoi (VNU-UED), through a survey of students' ICT capacity in teaching STEM and ER education, the study has conducted an investigation. Learners through interviews, questionnaires, and assessment of learning outcomes in both ICT capacity according to the levels of Knowledge Acquisition, Knowledge Deepening, Knowledge Creation, and capacity ICT in ER.

The capacity distribution chart of learners in Figure 1.7 shows that many students have weak Knowledge Creation, while Knowledge Deepening is good, ICT capacity in ER is quite scattered.

The student teacher's feedback after the course is compiled through questionnaires and calculated descriptive statistics and results as in Table 1.3.

Table 1.3 shows that the majority of teachers strongly agree with the questions. In particular, students commented that the lecturer has organized teaching that integrates ICT in teaching according to ER with clear and effective subject contents (average value is 4.5). Through the students' comments, it can be seen that the course has helped them improve both ICT in ER teaching and improve their professionalism. Although the number of students is not much, the course has shown that the training program for natural science teachers at the University of Education - VNU-UED has improved the capacity of teachers in both professional and technical areas, subjects, occupations, and ICT competencies in teaching STEM and ER.

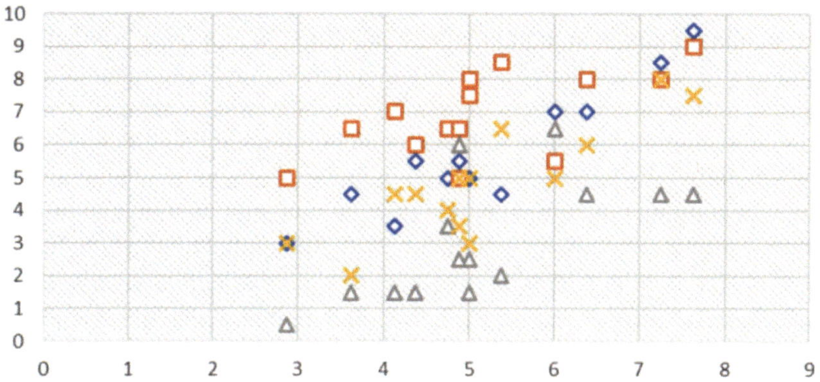


**FIGURE 1.7** Graph of students' ICT competency distribution.

*Note:* ◇: Knowledge acquisition; □ : Knowledge deepening; △ : Knowledge creation; and ✕ : ICT in ER.

**TABLE 1.3** Summary of Student Feedback After the Course

| Ord. | Item | No | Mean | Stv. |
|---|---|---|---|---|
| 1. | The course content improves both ICT competence and subject knowledge. | 50 | 3.7 | 1.1 |
| 2. | Course content helps learners improve ICT and ER. Skills. | 50 | 3.1 | 0.6 |
| 3. | The form of the course organization is suitable for students. | 50 | 3.3 | 0.6 |
| 4. | Subject content helps learners improve their interdisciplinary integration skills in ER. | 50 | 3.6 | 0.8 |
| 5. | Rich and useful learning materials. | 50 | 4.2 | 0.6 |
| 6. | Learners can understand most scientific knowledge. | 50 | 3.4 | 0.8 |
| 7. | The lecturers have organized the teaching of the subject content clearly and effectively. | 50 | 4.5 | 0.7 |
| 8. | The lecturers well organize activities to help learners improve their ICT skills in teaching according to ER. | 50 | 4.1 | 0.5 |
| 9. | Good support online learning system for self-study. | 50 | 4.5 | 0.7 |

## 1.8 CONCLUSION

According to this orientation, robotics science education is considered an effective tool for STEM education in schools. Many studies show that the learning process with robots has created opportunities for students to achieve results in both Physics, Biology, Geography, Mathematics, Science, Electronics, and Mechanics subjects, and important academic skills, such as research, creativity, collaboration, critical thinking, decision-making, problem-solving, and communication skills, and design skills and computational thinking. Robotic science education provides an opportunity for students to explore avenues of engineering and technology development, enabling real-world applications of engineering and technology concepts and helping to make concrete abstractions of engineering more concrete, science, and math, which is essential for STEM education in schools. In robotics science education, students must be the ones who directly use, design, and manufacture robots, even at the simplest level, not just consumers of products.

The implementation of teaching Integrating ER into the teachers training program at the University of Education–Vietnam National University Hanoi for developing students' ICT competence in teaching for students. Teachers aim to accelerate the process of organizing ER teaching in some high schools. In order to quickly train ER teachers, it is necessary to build teachers training programs integrating ICT in ER in a scientific manner, with a flexible teaching organization.

## KEYWORDS

- **educational robotics**
- **information and communication technology**
- **natural sciences**
- **pre-service natural science teachers**
- **real-world applications**
- **robotics**
- **STEM**

## REFERENCES

Adem, U., (2020). Using educational robotics as a cognitive tool for ICT teachers in an authentic learning environment. *International Education Studies, 13*(4). ISSN 1913-9020 E-ISSN 1913-9039 Published by Canadian Center of Science and Education. doi: 10.5539/ies.v13n4p27.

Alimisis, D., &Kynigos, C., (2009). Constructionism and robotics in education *Teacher Education on Robotic-Enhanced Constructivist Pedagogical Methods,* 11–26.

Alimisis, D., (2010). *Introducing Robotics in Schools: Post-TERECoP Experiences from a Pilot Educational Program.* Paper presented at the Proceedings of Intl. Conf. on Simulation, Modeling and Programming for Autonomous Robots (SIMPAR 2010) Workshops.

Alimisis, D., (2012). *Robotics in Education & Education in Robotics: Shifting Focus from Technology to Pedagogy.* Paper presented at the Proceedings of the 3rd International Conference on Robotics in Education.

Benitti, F., (2012). Exploring the educational potential of robotics in schools: A systematic review. *Computers & Education, 58*(3), 978–988.

Blikstein, P., (2013). Digital fabrication and 'making' in education: The democratization of invention. *FabLabs: Of Machines, Makers, and Inventors, 4,* 1–21.

Burke, B. N., & D.T. E., (2014). The ITEEA6E learning by DeSIGN(TM) model maximizing informed design and inquiry in the integrative stem classroom. *Technology and Engineering Teacher, 73*(6), 14–19.

Bybee, R. W., Taylor, J. A., Gardner, A., Van, S. P., Powell, J. C., Westbrook, A., & Landes, N., (2006). *The BSCS 5E Instructional Model: Origins and Effectiveness* (Vol. 5, pp. 88–98). Colorado Springs, Co: BSCS.

Christensen, R., & Knezek, G., (2017). Relationship of middle school student STEM interest to career intent. *Journal of Education in Science & Environment and Health, 3*(1), 1–13.

Chung, C. C., Lin, C. L., & Lou, S. J., (2018). Analysis of the learning effectiveness of the STEAM-6E special course—A case study about the creative design of IoT assistant devices for the elderly. *Sustainability, 10*(9), 3040.

Despoina, S., Esteve-González, V., & Mireia, U., (2021).An overview of teacher training programs in educational robotics: Characteristics, best practices, and recommendations. *Education and Information Technologies, 26,* 2831–2852. https://doi.org/10.1007/s10639-020-10377-z.

Eguchi, A., (2014). *Why Robotics in Education?-Robotics as a Learning Tool for Educational Revolution.* Paper presented at the Society for Information Technology & Teacher Education International Conference.

Huang, R. H., Zhou, Y. L., & Wang, Y., (2006). *Blended Learning: Theory into Practice.* Beijing: Higher, Education Press.

Jung, S., & Won, E. S., (2018). Systematic review of research trends in robotics education for young children. *Sustainability, 10*(4), 905.

Kim, C., Kim, D., Yuan, J., Hill, R. B., Doshi, P., & Thai, C. N., (2015). Robotics to promote elementary education pre-service teachers' STEM engagement, learning, and teaching. *Computers & Education, 91,* 14–31.

Komis, V., Romero, M., & Misirli, A., (2016). *A Scenario-Based Approach for Designing Educational Robotics Activities for Co-creative Problem Solving.* Paper presented at the International Conference EduRobotics 2016.

Owen, C., (2007). Design thinking: Notes on its nature and use. *Design Research Quarterly, 2*, 16–27.

Sokratis, T., & Theodosios, S., (2022). Exploring the features of educational robotics and STEM research in primary education: A systematic literature review. *Education Sciences, 12*, 305. https://doi.org/10.3390/educsci12050305.

*The Natural Science Pedagogical Student Training Program of University of Education.* Hanoi VNU; https://education.vnu.edu.vn/files/2021/Cac%20file%20pdf/1732-KHTN.pdf (accessed on 13 December 2023).

*UNESCO ICT Competency Framework for Teachers.* https://www.open.edu/openlearncreate/pluginfile.php/306820/mod_resource/content/2/UNESCO%20ICT%20Competency%20Framework%20V3.pdf (accessed on 13 December 2023).

Vimala, J. K., Figaro-Henry, S., Ramsawak-Jodha, N., & Zhanna, D., (2017). The development of teacher ICT competence and confidence in using Web 2.0 tools in a STEM professional development initiative in Trinidad. *Caribbean Teaching Scholar, 7.*

## CHAPTER 2

# Constructivist Learning in LMS Moodle for Students of Higher Educational Institutes

V. RACHEL

*Avinashilingam Institute for Home Science and Higher Education for Women, Coimbatore, Tamil Nadu, India*

## ABSTRACT

The major demand in higher education institutes is to provide the finest education to the maximum number of students at an affordable cost. In today's digital age, learning takes place at anytime and anywhere. So, it becomes mandatory to change the teaching-learning methods to the latest techniques. ICT applications in terms of E-learning have already brought tremendous change in teaching-learning methodology in higher education, and the learning management system (LMS) has an important role in it. Nowadays, higher educational institutes have Wi-Fi and internet facilities, so they can think of effectively incorporating the LMS-Moodle so that learning can take place anytime, anywhere. The future demand for higher education for construction and administering lies not in the existing physical campus when limited resources are given. Constructivists insist that a student must take a dynamic role in their education. LMSs can be used in constructivist learning so students can have the ability to work with real problems and circumstances. It shapes the teacher's systematic thinking, which students apply with suitable feedback to their own issues. It models the systematic thoughts of the teacher, which students apply

Intelligent Learning Paradigms and Student Empowerment: Digital Integration and Transformation.
Souvik Pal, Ton Quang Cuong, & R. S. S. Nehru (Eds.)

with suitable feedback to their problems. It also helps to create work with problems that are related to real scenarios.

## 2.1 INTRODUCTION

Online learning is likely to improve the outcomes of learning by engaging students more actively in learning with motivation (Twigg, 2003a, b). The tasks comprise virtual discussions, assessments like assignments, quizzes with immediate response where students can get instant support related to the work they do through the online portal of learning.

Many educational institutes have tried to bring in learning management systems (LMS) to aid the in-person learning procedure. LMS is nothing but a tool or web-based application to design, devise, and evaluate a particular learning process (Dougiamas & Taylor, 2003). In today's world of technology, the use of ICT tools including LMS has become imperative. The LMS includes several tools that provide higher educational institutes to be capable. To support the distance mode, it is effective and also enhances the conventional method of instruction. LMS is a portal where it can store, manage, and share its resources and knowledge (Al-Busaidi & Al-Shihi, 2010). The acceptance rate of LMS in higher educational institutes is very promising throughout the world. LMSs are online-based portals that have tools and resources to uphold learning that includes learning materials and multimedia resources needed for the study. Tools for assessment like online quizzes and assignments are available for students to attend quizzes and submit assignments. Email, chat for one-to-one communication, and discussion forums are there for effective communication between tutor and students and between peers. Tutors can use course administration tools to keep track of grades. Notices and course deadlines can be displayed. Learning management tools allow students to analyze their grades and have a check on their progress. Higher educational institutions in the USA have shown more than a 70% acceptance rate of LMS (Campus Computing Project, 2008). Nowadays teaching through LMS is common in higher educational institutes. Teaching through online involves skill sets, knowledge, and specialized training. The faculty development programs sometimes support or restrict the use of technologies among teachers.

The tools in LMS provide a thorough method to categorize activities and resources. The reading materials and handouts are uploaded digitally, thereby eliminating additional clerical work. The integration and incorporation of LMS are advantageous for faculty who are fervent users. It is also an advantage for faculty to adopt an LMS to support their instruction.

## 2.2 LEARNING MANAGEMENT SYSTEM (LMS)

A lot of interest is shown at present in E-Learning. E-Learning is not just the matter of keeping the course material in electronic form, and learner referring to that course material. Many tools are coming up for supporting the various activities of the e-learning process like communication, content creation, content delivery, etc. To keep a record of the various activities of e-learning process an LMS with an integrated set of e-Learning features is required.

LMS is a tool which is used to design, devise, and evaluate a learning process. Broadly we can classify the users of the LMS as learner, tutor, course designer and administrator. The learner needs to register for the various courses, learn from the required learning material provided by the LMS, undergo tests and practical, complete assignments, etc. The tutor can deliver learning materials, monitor student participation in quiz, assignment, discussion, and also assesses the performance of student. In order to do this a tutor needs to organize or plan a course based on prescribed syllabus and he/she has to establish a course calendar to monitor student progress. LMS provides course designer to create course content by supporting various content creation facilities. LMS also provides students to use communication tools such as chat (synchronous as well as asynchronous), discussion forum, audio, and video conferencing. Administrator is considered to be the super user of the LMS, who has the privileges for user/group management, server management, etc. Looking at the great market potential of this field, many key players are already in the market with their products pertaining to this field. There are a range of LMS on the market right now like Ariadne, DLS, Learning Space, Medit, Tool Book, Top-Class, Blackboard, Sakai, etc. These tools still could be improved to provide interoperability, scalability, and conformance to standards (EduTools, 2006). An effective LMS needs to simulate e-Learning environment for synchronous and asynchronous learning with effective collaboration. In addition to this, the LMS needs to support generalized capabilities to fit into diversified learning environments and multilingual support.

1. **Content Creation and Delivery Mechanisms:** The efficiency of any course highly depends on the contents of the course. The tool must support various formats for the uploading of the course contents.
2. **Assessment:** For online learning, assessment is an important tool. Various types of assessments are possible such as assignments, quizzes, and tests. These assessments can be organized and administered in many ways. Individual as well as group assignments can be given. LMS should allow the instructor to add assignments, tests, quizzes, and other student testing mechanisms. A feature such as online gradebook and automatic assessment relieves the instructor, to a large extent, from manual correction and grading of the student submissions. The facility of adding different types of questions to the test is also useful to the instructor while designing the course. Currently most of the tools support multiple-choice questions, fill in the blanks, true/false, etc. Descriptive type questions require manual evaluation. Research has been carried out for automatic evaluation of descriptive type questions. Tools must provide the provision to annotate the answers with instructor's comments which can be made available to the students. While comparing assessment capabilities, one should be concerned with the types of questions supported, generations of questions, feedback, tips, etc. It is also essential that an assessment system provide systematic tracking capabilities.
3. **Grading Capabilities:** Depending on the learner's performance, grading must be given as feedback to the student. An efficient feedback mechanism helps the learner to know his/her own performance with respect to other learners without revealing individual grades of other students. The grading system can be implemented effectively by using graphical comparisons like bar graphs or pie charts, etc.
4. **Collaboration:** Interaction may be considered as an important issue among the users in any type of learning. Collaboration impacts the way in which stakeholders share thoughts and ideas. Interaction among the learners may be in the form of chatting, posting queries to a discussion forum/bulletin board or through email. The interaction that takes place between the instructor and the learner may not take so many forms. Under e-Learning environment, there are

various tasks, which require the expertise of more than one stakeholder of same or different types. Implementation of communication with proper collaboration under learning environment enables an effective and efficient way of sharing expertise and resources. Here again the instructor can form small groups among students themselves in a forum for an exchange of queries, ideas, etc., for the purpose of discussion.

5. **Implementation:** These address the issues like ease of use, prerequisites of the learning system, and maintenance issues. The tool must have the least dependencies on platforms, operating systems, browsers, and databases. The less the dependency, the more is the ease of use on multiple platforms.
6. **Security:** The security includes the security for the course content, student tracking information; source code and ensuring that only registered learners take the test.
7. **Blended Learning:** There are so many different ways for people to learn. There should be an option in LMS that can combine classroom and virtual courses to have rigid and customized training.
8. **Administration Tools:** Administrators should be able to manage user registrations, profiles, describe roles like course creator, teacher, student, etc., assign tutors, and manage learning materials. Access rights have to be given to the administrators to access the database so that they can create quality and standard reports on the performance. The reports generated should have the entire team's work. The system should also give a schedule for students, tutors, and classrooms. The features should be convenient using user-friendly interfaces.
9. **Standards:** These should be adopted by LMS so that it can import and manage content that adheres to the standards in spite of the system that created it.

The above criteria are very fundamental to develop an effective LMS.

### *2.2.1 MOODLE*

Moodle's creator is Martin Dougiamas, when he was doing his postgraduate studies at the Curtin University of Technology in Australia. In the year 2002, he was the administrator of the university web and also the WebCT installation system administrator. Since he faced some problems with WebCT and to overcome that problem, he happened to develop Moodle. In the beginning stage of Moodle development, a class with few students used it and case studies were done. Following that, designers and contributors from all around the world added more features (Martin et al., 2004; Dougiamas, 2004; Koh, 2006). Moodle is perhaps the most user-friendly, flexible, and open-source LMS available worldwide. Moodle is an online learning environment that helps instructors to upload and distribute learning materials, conduct quizzes, discussion forums, enable students to upload assignments, in a friendly environment (Dougiamas, 2011; Cole, 2005; Wharekura-Tini, 2004). Moodle is developed in a user-friendly way that helps people to build good virtual courses. Also, it has excellent document maintenance, is very well secured, and has excellent management (Zenha-Rela et al., 2006; Cole, 2005). Because of Moodle's excellent features, it has a rigid development and a maximum community of users and is also possible to download and use it on any computer (Berry, 2005; Brandl, 2005; Al-Ajlan et al., 2008).

### *2.2.2 MOODLE ARCHITECTURE*

The Moodle architecture developed by Dougiamas is simple and that makes the strength of Moodle. Compared to other LMS, Moodle's architecture has a strong foundation because of its low blend and high reliability. These features of Moodle make the system easy, flexible, and very effective so users can access in an easy manner (Dougiamas, 2011).

### *2.2.3 ONLINE LEARNING ENVIRONMENT TOOLS OF MOODLE*

Technical skills are not needed for the teachers to create resources as tools are very powerful. These tools help the creators to analyze and choose the most suitable online learning product. One product cannot potentially satisfy the essentials that are needed for all purposes. The activity (Table 2.1) and resource (Table 2.2) are the main modules in an online learning platform (Dougiamas et al., 2002; Perrie, 2003). Moodle has an extensive series of activity modules which helps to create any type of course. These activity modules serve as a central point for Moodle users so they can share, discuss, and collaborate. Some of the current activities as in Moodle version 3.4 are as in Table 2.1.

**TABLE 2.1** Activity Modules

| SL. No. | Activity | Description |
|---|---|---|
| 1. | Assignments  | Student can submit the assignment by uploading file. |
| 2. | Chats  | Discussion on subject can be done in real time and peers can understand each other and, on the topic, covered. |
| 3. | Choices   | Tutors can use this feature to ask question on the topic discussed in classes. |
| 4. | Forums  | Forums is a place for discussion between teacher and students. |
| 5. | Glossary  | Definitions can be created using glossary. |
| 6. | Labels   | Text and graphics can be inserted. |
| 7. | Lesson 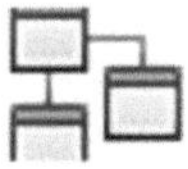 | Teacher can deliver learning materials in an interesting way. It contains multiple pages, and each page has a question and its possible answers. |
| 8. | Quizzes   | Quiz allows the teacher to assess the student by giving multiple choice/descriptive or short questions. |
| 9. | Resources  | Information related to the course can be added using resources. |

Moodle has so many different types of resources where users can add any kind of web-related materials into courses. Resources can be found from the course option. Some of the current resource activities as in Moodle version 3.4 are as in Table 2.2.

**TABLE 2.2** Resource Types

| SL. No. | Resource | Description |
|---|---|---|
| 1. | Text page | Page can be created using plain text. There are many formatting types available to convert plain text into enriched web pages. |
| 2. | HTML page | A complete single web page can be developed within Moodle, especially when users use WYSIWYG HTML editor. |
| 3. | Files and web pages | Files option allows uploading a file from the computer where the file is stored. Web pages can be used to link the pages. |
| 4. | Directory | Students can view the course related files from the directory and sub-directories. |

## *2.2.4 MOODLE USABILITY*

The interface of Moodle is very user-friendly. The front page (Figure 2.1) can be customized by clicking Edit settings under Settings. Editing can be done by turning editing on under Settings option. Full site name (in our study it is Computer Science-ADU), Front page summary (about the University and department), etc., can be added so it appears on the Moodle site's front page. There are so many themes available like Afterburner, Aerialist, Formal white, etc., which can be set for the site. The theme can be changed by clicking site administration-appearance-themes-theme selector. The default theme was used for our website. Logo (ADU logo) (Rachel et al., 2016) can be added on the front page which has the option to add a logo.

1. **Creation of Users:** This can be done using site administration option. Their username, password, email-id details should be added for creating users. Once the user logs into the Moodle, the personal details can be updated which is found under profile option. Only users play an important role in accessing the Moodle site. Around 100 users have been created who belong to BCA course. The register number of the student was username and as well as password.
2. **Course Creation:** Course creators can create courses by clicking Courses under Site Administration. There are no limitations for

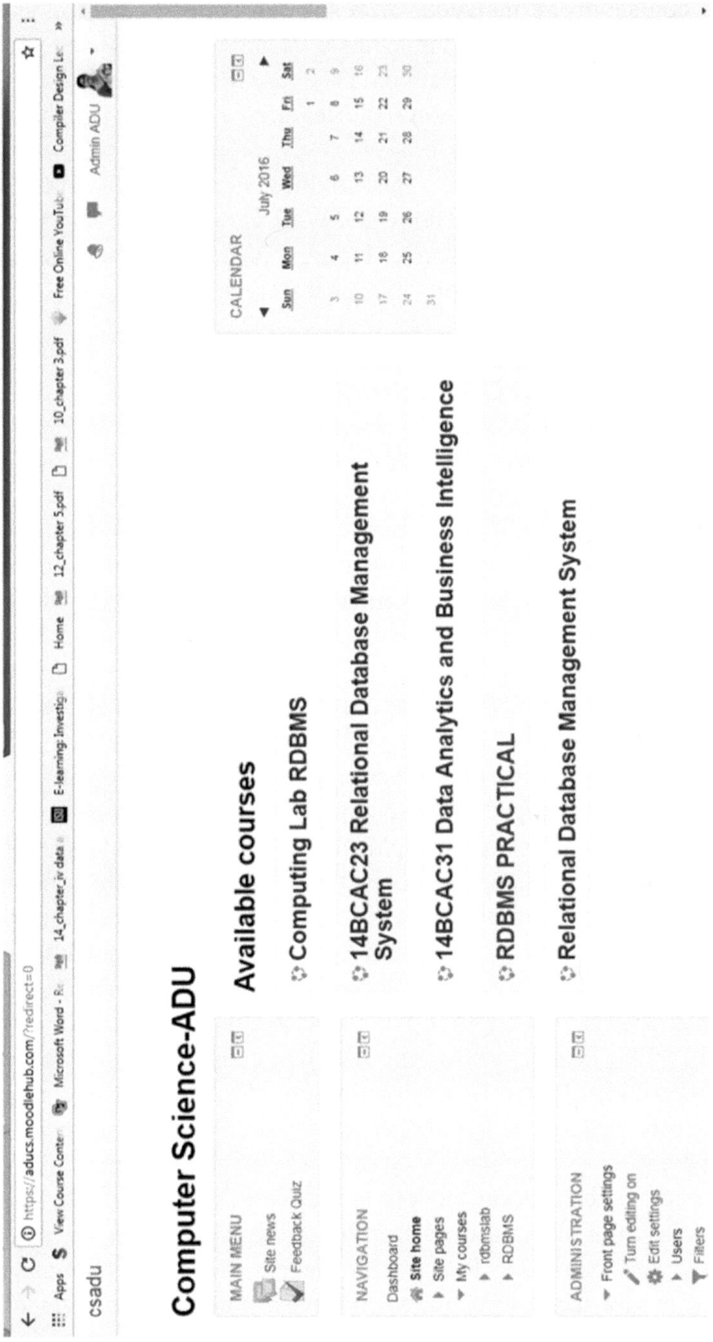


**FIGURE 2.1** Moodle front page.

courses to be included, even sub-categories of courses can also be included. Here the courses 'Data Analytics and Business Intelligence' and 'Relational Database Management System' were added. Figure 2.2 shows the learning materials that have been added under the course.

3. **Creation of Activities:** The activities or resources like Assignment, Forum, Chats, Quiz, Blogs, and Wiki, Glossary, and RSS Feed, etc., can be added as shown in Figure 2.3. For our study assignment, blog, forum discussion, quiz, chat were added.

## 2.3 CONSTRUCTIVIST LEARNING IN LMS

The teacher was more active and dominant, whereas the students were passive recipients of information. During the 1970s and 1980s, many educators began to question the teaching-learning process on the basis of behaviorist school. The students were not able to work in a group, build knowledge of their own, think divergently for seeking new knowledge, and inventing. Furthermore, the teaching-learning strategy was mechanical, stereotypic, and static, which ignored the critical and reflective thinking of students. As a result, constructivist pedagogy emerged in the world of educational scenarios as a protest, which believes that learning is knowledge construction by learners either independently or cooperatively when they are actively engaged in social experiences and activities.

Constructivism has philosophical, educational, and psychological origins. Constructivism opposes objectivism, which holds that a human can learn about external reality, whereas constructivism holds that the opposite is true. We can only know the truth as it is represented by human understanding. Individuals develop their own knowledge and meaning through their interactions with the environment, according to constructivism (Gale & Steff, 1995; Fosnot, 1996). The idea that people are builders, shapers, and designers inspired this construction metaphor. Knowledge, according to constructivists, is the consequence of individuals constructing reality (Brooks, 1990).

The use of behavioral models in learning theory began to give way to a method that depended on learning models and from the perceptive theory. Cognitive models focus on the students' learning processes. It also focuses on how the mind acquires, manages, stores, and corrects information. Learning emphasizes what learners know and how they gained it,

**FIGURE 2.2** Learning materials added under the course.

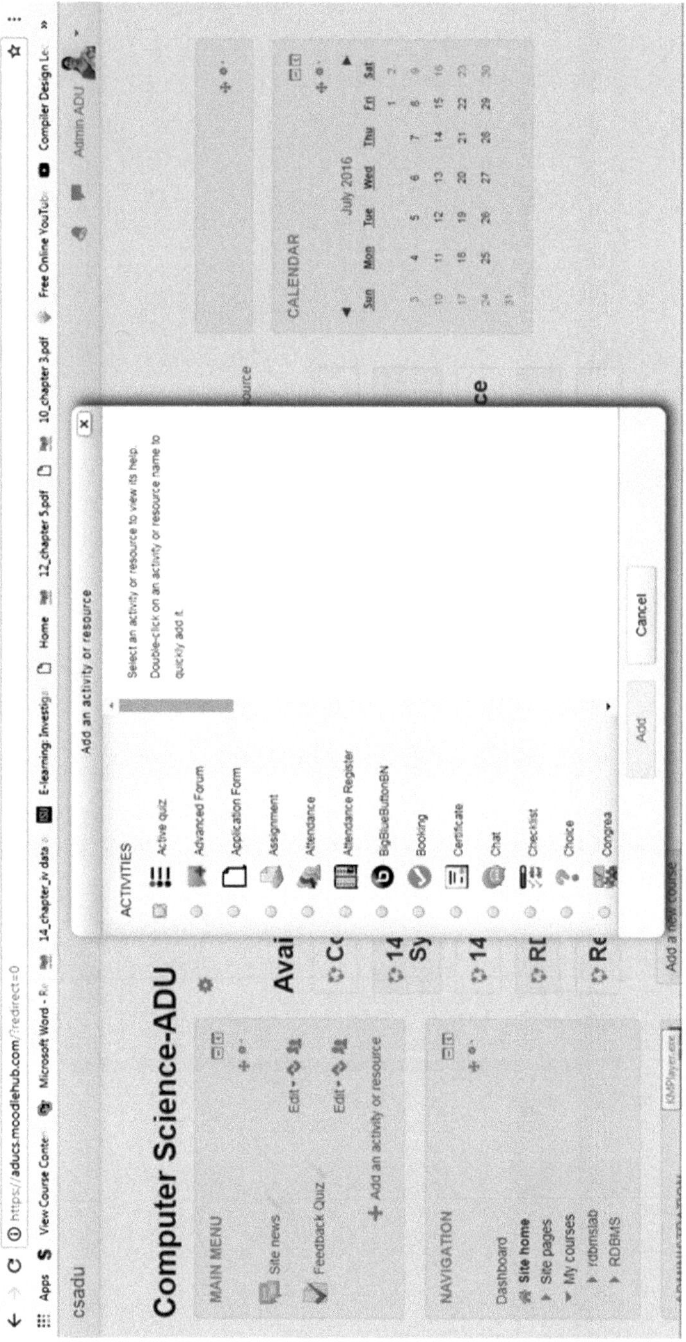


**FIGURE 2.3** Add an activity or resource.

instead of how they perform it (Jonassen, 1991b). Knowledge awareness is defined as intellectual action that encompasses coding and is ordered by the user. When it comes to the learning process, the learner is considered a very active participant.

Teachers, friends, students, administrators, and participants form the group of learners. Social constructivism uses teaching plans like quoting meanings with students, discussion inside the class, collaborative work, and evaluating meaningful activity over correct answers. From a constructivist point of view, the learners are dynamically involved in the meaning-making process. The students can study, examine, work in a team, share, build, and create based on what they already know (Dougiamas & Taylor, 2003).

If LMS is to be deployed to support learning, they must allow learners to interact with instructors and peers, as well as share ideas, form concepts based on prior knowledge, reflect on experiences, and construct knowledge. Students could use interactive tools including email, chat feature to communicate with students or with the teacher, discussion forums for discussing synchronously with the teacher or with peers, online classes, and features that help them to build knowledge.

### *2.3.1 LMS FEATURES SUPPORTING CONSTRUCTIVIST LEARNING*

LMS software has become a useful tool to deliver a course entirely. LMS software has several components that assist learning and its processes for students. Reigeluth et al. (2008) proposes four primary roles an LMS should include.

- Record maintenance;
- Organization;
- Training; and
- Evaluation.

The above four attributes can enable a teacher to adapt and individualize the learning materials and goals, thus enabling students to build a learner-centered experience. In this process, teachers become facilitators rather than knowledge sources (McCombs & Whisler, 1997). When done correctly, educators can develop a curriculum that fully embraces the constructivist learning model by successfully integrating an LMS system.

LMS is a fully incorporated software for learning, providing facilitators with a range of tools and resources for learners. Students are able to access learner-centered content that can be adjusted and individualized, and it helps in the construction of knowledge. These tools include a discussion forum, chat, assessments, learning materials, and the ability to integrate third-party applications APIs. The aim is to create student-centered learning environments where the students improve themselves from the activities they do and think rather than being told what to do. If the study's goal is to recommend new opportunities to learn or to improve the way in which existing learning plans are implemented, then the overall efficacy of learning environments is of vital concern, not whether they are more successful with or without computers.

## 2.4 LMS ACCEPTANCE

The LMSA tool (Rachel et al., 2018) (*refer* Appendix I) was used to assess the LMS acceptance by the students. Students felt LMS is friendly, flexible, and pleasant. Most of the students have felt that more mental effort is not required to interact with LMS. Accessing the activities like assignment, quiz, blog, and forum discussion were easy. They were able to easily download the learning materials, submit assignments, and attend quizzes. They were able to access LMS through their smartphones/iPads/tablets without any difficulty. Most of the students have said that they were able to handle technical difficulties easily. Most of the students have said that LMS helped them to achieve well both in continuous internal assessment and also in comprehensive examination. They said that they can submit assignments, attend quizzes, discuss in forums, create blogs, and download learning materials from anywhere anytime. Immediate marks and feedback after attending quizzes were very useful for the students so they were able to correct their mistakes. The attitude towards LMS was that the students needed all subjects to be learned through LMS. They felt very positive towards LMS. The students have felt that learning the subjects through LMS is more difficult than learning in a traditional classroom. Because of LMS ease of use and perceived usefulness, students feel that it is becoming more popular in universities and colleges. Most of the students intended to be users of LMS frequently in their learning activities, recommend other students to use LMS, intend to use LMS as part of their daily learning activities, and use LMS in the future if they get any opportunity. Students felt that they could use LMS without any manual for reference and feel confident using the LMS. Most of the students felt that LMS maintains privacy and security. The assignment material, quiz marks, and feedback of a student by a tutor are not accessible by other students.

## 2.5 INFLUENCE OF CONSTRUCTIVIST LEARNING

The knowledge of the internet and the adaptability to new technology were considered to decide the sample for this research. The undergraduate students of Computer Applications were taken as a sample for the study. Constructivist On-Line Learning Environment Survey (COLLES) (Taylor, 2000) (*refer* Appendix II) was developed to explore the quality of online learning environments like LMS. The COLLES helps in exploring the impact to which LMS enriches students' methods of knowing because it is founded on the concept of social constructivism. In this study, COLLES was used to assess the students' usage of the LMS activities like learning materials, Chat, Assignment, Quiz, and Discussion Forum, blogs on students' participation and performance in light of social constructivist pedagogical principles.

COLLES has a five-point Likert scale (Almost Never, Seldom, Sometimes, Often, and Almost Always). It has 24 statements clustered into six scales, each of which addresses the worth of online learning and is shown below.

1. **Relevance:** It implies how far online learning is relevant to students' learning.
2. **Reflection:** It focuses on whether online learning arouses students' vital deep thinking.
3. **Interaction:** It means how far students engage in online communication.
4. **Making Sense:** How well do students and tutors relate to each other's online communications?
5. **Tutor Support:** To what extent do mentors facilitate student participation in e-learning?
6. **Peer Support:** It raises the question of whether there is support provided by peers.

From the collected data, it was found that students' constructivist learning enables them to think for themselves and engage in the process of acquiring knowledge. Students felt that constructivist learning through

LMS played a significant role for them and helped them to achieve good academic scores and improve their professional practice. They felt that what they learn is important and also complements their studies well. Constructivist learning made the students think about how they learn and about their own ideas as well as their peers' ideas. Constructivist learning encouraged students to interact with their peers through chat, blogs, and forum discussions. This allowed them to explain their concepts to their peers, ask their fellow students to explain their concepts, and receive responses from other students. This interaction paved the way for better communication skills. Most of the students felt that they gained valuable insights from other students' messages, and other students gained valuable insights from each other's messages. The students gained valuable insights from the tutor's messages, and the tutor gained valuable insights from the students' messages. Students felt that tutors stimulated their thinking, encouraged them to participate in blogs, discussions, and quizzes. They felt that the tutor facilitated critical knowledge construction. Students feel happy when their fellow students encourage them to actively participate, appreciate their efforts and contributions, and support them when they find it difficult to learn.

## 2.6 IMPLICATIONS

- Constructivist learning approach through LMS helped the students to learn themselves by using the forum, blog, chat, quiz activities of LMS anytime anywhere and improve their achievement score.
- The tutor has to tailor the needs of the students in preparing learning materials, topics for forum discussion, blog, chat, and also in preparing questions for quizzes. Once prepared, it can be used for many years with updates.
- This study enables the student to construct knowledge and to work in a group, so there is better understanding and adjustment among students and also to build self-confidence during the learning process.
- This study highlights the change from teacher-oriented to learner-oriented, where the students are free to explore things on their own and learn.
- Constructivist learning enables the student to learn through understanding rather than by memorization process.

## 2.7 CONCLUSION

The information and communication technology (ICT) has effectuated enormously in the teaching-learning process in higher educational institutes to face new challenges every day. In India, only a few reputed higher educational institutes provide LMS, and it is used only to distribute learning materials and other constructivist activities like assignments, forum discussions, chats, blogs, and quizzes are not used. As LMS Moodle is open-source software, a greater number of higher educational institutes can use it as it improves educational quality. Efforts should be made to make LMS popular in higher educational institutes in India. The present study sought to explore Constructivist Learning in LMS Moodle for students at Higher Educational Institutes. The study showed that the majority of the students have accepted the new way of learning through LMS. The findings showed that there is a positive relationship between LMS acceptance and the comprehensive examination (end-semester assessment), and this shows that the students found LMS easy to use, very useful to them, have a positive approach towards using it, and their behavioral objective towards using it. The use of blogs, chats, forum discussions, and quizzes has made way for the constructivist principles of interaction, social, and situational among the students. The findings showed that students' constructivist learning helped the students to academically perform better compared to students who learned using the traditional lecture method. This showed that students were able to think on their own and engage in the knowledge acquisition process. The present findings hold that students have accepted the LMS. The LMS has made a big impact on student learning, and the constructivist learning facilities in LMS have made way for the students to think on their own and gain knowledge.

The challenges faced by higher educational institutes in India are to provide quality education at minimal cost. Here LMS plays a vital role in imparting knowledge to the students through its constructivist learning approach. Higher educational institutes in India should use LMS for higher education of the students where perfect access, flexible schedules, quality learning materials, and a complete delivery method are provided through it. The constructivist learning provides students with a flexible learning environment and enhanced achievement score. The findings in the present study show that students who used constructivist learning through LMS were student-centered and scored better compared to students who learned using the traditional lecture method. Higher educational institutes should incorporate constructivist-based LMS where qualities like innovation, interest, potentialities, collaboration, observation, prediction, fact-finding, discussion, and investigation develop among the students to enhance quality education.

## APPENDIX I

### ➢ Learning Management System Acceptance (LMSA) Tool:

| SL. No. | Questions | SA | A | D | SD |
|---|---|---|---|---|---|
| | **Perceived Ease of Use (PEU)** | | | | |
| 1. | I find LMS is easy and friendly to use. | | | | |
| 2. | LMS is flexible and interactive to learn subjects. | | | | |
| 3. | The interface is pleasant. | | | | |
| 4. | It is easy to become skillful in using LMS. | | | | |
| 5. | I find LMS not easy to use because of my lack of experience. | | | | |
| 6. | Interacting with LMS requires much mental effort. | | | | |
| 7. | The language used in LMS is easy to understand. | | | | |
| 8. | Accessing the activities (assignment, quiz, learning materials, forum) are easy. | | | | |
| 9. | Activities such as assignment, learning material, quiz, and forums in LMS are clear and understandable. | | | | |
| 10. | LMS is a package where learning materials, assignment, quiz, forums are all at one web portal. | | | | |
| 11. | It is convenient to download learning materials in .ppt, .doc, and .pdf format. | | | | |
| 12. | It is easier to listen to the audio-based learning materials. | | | | |
| 13. | It is easier to view the video-based learning materials. | | | | |
| 14. | Allows to access learning materials as many times as needed. | | | | |
| 15. | It is convenient to upload assignment as a file in any format (.doc, .pdf, and .ppt). | | | | |
| 16. | It is convenient to submit assignment by typing text in text editor. | | | | |
| 17. | LMS helps to add images easily in assignment preparation. | | | | |
| 18. | Hyperlinks in activities (assignment, quiz, learning materials, forum) are properly connected. | | | | |

**APPENDIX I** *(Continued)*

| SL. No. | Questions | SA | A | D | SD |
|---|---|---|---|---|---|
| 19. | Accessing links to the external web resources is easy. | | | | |
| 20. | It is convenient to attend multiple choice online quiz. | | | | |
| 21. | It is convenient to attend short answers in quiz. | | | | |
| 22. | It is convenient to attend descriptive answers in quiz. | | | | |
| 23. | Easy to participate in the survey. | | | | |
| 24. | Easy to communicate with other students through 'chat' feature. | | | | |
| 25. | Easy to communicate with other students through 'message' feature. | | | | |
| 26. | Easy to communicate with teacher through 'chat' feature. | | | | |
| 27. | Easy to communicate with teacher through 'message' feature. | | | | |
| 28. | LMS can be accessed anytime through internet from inside the campus. | | | | |
| 29. | LMS can be accessed anytime through internet from outside the campus. | | | | |
| 30. | LMS can be accessed through smart phones. | | | | |
| 31. | LMS can be accessed through iPad/tablet devices. | | | | |
| 32. | Easy to handle technical difficulties if arises. | | | | |
| | **Perceived Usefulness (PU)** | | | | |
| 1. | LMS improves my academic achievement (internal/external marks). | | | | |
| 2. | Has a positive effect on my learning. | | | | |
| 3. | LMS with the support of traditional teaching method helps me to learn better. | | | | |
| 4. | Learning materials uploaded are available throughout the semester and hence it gives flexibility to learn anytime. | | | | |
| 5. | LMS gives me learning materials and other information that I need at right time. | | | | |
| 6. | Helps in accessing unit wise 'learning materials' according to the syllabus. | | | | |
| 7. | The calendar in LMS helps to know the assignment submission date. | | | | |
| 8. | The calendar helps to know the quiz participation date. | | | | |
| 9. | Helps to improve questioning and answering performances in forum participation. | | | | |
| 10. | Submission of assignment, attending quiz, downloading learning materials can be done from anywhere. | | | | |

**APPENDIX I** *(Continued)*

| SL. No. | Questions | SA | A | D | SD |
|---|---|---|---|---|---|
| 11. | LMS allows me to complete assignment on time than would otherwise be not possible if submission done manually. | | | | |
| 12. | Feedback on assignment given by the teacher is very useful to learn further. | | | | |
| 13. | LMS allows me to participate in quiz on time than would otherwise be not possible. | | | | |
| 14. | Attending quiz helps to test the knowledge gained from learning materials distributed through LMS. | | | | |
| 15. | Attending quiz helps to test the knowledge taught in traditional teaching. | | | | |
| 16. | Knowing the immediate answer (feedback) at the end of the quiz helps to correct the mistakes. | | | | |
| 17. | Helps to know the marks immediately after submission of quiz. | | | | |
| 18. | News forum in LMS is useful to know the events. | | | | |
| 19. | RSS feed in LMS is useful to know the current news. | | | | |
| | **Attitude Toward Usage (ATU)** | | | | |
| 1. | Learning through LMS is a good idea. | | | | |
| 2. | LMS makes me to realize anywhere and anytime learning. | | | | |
| 3. | I feel positive towards LMS. | | | | |
| 4. | LMS has all the functions and capabilities required for a learning environment. | | | | |
| 5. | LMS has to be an essential part of this graduation program. | | | | |
| 6. | Wish all the subjects be taught by face-to-face/traditional learning method and supported through LMS. | | | | |
| 7. | Wish all the subjects be taught by face-to-face/traditional learning method only. | | | | |
| 8. | Wish all the subjects be taught through LMS only. | | | | |
| 9. | Interested in using LMS for all subjects. | | | | |
| 10. | LMS is useful only when teacher provides appropriate learning materials and relevant activities. | | | | |
| 11. | Believe I could become successful in using LMS. | | | | |
| 12. | Learning the subjects through LMS is more difficult than learning in a traditional classroom. | | | | |

**APPENDIX I** *(Continued)*

| SL. No. | Questions | SA | A | D | SD |
|---|---|---|---|---|---|
| 13. | The organization of information on the screens of LMS is clear and understandable. | | | | |
| 14. | LMS requires proficiency in information technology (IT). | | | | |
| 15. | Learning through LMS is acceptable. | | | | |
| 16. | LMS is becoming more popular in universities and colleges. | | | | |
| | **Behavioral Intention to Use (BIU)** | | | | |
| 1. | I intend to be a user of LMS frequently in my learning activities. | | | | |
| 2. | I like to use new learning methods other than traditional way of learning. | | | | |
| 3. | I intend to learn more about the features of LMS. | | | | |
| 4. | I would recommend other students to use LMS. | | | | |
| 5. | I intend to continue using LMS every semester. | | | | |
| 6. | I intend to use LMS as part of my daily learning activities. | | | | |
| 7. | I will use LMS in the future if I get any opportunity. | | | | |
| | **Self-Efficacy (SE)** | | | | |
| 1. | I could use the LMS if only I had the manual for reference. | | | | |
| 2. | I could use the LMS if I see someone else using it before trying it myself. | | | | |
| 3. | I could access learning materials on the LMS even if there is no one around to show me how to use it. | | | | |
| 4. | I feel confident using the LMS. | | | | |
| 5. | I have the necessary skills for using LMS. | | | | |
| | **Access Control (AC)** | | | | |
| 1. | The submission of assignment material by me is accessible only by the teacher. | | | | |
| 2. | I cannot see other student's assignment material. | | | | |
| 3. | I cannot see other student's assignment marks. | | | | |
| 4. | The feedback for assignment given by the teacher is accessible only by me. | | | | |
| 5. | I cannot see other's student's feedback given by the teacher. | | | | |
| 6. | I cannot see other student's quiz marks. | | | | |

## APPENDIX II

### ➢ Constructivist Online Learning Environment:

| SL. No. | Questions | Almost Never | Seldom | Sometimes | Often | Almost Always |
|---|---|---|---|---|---|---|
| | **Relevance** | | | | | |
| | In this online unit I prefer that | | | | | |
| 1. | My learning focuses on issues that interest me. | | | | | |
| 2. | What I learn is important for my professional practice. | | | | | |
| 3. | I learn how to improve my professional practice. | | | | | |
| 4. | What I learn connects well with my professional practice. | | | | | |
| | **Reflection** | | | | | |
| | In this online unit I prefer that | | | | | |
| 5. | I think critically about how I learn. | | | | | |
| 6. | I think critically about my own ideas. | | | | | |
| 7. | I think critically about other student's ideas. | | | | | |
| 8. | I think critically about ideas in the readings. | | | | | |
| | **Interaction** | | | | | |
| | In this online unit I prefer that | | | | | |
| 9. | I explain my ideas to other students. | | | | | |
| 10. | I ask other students to explain their ideas. | | | | | |
| 11. | Other students ask me to explain my ideas. | | | | | |
| 12. | Other students respond to my ideas. | | | | | |
| | **Making Sense** | | | | | |
| | In this online unit I prefer that | | | | | |
| 13. | I make good sense of other student's messages. | | | | | |
| 14. | Other students make good sense of my messages. | | | | | |
| 15. | I make good sense of tutor's messages. | | | | | |
| 16. | The tutor makes good sense of my messages. | | | | | |

**APPENDIX II** *(Continued)*

| SL. No. | Questions | Almost Never | Seldom | Sometimes | Often | Almost Always |
|---|---|---|---|---|---|---|
| | **Tutor Support** | | | | | |
| | In this online unit I prefer that | | | | | |
| 17. | The tutor stimulates my thinking. | | | | | |
| 18. | The tutor encourages me to participate. | | | | | |
| 19. | The tutor model's good discourse. | | | | | |
| 20. | The tutor models critical self-reflection. | | | | | |
| | **Peer Support** | | | | | |
| | In this online unit I prefer that | | | | | |
| 21. | Other students encourage my participation. | | | | | |
| 22. | Other students praise my contribution. | | | | | |
| 23. | Other students value my contribution. | | | | | |
| 24. | Other students empathize with my struggle to learn. | | | | | |

## KEYWORDS

- **constructivist learning**
- **environment tools**
- **higher education**
- **information and communication technology**
- **learning management system**
- **Moodle**
- **online learning**

## REFERENCES

Al-Ajlan, A., & Zedan, H., (2008). Why Moodle. *Proceedings of 12th IEEE International Workshop on Future Trends of Distributed Computing Systems (FTDCS)* (pp. 58–64).

IEEE Press, Kunming, China. https://www.researchgate.net/publication/232615507_Why_Moodle (accessed on 13 December 2023).

Al-Busaidi, K. A., & Al-Shihi, H., (2010). *Instructors Acceptance of Learning Management Systems: A Theoretical Framework.* IBIMA Publishing Communications of IBIMA. Retrieved from: https://ibimapublishing.com/articles/CIBIMA/2010/862128/862128.pdf (accessed on 13 December 2023).

Berry, M., (2005). *An Investigation of the Effectiveness of MOODLE in Primary Education.*

Brandl, K., (2005). Are you ready to "MOODLE"? *Language Learning and Technology, 9*, 16–23. University of Washington. https://research.moodle.org/100/1/Brandl%20%282005%29%20Are%20you%20ready%20to%20%27%27Moodle%27%27.pdf (accessed on 13 December 2023).

Brooks, J. G., (1990). Teachers and students: Constructivist forging new connections. *Educational Leadership, 47*(5), 68–71. https://eric.ed.gov/?id=EJ402402 (accessed on 13 December 2023).

Campus Computing, (2008). *The 2008 Campus Computing Survey.* Encino, CA: The Campus Computing Project.

Cole, J., (2005). *Using Moodle: Teaching with the Popular Open-Source Course Management System.* ISBN: 0596008635, O'Reilly. https://www.researchgate.net/publication/220694026_Using_Moodle_teachingwith_the_popular_open_source_course_management_system (accessed on 13 December 2023).

Daniels, H.,(2010). Reflections on points of departure in the development of socio cultural and activity theory. In: Van, O. B., Wardekke, W., Elber, E., & Van, D. V. R., (eds.), *The Transformation of Learning* [Kindle Edition]. Cambridge: Cambridge University Press. https://www.researchgate.net/profile/Rupert_Wegerif/publication/236950592_Reason_and_Dialogue_in_Education/links/00b7d530118ac6ba8f000000.pdf#page=74 (accessed on 13 December 2023).

Dougiamas, M., & Taylor, P., (2002). Interpretive analysis of an internet based course constructed using a new courseware tool called Moodle. In: *HERDSA 2002 Conference*, (Perth, Australia), Curtin University of Technology. https://www.researchgate.net/profile/Peter_Taylor11/publication/246515358Interpretive_analysis_of_an_internetbased_course_constructed_using_a_new_courseware_tool_called_Moodle/links/0c960529ee85a5a57a000000/Interpretive-analysis-of-an-internet-based-course-constructed-using-a-new-courseware-tool-called-Moodle.pdf (accessed on 13 December 2023).

Dougiamas, M., & Taylor, P., (2003). Moodle: Using learning communities to create an open-source course management system. *Proceedings of the EDMEDIA 2003 Conference*, Honolulu, Hawaii. Retrieved from: https://researchrepository.murdoch.edu.au/id/eprint/36645/1/Moodle%20Create.pdf (accessed on 13 December 2023).

Dougiamas, M., (2011). Retrieved from: http://www.MOODLE.org (accessed on 13 December 2023).

EduTools, (2006). *Course Management Systems.* EduTools. Retrieved from: https://www.edutools.info/about/ (accessed on 13 December 2023).

Ellis, R. K., (2001). LCMS roundup. *Learning Circuits* (Vol. 8, No. 2). ASTDs Sources for E-learning; https://www.exactls.com/news/lcms-technology-in-todays-elearning-ecosystem/ (accessed on 13 December 2023).

Fosnot, C. T., (1996). Preface. In: Fosnot, C. T., (ed.), *Constructivism: Theory, Perspectives and Practice* (p. 9). New York: Teachers College, Press. https://eric.ed.gov/?id=ED396998 (accessed on 13 December 2023).

Greenberg, L., (2002). LMS and LCMS: What's the difference. *Learning Circuits, 31*(2). https://www.researchgate.net/publication/264858045_LMS_and_LCMSWhat's_the_Difference (accessed on 13 December 2023).

Jonassen, D.,(1991). Evaluating constructivist learning. *Educational Technology, 31*, 28–33. https://eric.ed.gov/?id=EJ433315 (accessed on 13 December 2023).

Koh, K., (2006). *MOODLE as a Course Management System*. eslweb.org, Retrieved from: http://cdn.intechopen.com/pdfs/27926/InTechA_comparative_study_between_e_learning_features.pdf (accessed on 13 December 2023).

Martin, C., Morris-Cotterill, N., & Smith, M., (2004). *Open-Source Software for the Education Market*. Eduforge. Retrieved from: http://eduforge.org (accessed on 13 December 2023).

McCombs, & Whisler,(1997). *The Learner-Centered Classroom and School: Strategies for Increasing Student Motivation and Achievement*. San Francisco: Jossey-Bass.

Perrie, Y.,(2003). Virtual learning environment. *The Pharmaceutical Journal, 270*, 794, 795.

Peter, T., et al., (2000).Assessing the efficacy of online teaching with the constructivist on-line learning environment survey. *Teaching and Learning Forum*. https://researchrepository.murdoch.edu.au/id/eprint/8750/1/TL_Forum_2000__Taylor_and_Maor_-_the_Constructivist_On-Line_LearningEnvironmentSurvey.pdf (accessed on 13 December 2023).

Rachel, V., & Parthasarathy, M., (2016). Learning management system using open-source Moodle for computer science students in higher educational institute. *International Journal of Computer Science & Engineering Technology (IJCSET)*.

Rachel, V., & Parthasarathy, M., (2018).Acceptance of learning management system among undergraduate computer science students using extended technology acceptance model. *Shanlax International Journal of Education*.

Reigeluth, C. M., Watson, W. R., et al., (2008). Roles for technology in the information-age paradigm of education: Learning management systems. *Educational Technology, 48*(6), 32–40. http://www.edtechlearning.org/wp-content/uploads/2017/01/lms-and-constructivism.pdf (accessed on 13 December 2023).

Steffe, L. P., & Gale, J., (1995).*Constructivism in Education*. Hillsdale, NJ: Lawrence Erlbaum., http://emis.muni.cz/journals/ZDM/zdm982r2.pdf (accessed on 13 December 2023).

Twigg, C., (2003). Improving learning and reducing costs: New models for online learning. *EducauseReview, 38*(5), 28–38. https://www.unf.edu/uploadedFiles/ aa/acadaffairs/provost/Twigg%20online%20learning.pdf (accessed on 13 December 2023).

Twigg, C., (2003). Improving quality and reducing cost: Designs for effective learning. *Change, 35*(4), 22–29. https://www.tandfonline.com/doi/abs/10.1080/00091380309604107 (accessed on 13 December 2023).

Vishal, P., (2003). *Learning Management System and Learning Content Management System: An Overview*. Workshop on Content Development and Standards in e-learning. Hyderabad: CDAC.

Watson, W. R., & Watson, S. L., (2007). An argument for clarity: What are learning management systems, what are they not, and what should they become. *TechTrends, 51*(2), 28–34. https://hal.archives-ouvertes.fr/hal-00692067/document (accessed on 13 December 2023).

Wharekura-tini, H., & Aotearoa, K., (2004). *Technical Evaluation of Selected Learning Management Systems*. Master's thesis, Catalyst IT Limited, Open Polytechnic of New Zealand.

Zenha-Rela, M., & Carvalho, R., (2006). Works in progress: Self-evaluation through monitored peer review using the Moodle platform. *Proceedings of the 36th Annual Education Conference* (pp. 26, 27). San Diego, CA, Univ, IEEE. https://www.researchgate.net/publication/224061122_Work_in_Progress_Self_Evaluation_Through_Monitored_Peer_Review_Using_the_Moodle_Platform (accessed on 13 December 2023).

## CHAPTER 3

# Future University Transformation Through Innovation and Inclusion: New Global Directions for Higher Education

SANDRA PAREDES[1] and R. S. S. NEHRU[2,3]

[1]*Assistant Professor, School of Humanities and Education, Tecnologico de Monterrey, Mexico*

[2]*Assistant Professor, Department of Education, Sikkim University, Gangtok, Sikkim, India*

[3]*Post-Doctoral Scholar (DLit, in Education), Sambalpur University, Sambalpur, Odisha, India*

## ABSTRACT

People, universities, and governments have dealt with different problems and setbacks. However, research has helped reduce the destructive effects of COVID-19 around the world, and people have come to trust science and universities as good places to get information. When looking at India and Mexico as examples of global higher education, you can see the current system, how it has changed along the lines of innovation and inclusion, and what the future holds. Inequalities have been exposed and worsened by the outbreak. Now is the time to reorganize international education so that less-developed regions and underserved populations have equal and fair access to high-quality education. Higher education's mission has become more critical than ever before. Moreover, as top priorities, we must address these concerns and establish significant collaboration, such

Intelligent Learning Paradigms and Student Empowerment: Digital Integration and Transformation.
Souvik Pal, Ton Quang Cuong, & R. S. S. Nehru (Eds.)

as collaborative laboratories and big research initiatives. We should be more transparent and united in dealing with global threats and issues at this time.

We have attempted to comprehend the system, its regulation, change, opportunities, and problems and provide essential recommendations in this chapter. This qualitative conceptual study uses secondary data from websites, research papers, journals, articles, polls, and government publications. Discussions with specialists in higher education are included in this study. Analysis and difficulties are based on a detailed examination of the Indian and Mexican regulations, transformations, and policy papers for a futuristic vision in global higher education. It is critical to rethink monetary funds, access, equality, and equity. India's and Mexico's higher education needs a systematic approach; This study examines regulations, SWOT analysis, and problems in global higher education; The study produced creative solutions.

## 3.1 INTRODUCTION

Most innovative universities use distance learning to speed up, save money, and give students more freedom with traditional tasks. New universities use the terms "distance teaching," "remote education," and "online learning" to talk about the same thing: letting students of all ages learn without going to class in person. This first benefit allows learners and instructors to be flexible; distance classes may be more comfortable. Part-time students can keep working and advance in their careers. Also, some students may lack concentration in the mornings but be more productive in the afternoons or at night. This teaching method allows students and instructors to change their schedules. Despite email availability, some of the 30 students in a lecture hall may need to express how they are learning. There is much flexibility with distance education. The COVID-19 pandemic highlighted the adaptability and ease of distance learning. As well as managing time multitaskers included skill acquisition in areas like online research, video conferencing, and discussion boards, as well as quicker learning results, are all possible due to the accessibility of existing learning materials. Students can save money on transportation and food because this teaching method requires fewer fixed costs for the university. Distance learning saves money for both universities and students. This affordability improves technological literacy and lowers education costs per capita, improving economic competitiveness.

According to Ahedo (2016) and Stone (2019), colleges risk losing sight of their essential mission of educating students in a humanistic and truth-seeking manner. For these authors, the contemporary university should remember that teachers must transmit knowledge in a way that incorporates all knowledge and is not fragmented. According to Goyal (2011) and Pauwels (2020), students now share their learning stories via blogs, YouTube, Instagram, TikTok, and other social media platforms. Internet news. In a Gallup poll, young people chose 'boring' as their top term to describe college, followed by 'weary' inclined to choose descriptors "above average" of learning and currently in learning where results increase dedication drops (Ramsay, 2020).

- Problem-solving thinking;
- Collaboration;
- Adaptability;
- Initiative and business;
- Communication;
- Data mining;
- Inquiry and fantasy.

According to other research, addressing the human resources and entrepreneurship crises requires nurturing human potential in a style of university education that allows for individual learning results. The university's influence will be extended (Feliz, 2005; Jonker et al., 2020; Toraman et al., 2020). Educational goals should always be lifelong learning, global engagement, and metacognition. Interaction is emphasized. Learners interact with the content, each other, and teachers (Dede & Richards, 2020).

A study of higher education students' dedication, interaction, and participation suggested they should be concerned with pragmatic possibilities where they use their academic knowledge by interacting with peers. The challenge is disseminating knowledge adept at discoursing global and essential concerns (Arocena & Sutz, 2001; Nursalam, 2020). "The new generation of university students appears to favor an educational paradigm based on activity and engagement," argue Flynn & Vredevoogd (2010).

Created the phrase "Digital Natives" in 2001, prefer small group discussions, frequently conducted on digital platforms, to massive lecture halls. According to this source, pupils prefer search engines over library analysis (Sanchiz et al., 2020).

According to authors like Philip & Zakariya (2020), the demand for experiential learning messages educators. Faculty-student interaction has recently evolved study co-designed courses where the student helps specify the learning outcomes and the skills. The faculty will be in charge of certifying their progress. The faculty will be able to construct multi-disciplinary and disciplinary study programs. The most critical thing is to transform the problematic curriculum into a rich and diverse one.

## 3.2 EAST AND WEST TRENDS IN FUTURE HIGHER EDUCATION

Following Japan's lead, regional trends in higher education have grown increasingly prominent globally. In Southeast Asian countries like South Korea, Singapore, China, Hong Kong, and Taiwan, there are more universities. The post-Confucian systems have achieved three goals, according to Hawkins, Mok, & Neubauer (2018): and the post-Confucian systems have achieved three goals.

- Rapid growth in interest and involvement;
- The brisk pace of scientific progress;
- The accelerated merger of elite educational institutions.

The higher education system or university research has progressed at this rate, according to Moore et al. (2019); Tan et al. (2007); and Walkinshaw et al. (2009). Hou (2015) asserts that Asian universities have adopted a "glocal" (global, national, and local) strategy to facilitate student mobility and recognition. East Asia and Singapore governments have strongly emphasized developing WCUs, with the latter taking their status and research models mainly from the United States (USA), the United Kingdom (UK), and Western Europe. Akin to Japan's imperial institutions, China's Peking University (founded in 1898) and Korea's Seoul National University (1946) all have endowments for specific purposes. The Hong Kong University of Science and Technology (HUST), which opened its doors in 1991, is one example of a successful modern model (2009).

1. Develop innovative leadership and entrepreneurship skills that will lead to technologies that meet societal needs, in line with the UN's latest global goals.

This trend represents both a challenge and an opportunity for Australia, whose geographic location and Asian-influenced demographics may allow it to develop its research capacity further, as Brennan & Zip (2019), and cultural capacity to interact with the systems of the region. Does a nation believe that a future university will be a force for social change? This list will be centered on new institutions or how universities can update their vision and mission statements to reflect a particular stage of societal development. Here is our model for "Five Dimensions for Innovative Universities.

i. **New Domains/Disciplines:** Biotechnology, medical technologies for endoscopic interventions, human genomic analytics, and specialization in different kinds of cancer research, space travel, gravity, and outer space meteorology should be judged based on their importance.
ii. **Educative Focus:** The professional and scientific perspectives are essential. Professional, and differentiating these two aspects. Many universities are transitioning to a two-tier system.

2. Develop innovative entrepreneurial leadership skills that can lead to the intervention of technologies that meet societal needs, in line with the UN's last global goals.
3. Mastering soft skills like peace and tolerance, flexibility, and conflict resolution can improve people's quality of life and well-being.

A university's reputation is an asset that can be used to market the school, get more students, and raise money. For students, society, and international rankings, it is essential that institutes are known for their long-term quality. There are, for example, learning support systems on the web, MOOCs (massive open online courses), and mobile learning through smartphones. Both educators and students have an ongoing need for training in the use of digital tools like Twitter and blogging. The technology used in universities is a prime example.

Didactics Pedagogy Supported by AI/ICT: Pedagogical models that allow new web- or cloud-based media are needed for mediated course delivery and remote assessment. "A Story with Gamification" is an excellent way for teachers to get students involved and help them take charge of their learning.

Using the top five dimensions of innovation, a future university can be put into three categories: high, medium, or low ambition. The goal of this concept study is to make a new university that prepares students for the technology and leadership roles of the future in a society that is changing. It is still working on its mission statement, but it must be up to date.

The new society's readiness:

- Boost the economy's competitiveness.
- Mastering soft skills peace and tolerance, adaptability, and the ability to resolve conflict can improve the quality of life and well-being of the people.
- Ecological and environmental awareness.
- Through research and lifelong self-training, students can get, make, and use new technologies based on their and other societies' needs.
- Cultivate creative leadership and entrepreneurial expertise to bring technologies that serve society's needs, in line with the United Nations' most recent global goals.

Choosing between a "new old university" and a "new university" is necessary when starting a new one; The second benefit of not adhering to the rigid structures of conventional universities is earning a better reputation. Even after receiving full accreditation from national authorities, it took a good two decades for many polytechnic high schools to be recognized as "full universities" in many parts of the world.

An excellent illustration of a category is FUH. Since its establishment in 2000, its reputation and levels of student satisfaction have steadily increased. It is growing its network of international exchanges. Any future university might apply a similar framework for close collaboration. University-Society Relations and Collaboration Center (CRC).

To connect corporations, regional governments, industry, and citizen organizations with collaborative research and trustee research programs. The CRC encourages teachers and students to get involved in their local communities to help the institution build a society for the 21$^{st}$ century.

Austria's Internet Institute Wien is a think tank with the mission of creating world-class centers for social innovation by connecting individuals, groups, and businesses committed to making the world a better place via the use of science and technology. The "Future University" is the emphasis of its academic program (AP), "building innovation and technological capacities of universities."

## 3.3 A NEW MODEL OF FUTURE UNIVERSITY

The university of the future is drawn as a hybrid ecosystem of innovation where bottom-up and top-down models are combined with three critical aspects: priority to the development of the faculty, increase of university-company collaborations, and effective mediation between entrepreneurs and innovations as proposed by Heaton, Siegel, & Teece in 2019. For its part, Ahedo (2016) establishes that the growing preference of students for experiential learning favors this model and is reflected in a growing demand for APs that develop practical skills (Figure 3.1).

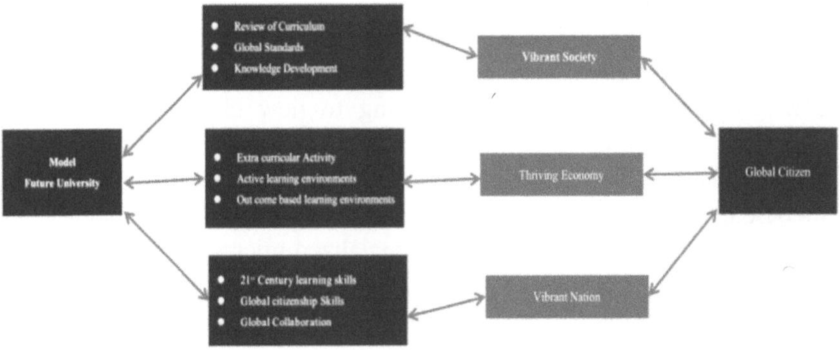


**FIGURE 3.1** Future university model.

In the so-called "new university model," the "negotiated curriculum" is another trend that is gaining popularity. In this model, learners can make decisions based on creating a personalized and relevant training path that lets them stay in charge of their learning. As a result, he is assumed to be not only a reader and writer, but also a creative planner and executor of his learning. The permanent link between activity and experimental and hybrid learning will be ideal in designing higher education courses for the 21st-century graduate, where memorized learning will be insufficient, according to Helyer (2011); and Wilson (2013). Learning can quickly occur outside the classroom and become more meaningful if it takes place in natural work settings. This type of action-oriented learning has been privileged in the UK for 25 years. For this reason, the study carried out by the Academic Research Center of the University of Phoenix in 2011 concluded that the skills indicated by employers, students, and universities required in future graduates would be the following:

- Critical thinking for decision making;
- Social intelligence;
- Innovative thinking;
- Multicultural competence;
- Computational thinking of data interpretation;
- Ability to use new means of communication and interaction;
- Transdisciplinary;
- Approach to design;
- Knowledge management;
- Virtual collaboration ability.

The combination of economic forces, more excellent candidates, and new demands from employers suggest that university graduates must constantly develop and grow, adapting to new challenges. The work experience implemented in higher education programs represents a growth opportunity. Similarly, how higher education graduates will enter the labor market is changing: an increasing number of them will establish their businesses, and others will work in specialized micro-enterprises or under various short-term contracts; that is why learning practical skills will equip them with the skills required to cope with these changing environments, following Kaufman (2019).

Because of today's complicated society, the chance to design the learning process is critical. This approach stems from eight years of pedagogical innovation-focused didactic experiments by University College of North Denmark teachers and Cornwall College centered on self-directed learning and problem-solving learning. Students can make decisions in specific curriculum areas for more meaningful, relevant, and successful learning. It also responds to the future education demands of society and the workplace. Students who actively created their learning processes showed stronger self-management and self-regulation of learning, supported continual issue-solving, and favored their transformation processes.

One of the main challenges of this learning approach is a greater demand for student and teacher involvement since the former must develop self-direction skills and experience periods of uncertainty in the design process. The latter must be open and willing to letting go of control of the process and accepting the participation of the student, at the same time that it must be sufficiently explicit in the establishment of formal objectives and curricular demands, which, according to Wong & Chiu (2019), gives rise to a new type of relationship between student and teacher.

The issue of learning space has become a challenge for colleges worldwide; Park & Choi (2014) say that the Student-Centered Experiential Learning Environment for Undergraduate Programs was designed to assist students in learning how to solve issues, comprehending concepts, cultivating a more positive attitude toward education, and experiencing a lower percentage of academic failure. More than 250 universities in the US have redesigned classrooms to improve learning. It has so far spread to the University of Tokyo and the Israel Institute of Technology. Similar to the Technology Enabled Active Instructional Project at MIT, which reconfigured classrooms (TEAL), Dori & Belcher (2004), and Sandi et al. (2020) reported that this project uses multimedia software to simulate and visualize desktop trials and internet-based tasks.

The leaders of the most powerful countries are aware that science and technology are crucial for the future of their nations. However, Nussbaum (2016) declares that the Arts and Humanities are not left aside in the university of the 21st century since he considers them a source of crucial skills for the healthy growth of nations and their cultures, including critical thinking, the ability to transcend the local environment, and to face global problems as citizens of the world. Similarly, Huye (2015) and Garrett (2013) argue that exposing students to the arts improves their academic performance. Skorton (2019) adds that they become capable of evaluating content and connecting it with real-world problems.

A study of political and business leaders found that fine arts education helped encourage creativity, curiosity, imagination, and evaluation skills, considered essential leadership skills. A study conducted at the University of Michigan (Parker et al., 2013) revealed that those graduates with outstanding results from careers related to science, technology, engineering, or mathematics (STEM) had been exposed to the arts eight times more than those who did not achieve outstanding performance.

In 2015, as a result of studies carried out (Piro, 2010; Boy, 2013; Park & Ko, 2012) and of the report on the economic impact of arts and culture published in 2014 by the United States Chamber of Economic Analysis, According to statements made by Setiawan, educational researchers advocated for changing the acronym STEM to STEAM, putting emphasis on art and design in the middle of STEM because they are thought to be catalysts for the imagination, creativity, and innovation skills needed by students.

The University of the future then, and now following, will have to respond to multiple questions related to changes in the type of students, more flexible teaching, cooperation between universities and with other centers, interdisciplinary, specialization, mobility, and new forms of management in the face of the following challenges.

- Increasing predominance, in general, of the teaching function over that of research and cooperative research (with other universities or national or international research centers) over the individual.
- Students will change: the training of adults to learn throughout life will have greater weight due to the intellectual concerns of the growing population of retirees.
- Greater flexibility in choosing the study program (curriculum) and following the learning process (face-to-face/online; at home/work/class).
- Growing cooperation between universities on a national and international scale to offer prestigious products, taking advantage of each university's best.
- Increase interdisciplinary programs and collaboration with extra-university institutions (companies, foundations, public, and private teaching, and research centers).
- Need for specialization for each university in an environment of increasing competition with other higher education centers (public, private, corporate, national, or international universities).
- Profound organizational transformation to respond to these demands for change.
- Prioritize the mobility of teachers and students and language training (especially in English).

The location of learning and whether it occurs in person in conventional classrooms or virtually through a device will be less significant in the future because learning will occur in both settings indistinctly under the direction of the teacher. The most important thing would be to understand how, why, and what the person does with his new knowledge.

For all the above, the redefinition educational model of a university that aims to train the necessary leaders in our country and world must be based on its history, values, and mission. They require the teaching tasks to be narrowed to research and technology transfer (Davidson & Goldberg, 2009; Novak, 2019) and institutional vision, with a systemic projection in all fundamental academic processes.

## 3.4 FUTURE UNIVERSITY PARADIGMS

### *3.4.1 THEMATIC TEACHING WILL REPLACE DISCIPLINE-BASED INSTRUCTION*

The education at traditional universities is based on disciplines, not on themes. Compare this to world-famous Western universities like the University of Texas at Austin (USA), Durham University (UK), Heriot-Watt University (Scotland), and RMIT University in Melbourne (AUS) where faculty actively promote theme-based rather than discipline-based teaching. The proposed university model uses thematic learning to change how people are taught. For each subject, a central theme is chosen.

For example, artificial intelligence (AI) and new technologies like robotics would be adopted as modules for nanotechnology because they are not as up to date. In drug delivery and computational modeling, it is essential to be able to work at nanoscales. Nagoya University in Japan has also tried to bring together nanotechnology and robotics. There are also research courses in intelligent systems and nanoscience that you can take at the University of York. Even traditional universities with much technology still need this level of development.

The idea of sustainability will also go into making the disciplines. Climate change, global warming, and cutting down trees are recent environmental problems. There are also these environmental problems in places where universities only use old teaching methods. For example, oil refineries in the Gulf region pollute the air and water (Ouda et al., 2016). When many people are living in cities, there is also much trash that needs to be taken care of. These are just a few things students in these countries should be aware of. US universities like West Chester University (West Chester, Pennsylvania, USA), Metropolitan State University (Saint Paul, Minnesota, USA), and the University of Utah (Salt Lake City, Utah, USA) know that interdisciplinary teaching is vital for sustainability (Gosselin et al., 2016).

Environmental issues are addressed in science courses. The proposed model for universities would also teach students to care about the environment. The environment will be considered for STEM courses like robotics, AI, and HCI. Students will learn how to make control systems that use less energy and get more done in these classes. Students will also learn ways to industrialize silicone and sand with little energy but high output. In countries where people do not care as much about the environment, a mix of these courses could be offered to raise awareness across different fields. Some countries' promises on these issues are hidden in signed agreements and folders. The new university model we suggest here aims to fix these problems by using new teaching and research methods.

Some countries, especially those with the money to do so, need to change how they teach, so they build a new university. So, accepting our idea is just a matter of politics. The Saudi Vision 2030 wants to create a "thriving economy," "vibrant society," and "ambitious nation" (Investment, 2016; Gazette, 2016). Vision 2030 says that the only way to reach these goals is to change how people are educated. Also, a country's natural wealth is its children and grandchildren, who will help it get richer. Preparing can only be done by giving these people the right educational tools and strengthening the tertiary education sector. Some countries seem socially and culturally behind their peers (Alnahdi, 2014). The goal is to make a university that actively looks for knowledge that crosses religious and cultural lines and will help make a fundamental change to an economy based on knowledge.

## 3.5 NEW TECH AND SOFT SKILLS TRENDS

A good university has many places to do research. For example, Singaporean universities are known for their research in STEM (Tan & Ang, 2017). With the proposed model, research centers would be set up for degree programs like Bioengineering, Radiology, Simulation, and Biotechnology. New technologies like remote surgery, technology forensics, retinal recognition, voice banking, and branchless financial institutions could be the focus of research projects. Research-intensive facilities would be prioritized in the proposed model to help students understand, make, and use new technologies.

The suggested university model tries to reach these goals by encouraging innovative leadership and entrepreneurship. The sustainable development goals (SDGs) for 2030 focus on a changing society, an economy that is doing well, and a country that wants to do its best. Students will benefit from the acquisition of both academic and "soft skills" through the use of these strategies. Countries with more conservative higher education systems should follow suit.

As was already said, students will learn how to design creative technology that meets societal needs like sustainability. Buildings and transportation use intelligent materials, like the solar cars designed at the Masdar Institute and MIT. The UAE has made progress in this area. A good education at university will also help them become involved and happy members of society. Investment in STEAM (Science, Technology, Engineering, Arts, and Mathematics) research facilities and leadership development programs will inspire the next generation to envision grand goals for their country. As seen in current global organizations, next-generation networking and cloud computing would also be used for international collaboration to help Vision 2030's goal of an ambitious nation come true.

A good university helps students grow as people by teaching them soft skills and good values like peace and tolerance for everyone, no matter what caste, color, creed, or religion they are. Soft skills are what you need to be able to get along with other people. In conservative countries, moral police make it hard for students to talk to each other well (male or female, cultural differences within one society, etc.). In the past, some countries did not have one campus for both men and women. Instead, they had separate campuses (Al-Bakr et al., 2017). For example, men and women attend King Abdullah University in Saudi Arabia.

In our proposed university model, eliminating segregation will make it easier for male and female students to talk to each other. So, students will learn more about how to act in workplaces where people of different races work together. This training in soft skills will help them a lot after they leave the proposed university. Adventure education (AE) classes in the outdoors would also help these students build their "soft skills." These courses' activities or events are interactive and based on essential learning themes. These give students a chance to think about how they learn independently. So, the suggested activities will help students think about the most important things they have learned and inspire others.

Students will learn how to talk to people who are hard to get along with, be flexible in their relationships, and be tolerant of others. Courses in teamwork, problem-solving, and the value of being a strong but approachable leader have recently been incorporated into degree programs at prestigious institutions around the world, such as the University of Birmingham.

Action research projects and AE courses will be part of the proposed university, which will help students learn more soft skills. They will be used in classes such as programming artificial life and the impact of ICT enabled e-health degree programs, which began in Japan. Soft skills will encourage nursing students to create programs that help them communicate with and help patients who are hard to deal with.

Universities in Malaysia, like private colleges in Georgetown and Penang, emphasize developing soft skills (Aithal & Suresh, 2015). Teachers can help students develop soft skills by actively encouraging them to think creatively. The proposed model for universities will emphasize the role of teachers in helping students develop "soft skills." This will be done by giving training to university faculty. Some of the things discussed in the training sessions include how students can be creatively motivated to grow professionally and personally. The faculty will also be asked to change their courses to include more "soft skills." So, the proposed model helps students develop their soft skills by giving them AE courses and training the teachers in soft skill development.

## 3.6 INTERNSHIPS IN GLOBALIZATION AND WORKPLACE COOPERATION

In addition to these activities, the proposed university will offer courses and seminars designed to equip students with the skills they'll need to assume leadership roles in the business world. Students will see how their classroom knowledge is put to use in the real world on field trips to local businesses and research facilities. It will also be crucial to provide students with stimulating internships at global and multinational companies so that they can acquire the skills they'll need to serve society after graduation.

### *3.6.1 INDIA CONTEXT*

India has traditionally focused on holistic growth that leads to self-realization and emancipation. It is not the amount of data that's crammed into your head and then forgotten about for the rest of your life. Education, to him, was the process of developing character, mental fortitude, and intellect, finally leading to self-sufficiency. Moreover, it is not just about the individuals. We must rethink Higher Education in India by preserving our rich heritage while remaining focused on the present. Ancient India, which rose to become Vishwaguru, left us with a tried-and-true method of teaching and learning. We need to show how vital our indigenous past is worldwide.

Every entity in the cosmos requires a meaningful, pleasant, healthy, and resonant life, according to Indian philosophy; the ultimate goal of higher education is to generate universal beings with healthy interdependence and integration. Pedagogy includes teaching-learning procedures that are acceptable. Incorporating collective wisdom through reflective dialogue is the most effective technique to teach and retain knowledge. It is also necessary to shift from teacher-designed and teacher-driven pedagogy to learner-designed and learner-driven education. Open education resources (OERs) and the Indian platform SWAYAM (study webs of active learning for young aspiring minds) is the MOOCs are already widespread, and quick response codes (QRCs) can lead to even more. Since COVID-19, when social separation became the "new normal," more people have used the internet and technology for remote learning. When using the internet, it is essential to use the best tools.

Teachers must be eager, innovative, adventurous, and well-equipped to teach using technology. Teachers should be inherently enthusiastic about their work. Universities must have a well-developed infrastructure and appropriate content that are freely accessible online. It encourages children to identify with a worthwhile purpose that will assist them in surviving and succeeding. The association between higher education and the "real world" is enhanced. Industry, institutions, and society must work together more closely. Needs of local and global businesses. At the same time, theoretical and practical knowledge merged. Educating students and the public that all jobs, whether blue, white, pink, or gold-collar, should be treated with respect is essential if higher education is to fulfill its social purpose. To address societies and the country's demands, create multi-faculty institutions that integrate disciplines such as agriculture, community participation, value education, sports, skill development, and core courses. Create a list of long- and short-term objectives. Long-term goals include fostering responsible citizenship, social consciousness, inclusiveness, and cultural integration. Higher education in India should cater to the various demands of all students. When accepting students, higher education institutions (HEIs) should encourage diversity while respecting individuality. Admission should be based on students' unique ideas and points of view, not their performance on qualifying examinations or entrance tests. Universities in India offer a unique chance to promote multilingualism and build cross-cultural bridges, opportunity universities should take advantage of. Universities were required to go through challenges to resolve legacy issues. The outbreak of COVID-19 compelled institutions worldwide to transfer their courses online. Despite the numerous obstacles, digital transformation can solve problems.

Colleges can provide selection using digital technology as available personal instruction. It overcomes obstacles a teacher and the rigidity construct course the skills that seek. The emphasis on students differs from India's usually strict curriculum structure and the traditional approach to in-class learning. According to Sancheti, many institutions founded to focus solely on medical or technical education cannot deliver multidisciplinary education. Employers today demand that graduates have a wide range of skills. Allows work to deliver courses that would otherwise be unavailable to their employees.

Digital technologies are used to remedy systemic issues. Indian institutions face a teacher shortage, yet a single pupil. The primary challenge for India is access to them, particularly in rural areas. Dr. Joseph Nellanatt's experience as pro-vice-chancellor and director of remote learning at Assam Don Bosco University. "We have had classes, examinations, and even our convocation online, and the connectivity and bandwidth difficulties are genuine," he said.

### *3.6.2 MEXICO CONTEXT*

The World Health Organization officially declared COVID-19 a pandemic on March 11, 2020, requiring all countries to develop responses to halt the disease's spread. These responses included closing total or partial trade, confining people, and closing schools at all levels and fields, which resulted in numerous changes to the lives of people and institutions, disrupting the dynamics and pre-established ways of acting. The internationalization field, which is firmly based on the mobility of university community members, was one of the most affected aspects of HEIs. Various studies reveal that actions of student mobility represented, before the pandemic, the activity of priority internationalization in different parts of the world, with almost 6 million annual students crossing borders for undergraduate studies, a record, researchers, and academic staff attached to HEIs on temporary stays around the world (Rumbley, 2020; Marinoni, 2019).

One of the examples that illustrate strategies achieved by some universities in Mexico, specifically regarding internationalization to promote global citizenship, is Tecnológico de Monterrey; this technology-based university has changed its vision to 2030 and framed it into five principles.

- Innovation is a change that makes things better;
- Integrity has both freedom and responsibility;
- Collaboration: we reach the goal as a group;
- Put other people's needs before; and
- Working for a sustainable world is part of being a global citizen.

Global classroom emerged as the only strategy that allowed internationalization and global citizenship experience during the pandemic; it can be defined as a collective learning experience based on challenges through a digital environment, allowing collaboration and the selected challenges' global social impact. Always putting people first and contributing to solving different problems in the involved communities, regularly between two groups from two universities located in different countries. This kind of international collaboration aimed to generate internationalization experiences with significant learning, linking the students of both institutions to multicultural, collaborative, and inclusive knowledge. Several successful collaborations between Tecnológico de Monterrey and other universities worldwide have occurred; collaborations such as the one generated by Sabaté (2021), Human flourishing: global classroom, during the international lockdown between Mexico and Spain provide hope for an uncertain future and health conditions.

Hybrid schemes are here to stay, even when they know they will not completely replace face-to-face. It is anticipated that the virtualization of teaching, and therefore internationalization strategies in the classroom, will have positive impacts in the medium and long term by allowing students from non-traditional segments to join the efforts of internationalization. However, work is needed to identify better practices, massify teacher training for virtual education and stimulate the effective use and integration of new technologies, as well as resolve issues related to national policies on virtual education and cross-border quality assurance in teaching-learning processes, participant satisfaction, and creation of learning environments.

Learning that is effective and interactive (Amemado, 2020; Altbach & de Witt, 2020).

## 3.7 CONCLUSION

The unemployment rates among college graduates in the Gulf (mostly citizens) and Africa are frightening (about 20%). Politicians and leaders attribute the situation to a lack of industrial prospects and try to develop new employment opportunities. We believe that the majority of these graduates are unqualified for business roles. Even unemployed master's degree holders are likelier to work as waiters or salespeople. In several countries, illegal immigration to Western nations is attempted. Most illegal immigrants falsely claiming refugee status are deported from their home nations. The criminality of recent graduates has increased, but their social tolerance has stayed unchanged. Research indicates sadness and acute poverty when students cannot afford to support their families or are the sole providers for their families. Poverty and social well-being may be disrupted, affecting politicians seeking answers.

According to our estimates, the industry's desired employment input does not correspond to the universities' output. Because they are mismatched, they are not effective, efficient, or competitive in the workplace. In some countries, this creates a negative snowball effect on society. The source of the problem is the conventional university model of student teaching and research. They are unable to produce enough because they lack the necessary knowledge, abilities, and experience to enter the market in a timely manner, as well as the ability to use and understand modern technologies. This chapter details and provides examples of the ways in which conventional educational systems in some countries fall short. We advocated for new methods of instruction and study that would better prepare students for their first years of university. New methods and perspectives are needed to build students' minds in this age of unprecedented technological advancement and digitalization at universities. To succeed in today's competitive and rapidly evolving society, established universities must adjust their goals and priorities.

Our new model of university sells skills for lifelong learners equipped with cutting-edge technologies and knowledge, whereas traditional universities sell degrees. Our model utilizes coop programs, field learning, and international internships to create a global network of students. This model does not claim to be the first of its kind; instead, it is an attempt to put together a puzzle widely disseminated. This chapter aims to integrate new approaches into a single model. Reform is our advice to traditional university decision-makers. We told them that they should be socially responsible for the people in their country by going above and beyond their basic social needs. We examined the educational systems of five countries with successful reforms. In terms of adapting to change, they can show how traditional universities can do it. Traditional universities are a burden on society. Illegal immigration also affects other countries; the change will occur.

## KEYWORDS

- **globalization**
- **higher education challenges**
- **Indian higher education**
- **knowledge-based society**
- **self-sustaining workforce**
- **transformation**
- **university paradigms**
- **workplace cooperation**

## REFERENCES

*(PDF) Online Learning in Australian Higher Education: Opportunities, Challenges, and Transformations*. Available from: https://www.researchgate.net/publication/335108363_Online_learning_in_Australian_higher_education_Opportunities_challenges_and_transformations (accessed on 13 December 2023).

Ahedo, J., (2016). La universidad: Una escuela al servicio de la verdad. *Revista Complutense deEducación, 27*(2). https://doi.org/10.5209/rev_RCED.2016.v27.n2.46604.

Aithal, P. S., & Suresh, P. M., (2015). Enhancement of graduate attributes in higher education institutions through stage models. *International Journal of Research in Business Management, 3*, 121–130.

Al Zahrani, M., & Ismaiel, N. M., (2018). The effectiveness of a proposed program to develop meta-learning awareness and its effect on the writing achievement of Saudi EFL Students at Taif University. *Revista Quid., 1*, 2732–2748.

Alabama, F., (2016). Factors underlying low achievement of Saudi EFL learners. *International Journal of English Linguistics, 6*, 1–7. https://doi.org/10.5539/ijel.v6n3p21.

Al-bakr, F., Bruce, E. R., Davidson, P. M., Schlaffer, E., & Kropiunigg, U., (2017). Empowered but not equal: Challenging the traditional gender roles as seen by University Students in Saudi Arabia. *FIRE: Forum for International Research in Education, 4*, Article 3. https://doi.org/10.18275/fire201704011083.

Alhaisoni, E., (2012). Language learning strategy use of Saudi EFL students in an intensive English learning context. *Asian Social Science, 8*, 115–127. https://doi.org/10.5539/ass.v8n13p115.

Alnahdi, G. H., (2014). Educational change in Saudi Arabia. *Journal of International EducationResearch, 10*, 1–6. https://doi.org/10.19030/jier.v10i1.8342.

Amado, D., (2020). COVID-19: An unexpected and unusual driver to online education. *International, Higher Education*, (102), 12–14.

Arocena, R., & Sutz, J., (2001). *La Universidad Latinoamericana Del Futuro. Tendencias*-Escenarios-Alternativas. México: Editorial UDUAL. Recuperado a partir de http://beu.extension.unicen.edu.ar/xmlui/handle/123456789/197 (accessed on 13 December 2023).

Azman, H., (2016). Implementation and challenges of English language education reform in Malaysian Primary Schools. *3L: Southeast Asian Journal of English Language Studies, 22*(3).

Boy, G. A., (2013). From STEM to STEAM: Toward a human-centered education, creativity & learning thinking. In*: Proceedings of the 31st European Conference on Cognitive Ergonomics,* (No. 3). ACM.

Brennan, M., & Zipin, L., (2019). Seeking an institution-decentring politics to regain purpose for Australian university futures. In: *Resisting Neoliberalism in Higher Education* (Vol. II, pp. 271–292). Palgrave Macmillan, Cham.

Davidson, C. N., & Goldberg, D., (2009). *The Future of Thinking. Learning Institutions in a Digital Age.* Boston, MA: The MIT Press. URL: https://library.oapen.org/bitstream/handle/20.500.12657/26031/1/8517.pdf (accessed on 13 December 2023).

Dede, C. J., & Richards, J., (2020). *The 60-Year Curriculum: New Models for Lifelong Learning in the Digital Economy.* Routledge.

DeWitt, A. J., (2021). *A Phenomenological Study Examining the Challenges and Strategies of Students Who are Parents in the Higher Education Setting.* (Publication No. 2858) [Doctoral dissertation, Liberty University]. Liberty University Digital Archive.

Dori, Y. J., & Belcher, J., (2004). How does technology-enabled active learning affect undergraduate students' understanding of electromagnetism concepts? *The Journal of the Learning Science, 14*(2), 243–279.

Eames, C., & Bell, B., (2005). Using sociocultural views of learning to investigate the enculturation of students into the scientific community through work placements. *Canadian Journal of Science, Mathematics, and Technology Education, 5*, 153–169.

Feliz, U., (2005). E-learning pedagogy in the third millennium: The need for combining social and cognitive constructivist approaches. *ReCALL: The Journal of Eurocall* (Vol. 17, No. 1, pp. 85–100). Cambridge University Press.

FICCI *Higher Education Summit & Exhibition 2021|Higher Education Exhibition|Conference|Event|B2B|New Delhi India.* (n.d.). www.ficci-Hes.com Retrieved from: https://www.ficci-hes.com (accessed on 13 December 2023).

Flynn, W. J., & Vredevoogd, J., (2010). The future of learning: 12 views on emerging trends in higher education. *Planning for Higher Education, 38*(2), 5.

Freer, C., (2017). *Concerts, Cinemas and Comics in the Kingdom: Revising the Social Contract After Saudi Vision 2030*. Middle East Centre Blog.

Friedman, T. L., (2005). *The World is Flat: A Brief History of the Twenty-First Century*. New York: Farrar, Straus, and Giroux.

Gadhoum, Y., (2022). A proposed model of a future university in the artificial intelligence transformative society era: From why to how. *Creative Education, 13*, 1098–1119. doi: 10.4236/ce.2022.133069.

Garrett, C. E., (2013). Promoting student engagement and creativity by infusing arts across the curriculum: The arts integration initiative at Oklahoma City University. *About Campus, 18*(2), 27–32. doi: 10.1002/abc.21115.

Gazette, S., (2016). *Full Text of Saudi Arabia's Vision 2030*. Saudi Gazette.

Gosselin, D., Burian, S., Lutz, T., & Maxson, J., (2016). Integrating geoscience into undergraduate education about environment, society, and sustainability using place-based learning: Three examples. *Journal of Environmental Studies and Sciences, 6*, 531–540.

Goyal, N., (2011). Forbes: January 11, 2013. In: *Defense of Skipping College and Enrolling in the Real World*. Recuperado de: https://www.forbes.com/sites/carolinehoward/2013/01/11/in-defense-of-skipping-college-and-enrolling-in-the-real-world/#656b0c2d1fd2 (accessed on 13 December 2023).

Hallinger, P., (2010). Making education reform happen: Is there an "Asian" way? *School Leadership and Management, 1*, 401–418. https://doi.org/10.1080/13632434.2010.502524.

Hawkins, J. N., Mok, K. H., & Neubauer, D., (2018). The many faces of Asia Pacific higher education in the era of massification. In: *Massification of Higher Education in Asia* (pp. 1–8). Springer, Singapore.

Heaton, S., Siegel, D. S., & Teece, D. J., (2019). Universities and innovation ecosystems: A dynamic capabilities perspective. *Industrial and Corporate Change, 28*(4), 921–939.

Helyer, R., (2011). Aligning higher education with the world of work. *Higher Education, Skills, andWork-Based Learning, 1*(2), 95–105.

Hou, Y. C., Morse, R., Ince, M., Chen, H. J., Chiang, C. L., & Chan, Y., (2015). Is the Asian quality assurance system for higher education going global? Assessing the impact of three types of program accreditation on Taiwanese.

Huye, H., (2015). Using poetry and arts analysis to evoke critical thinking and challenging reflection in senior-level nutrition students. *Journal of Nutrition Education and Behavior, 47*(3), 283. doi: 10.1016/j.jneb.2015.01.007.

Jonker, H., März, V., & Voogt, J., (2020). Curriculum flexibility in a blended curriculum. *Australasian Journal of Educational Technology*.

Kaufman, K., (2019). What skills do 21st century high school graduates need to have to be successful in college and life? In: *STEM Education 2.0* (pp. 337–349). Brill Sense.

Kinninmont, J., (2017). *Vision 2030 and Saudi Arabia's Social Contract: Austerity and Transformation*. Chatham House.

Marinoni, G., (2019). *Internationalization of Higher Education: An Evolving Landscape, Locally and Globally: IAU 5th Global Survey*. DUZ Verlags-und Medienhaus GmbH.

Moore, K., Coates, H., & Croucher, G., (2019). Measuring international higher education productivity: Lessons from nine countries in Asia. In: *Higher Education Forum* (Vol. 16, pp. 69–84). Research Institute for Higher Education, Hiroshima University.

Novak, J. I., (2019). Self-directed learning in the age of open source, open hardware and 3D printing. In: *Ubiquitous Inclusive Learning in a Digital Era* (pp. 154–178). IGI Global.
Nursalam, N., (2020). Glocal vision to deconstruct internationalization in Indonesian higher education. *Journal of Social Studies Education Research, 11*(1), 137–152.
Nussbaum, M. C., (2016). *Not for Profit: Why Democracy Needs the Humanities (Updated Edition).* Princeton, NJ: Princeton University Press.
Ouda, O. K., Raza, S. A., Nizami, A. S., Rehan, M., Al-Waked, R., & Korres, N. E., (2016). Waste to energy potential: A case study of Saudi Arabia. *Renewable and Sustainable Energy Reviews, 61,* 328–340. https://doi.org/10.1016/j.rser.2016.04.005.
Paine, S. L., & Schleicher, A., (2011). *What the US Can Learn from the World's Most Successful Education Reform Efforts.* McGraw-Hill Research Foundation.
Park, E. L., & Choi, B. K., (2014). Transformation of classroom spaces: Traditional versus active learning classroom in colleges. *Higher Education, 68*(5), 749–771. https://doi.org/10.1007/s10734-014-9742-0.
Park, N., & Ko, Y., (2012). *Computer Education's Teaching-Learning Methods Using Educational Programming Language Based on Steam Education.* In IFIP.
Parker, K., Roraback, E., & LaMore, R., (2013). *A Young Picasso or Beethoven Could be the Next Edison.* Research Study. Michigan State University. Retrieved from: http://msutoday.msu.edu/news/2013/a-young-picasso-orbeethoven-could-be-the-next-edison/ (accessed on 13 December 2023).
Pauwels, L., (2020). A multimodal model for exploring the material culture of digital networked platforms and their practices. In: *The SAGE Handbook of Visual Research Methods/Pauwels, Luc [edit.]* (pp. 553–573).
Philip, A. V., & Zakkariya, K. A., (2020). Effective engagement of digital natives in the ever-transforming digital world. In: *Digital Transformation in Business and Society* (pp. 113–125). Palgrave Macmillan, Cham.
Piro, J., (2010). Going from STEM to STEAM. *Education Week, 29*(24), 28–294.
Ramsay-Jordan, N., (2020). Preparation and the real world of education: How prospective teachers grapple with using culturally responsive teaching practices in the age of standardized testing. *International Journal of Educational Reform, 29*(1), 3–24.
Rumbley, L. E., (2020). *Coping with COVID-19: International Higher Education in Europe.* Amsterdam: The European Association for International Education (EAIE).
Rust, V. D., & Kim, S., (2012). The global competition in higher education. *World Studies in Education, 13,* 5–20. https://doi.org/10.7459/wse/13.1.02.
Sabaté, (2020). *Human Flourishing: Global Classroom During International Lockdown, México-España.* Revista del Congrés Internacional de Docència Universitària i Innovació (CIDUI), (5).
Sanchiz, M., Amadieu, F., Paubel, P. V., & Chevalier, A., (2020). User-friendly search interface for older adults: Supporting search goal refreshing in working memory to improve information search strategies. *Behavior & Information Technology, 39*(10), 1094–1109.
Skorton, D., (2019). Branches from the same tree: The case for integration in higher education. *Proceedings of the National Academy of Sciences, 116*(6), 1865–1869.
Stone, C., (2019). Online learning in Australian higher education: Opportunities, challenges, and transformations. *Student Success, 10*(2), 1–11. doi: 10.5204/ssj.v10i2.1299.
Swandi, A., Amin, B. D., & Muin, F., (2018). 21st century physics learning in senior high school through interactive computer simulation to enhance students' achievement.

In: *International Conference on Mathematics and Science Education of Universitas Pendidikan Indonesia* (Vol. 3, pp. 130–135).

Tabrizi, S., & Kabirnejat, M., (2017). Smart school: A comparative research between two Islamic countries, Malaysia and Iran. *Journal of Advances in Humanities and Social Sciences, 3*(1), 58–68.

Taleb, Z., & Hassanzadeh, F., (2015). Toward smart school: A comparison between smart school and traditional school for mathematics learning. *Procedia-Social and Behavioral Sciences, 171*, 90–95. https://doi.org/10.1016/j.sbspro.2015.01.093.

Tan, C., (2015). Education policy borrowing and cultural scripts for teaching in China. *Comparative Education, 2*, 196–211. https://doi.org/10.1080/03050068.2014.966485.

Tan, O. S., & Ang, R. P., (2017). Universities, research, innovation, and enterprise. In: *Lee Kuan Yew's Educational Legacy* (pp. 89–102). Springer. https://Doi.Org/10.1007/978-981-10-3525-8_8.

Toraman, Ç., Özdemir, H. F., Kosan, A. M. A., & Orakci, S., (2020). Relationships between cognitive flexibility, perceived quality of faculty life, learning approaches, and academic achievement. *International Journal of Instruction, 13*(1), 85–100.

Walkinshaw, I., Fenton-Smith, B., & Humphreys, P., (2017). EMI issues and challenges in Asia-Pacific higher education: An introduction. In: *English Medium Instruction in Higher Education in Asia-Pacific* (pp. 1–18). Springer, Cham.

Wong, B., & Chiu, Y. L. T., (2019). Let me entertain you: The ambivalent role of university lecturers as educators and performers. *Educational Review, 71*(2), 218–233.

## CHAPTER 4

# A Systems Architecture of an Immersive Technology-Based Healthcare Education System

MOHAMMAD NASFIKUR R. KHAN, KARI J. LIPPERT, and ROBERT J. CLOUTIER

*Systems Engineering, The University of South Alabama, Mobile, USA*

## ABSTRACT

Immersive technology allows users to immerse themselves in virtually created environments. The emergence of immersive learning also signifies the emergence of new learning technologies based on virtual reality (VR), augmented reality (AR), and spherical videos. The use of VR and AR in medical education is still relatively new. By moving education beyond more static presentations, these technologies enhance medical education. Firstly, these technologies offer a unique opportunity for today's learners to interact with medical practice in ways they couldn't before. Besides, this allows the medical learners to get closer to the competencies they require to become stellar physicians. The chapter describes an immersive, technology-based healthcare education system geared toward both educators and learners. Technology is used to deliver healthcare training that improves patient care through the Immersive Health Care Training System. Depending on the user's needs, medical personnel can receive feedback and data from the system. It first discusses the objective of the system, then an operational concept is developed, a stakeholder analysis

Intelligent Learning Paradigms and Student Empowerment: Digital Integration and Transformation. Souvik Pal, Ton Quang Cuong, & R. S. S. Nehru (Eds.)

is presented, a few use cases are illustrated with sequence diagrams, the system's physical and logical architectures are explained, traceability is demonstrated, and parametric diagrams are illustrated.

## 4.1 INTRODUCTION

A computer-generated world can be accessed through immersive technologies. This technology may be used in the field of medicine. On the other hand, immersive technology is still a relatively young field in the medical field. A few VR software systems are now available for doctors and medical personnel to learn. The use of VR may be extended to therapy for blindness, psychological disorders, amblyopia cure, rehabilitation training, personalized fitness training, and educational purposes (Khan & Lippert, 2022a, b).

This chapter proposes an immersive healthcare-based education system that assists healthcare professionals in providing medical care to students. Moreover, this chapter addresses a few important issues regarding the immersive technology-based medical system:

- Define virtual reality (VR).
- Define augmented reality (AR).
- What are the uses of VR in medical education?
- How to implement AR in healthcare systems?

The technology may be utilized with various devices, including immersive glasses, sensors, and wristwatches (Johnson & Paul, 2009). Educators and learners can access the system according to their needs. This system allows educators to upload their content according to their preferred time (Johnson & Paul, 2009; Haller et al., 2009). On the other hand, the learners can access these contents according to their needs. Along with this, users can exchange data with them, receive feedback, communicate with the professionals, surgical assistance, psychological knowledge exchange, and finally, emergency access system (Ustun et al., 2020). This chapter begins with a background description of the system, next moves on to stakeholder analysis, then to developing the operational concept in order to extract user desirements and system requirements through use cases, and finally through the block definition diagram explain the system architecture.

## 4.2 BACKGROUND

### *4.2.1 VR*

In their definition of VR, Zhang et al. describe a computer-generated simulation of a three-dimensional world (Zhang et al., 2018). The VR technology described by Sacks et al. allows users to experience a virtual world with computer-based operating systems and other technologies (Rafael, Amotz, & Ronen, 2013). Different devices enable people to interact with this simulated alternate world, which increases their sense of realism (Wiederhold & Giuseppe, 2012). VR technology has revolutionized how teachers train and students learn, according to Gadelha (Rafael, Amotz, & Ronen, 2013). Teachers can leverage it to focus on students instead of teaching them. Through being engaged in a virtual world in which they engage in a variety of activities, learners become active learners via the multimedia cone of abstraction (MCoA), a model of active learning based on Dale's cone of experience (CoE) (Rene, 2018). It replaced the CoE's foundation level, "Direct Purposeful Experiences," the most abstract level, showing that it can deliver highly realistic representations of things that learners might interact with and benefit from. If students receive timely feedback and the chance to improve at their own pace, they can understand work or concepts (Baukal, Ausburn, & Ausburn, 2013).

As many times as needed, learners can practice what they have learned in VR until they are able to complete the tasks. In addition, it encourages people to keep working hard to improve their skills (Bloom, 1974). A virtual learning environment can also provide students with timely feedback on their present proficiency. By using visual programming, students can construct a virtual learning environment suited to their needs and visualize where they need to focus to master a skill or activity (Sánchez-Cabrero et al., 2019).

#### *4.2.1.1 VR IN HEALTHCARE EDUCATION*

In healthcare education, simulation training has been shown to improve knowledge acquisition and competency (Norris, Spicer, & Traci, 2019). VR training can help healthcare professionals teach medical students to avoid situations that could lead to poor outcomes in a patient-practitioner relationship. For medical students, VR technology has the potential to be a valuable interactive, experiential tool that can help them to develop the skills needed in a real-life scenario, as well as a cost-effective approach to repeatedly practicing simulated clinical scenarios in healthcare (Marie-Stéphanie et al., 2019). By using VR, students can practice without fear of making real-life mistakes, prepare for diagnosing sickness indicators, and even perform complicated procedures.

By providing a suitable training method, VR simulations eliminate the need for cadavers or animals to gain professional knowledge and create crucial practical skills in medicine. While there is still room for improvement for the haptic (touch) sense, procedural, visual, and aural senses can be trained by using this method. Trainee surgeons can experience a variety of surgeries and procedures through the VR system, including endoscopic surgery, laparoscopic surgery, neurosurgery, and epidural injections (King et al., 2018). According to Vaughan et al. (2016), orthopedic VR training simulators provide surgeons with an excellent platform to develop and improve their skills in a safe, risk-free, realistic operating room.

For doctors with less experience in surgery, VR simulations may be an effective tool to teach essential procedures for orthopedics and other types of surgery. Patients and their primary caregivers may respond better to traditional instructional approaches, such as giving a verbal presentation of information or providing written materials (Vaughan et al., 2016). Interacting with a patient should be tailored to their language ability, ethnicity, socioeconomic background, level of education, and cognitive ability. There is evidence that these patient characteristics influence risk factors and patient outcomes (Vaughan et al., 2016).

For relevant and understandable patient knowledge, education must be designed to meet the specific needs of patients who experience acute or chronic conditions (Khan, Shakir, Nadi, & Abedin, 2022). To reduce recurrent strokes and maximize rehabilitation, Thompson-Butel et al. developed customized VR rehabilitation sessions for stroke survivors and their primary caregivers. In their study (Thompson-Butel et al., 2019), the researchers assessed whether or not VR sessions were effective in providing post-stroke education. This study found that the use of VR sessions resulted in "various significant improvements in technical expertise in areas such as neurodevelopment and physiology, cognitive impairment and healing, and stroke-specific instructions such as personalized stroke risk factors, as well as acute therapy advantages" for the victim and their caregivers (Hoffmann & McKenna, 2006).

Several studies have examined the current state of VR simulations in dentistry training (Roy et al., 2018). Their research suggests that VR equipment can be utilized in dentistry education to provide opportunities for flexibility and self-learning. VR devices enable learners to participate in their education in a variety of ways: They can perform simulations whenever and wherever they want, and they can keep track of and revisit their work after they have completed it. Moreover, incorporating VR technology into the classroom reduces anxiety and boredom and enhances student engagement and retention. In addition, students from all dental disciplines may benefit from more efficient and realistic pre-clinical practices with VR due to its rapid technological advancements (Roy et al., 2018).

### 4.2.2 AR

AR is currently the most popular technology trend, and it's only going to grow as handheld devices capable of displaying AR become more accessible around the globe. It is defined as multimedia that combines virtual and real elements, enables real-time interaction, and maps three-dimensionally. The first condition contrasts AR with VR; computer-generated models in live-action movies are contrasted with it in the second, and annotations and overlays on video are contrasted with it in the third (Felnhofer et al., 2015).

The design and development of computer-mediated communication target specific communication outcomes. In this context, it is useful for designers and developers of mediating technologies to have a theory of human communication behavior. Since the 1980s, AR has been on the market, but its development is still in its infancy due to the lack of adequate technology, social acceptance, usability, money, and time, as well as a lack of knowledge of what is possible with AR in education. Moreover, in addition to these three fundamental criteria, traditional AR applications must also combine virtual and real-world information, be interactive, and be 3D registered (Ferrer-García et al., 2017).

#### 4.2.2.1 AR IN EDUCATION

AR virtual learning content can be viewed on a variety of devices, including head-mounted displays (HMDs), computers with web cameras, handheld or mobile devices (HHDs), and Kinect. Several literature reviews have indicated that users and researchers are interested in mobile AR applications that can be used across multiple domains (Riches et al., 2021). As a result, mobile devices are beneficial in the learning process since they allow for easy following of trends on the go. Using marker-based AR learning, we can extract virtual content embedded in markers, as shown in Figure 4.1.

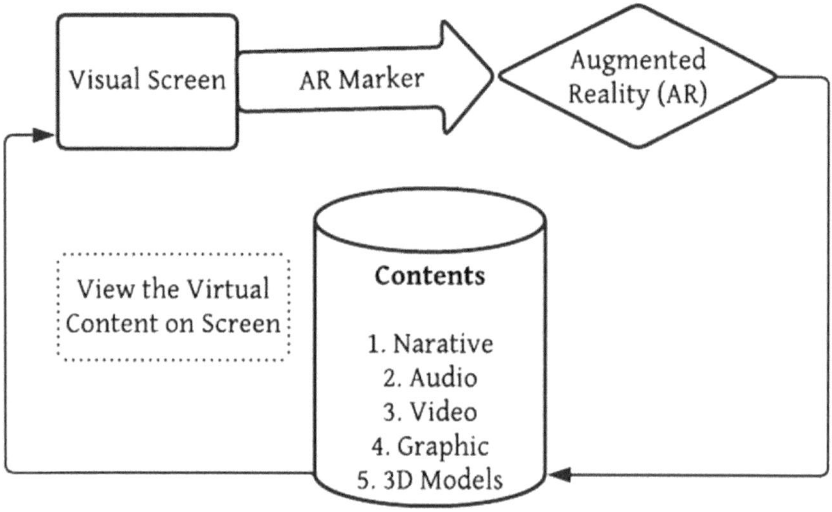


**FIGURE 4.1** AR using markers.

As shown in Figure 4.2, location-based AR utilizes the global positioning system (GPS) and Wi-Fi positioning system to extract virtual content from real-world objects, buildings, and locations.

Several studies have demonstrated the ability to learn from markers based on AR, such as (Riches et al., 2021). When a student is using markers, he or she is more likely to complete their learning. An AR-based learning approach is based on location, according to a study conducted by Riches et al. (2021) and Gamito et al. (2017). Location-based AR allows users to explore virtual content using their mobile devices. The inability to distinguish between reality and virtual, and the inability to interpret content, are among the problems that could arise from the inadequate development of mobile-based AR applications.

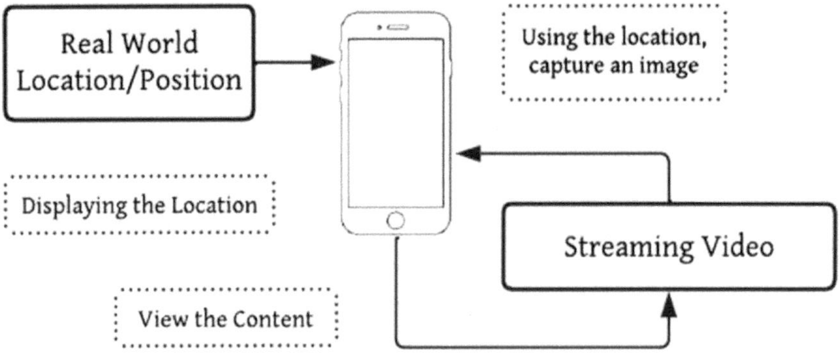


**FIGURE 4.2** A portable device-based AR.

Technological advancements enable the improvement of all aspects of human life, but health will suffer the greatest consequences. There is a need to rethink healthcare studies due to the healthcare crisis. Effective use of technology can improve the efficiency of healthcare organizations (Negro et al., 2019). AR has proven effective in providing enhanced healthcare to patients. This technology is expected to have a significant effect on the healthcare field (Riva et al., 2016). The reason for this is that AR makes use of sensors, displays, and embedded electronics.

## 4.3 STAKEHOLDERS

This section contains a list of all stakeholders of the system. Stakeholders include any individual, entity, or subsystem with an interest in, an effect on, a relationship with, or considerable influence over a system. There are two types of stakeholders considered for the system of interests: active and passive stakeholders. A system of interest will have active stakeholders that include users, companies, and other systems that will actively interact with it after it is operational and in use. The success of a system can be influenced by individuals, organizations, policies, procedures, and guidelines which may be considered passive stakeholders (Kirmse et al., 2021). Participants include the users (learners and educators), management (funding and management authority), experts, and technical support personnel, as well as those involved with hardware and software maintenance. The state government is a passive stakeholder, in addition to developers and researchers, local and international markets, and consumers and users of VR and portable devices. Table 4.1 lists the active stakeholders, whereas Table 4.2 lists the passive ones.

**TABLE 4.1** Roles and Responsibilities of Active Stakeholders

| Stakeholders | Responsibilities |
|---|---|
| Learner | A learner will run the system to learn from the educators. He or she also can use the system according to his or her needs. |
| Educator | An educator will run the system to teach and collaborate with the learners. He or she also can upload the teaching contents according to his or her needs. |
| Administrators | The system's funding and management will be overseen by administrators. |
| Service providers | The system will be serviced by medical providers (like doctors, nurses, and pharmacists). |
| Expert personnel | Expert professionals and lab technicians will help to run the collaboration without any major flaws. |
| Maintenance | Maintainers oversee the repair and upgrade services for the VR devices and software. |

**TABLE 4.2** Roles and Responsibilities of Passive Stakeholders

| Stakeholders | Functions |
|---|---|
| Designers | In possession of the system's development, distribution, and maintenance. |
| Research and development officers | Investigation period statistics and support with modifications for the designers. |
| Local clients | Capturing local clients will help capture the local market. |
| Global market | Globally, the system will be introduced on the international market. |
| VR devices | Immersive, virtual experiences will be created using VR devices. |
| Other devices | The VR device can be connected to other devices to collate, store, and exchange data. |
| Government authorities | Medical regulations and guidelines are regulated by a variety of government authorities. |

Figures 4.3(a) and (b) represent active and passive stakeholders, respectively. The stakeholders were classified into two categories: active and passive. Organizations, users, and maintenance are the three categories of engaged or involved stakeholders.

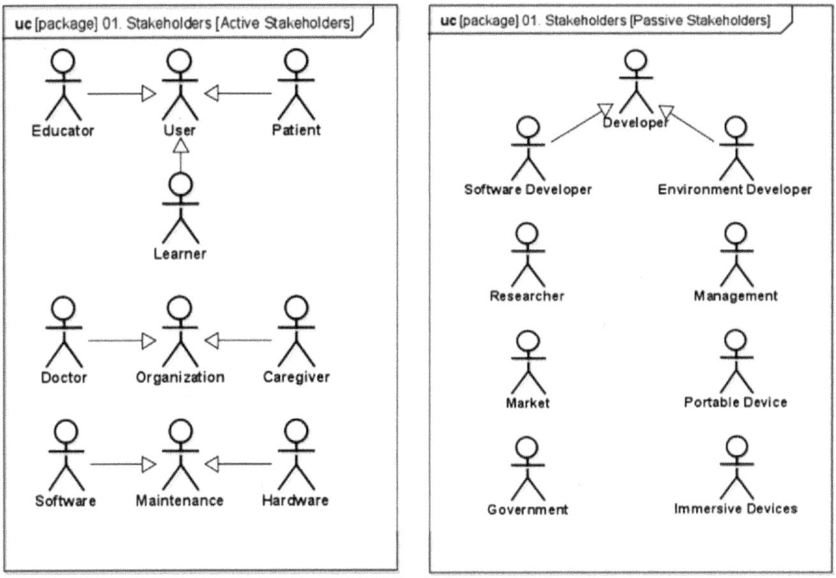


**FIGURE 4.3** Illustration of active and passive stakeholders.

### *4.3.1 DESIREMENTS OF THE STAKEHOLDERS*

A desire or need expressed by a stakeholder that a current system cannot meet is the starting point for developing a new system. When stakeholder expectations are only desired rather than required, those are referred to as stakeholder desirements. Research shows that the stakeholders for a VR medical system are looking for specific features fundamental to their preconceived notions. This section focuses on capturing stakeholder desires, expectations, and requirements representing the foundation of system validation–what system they want.

Figure 4.4 represents a sample of stakeholder desirements. Some desires are based on a VR implementation and utilize multiple sensors and devices. Uses include therapeutic solutions, healthcare for children, surgical aid, training for medical support staff and users, premedication, robotic surgery, psychiatric counseling, and autism therapy. The cultural requirement expresses the concern for patient differences. Additional system requirements (not shown here) include data security, privacy concerns, etc.

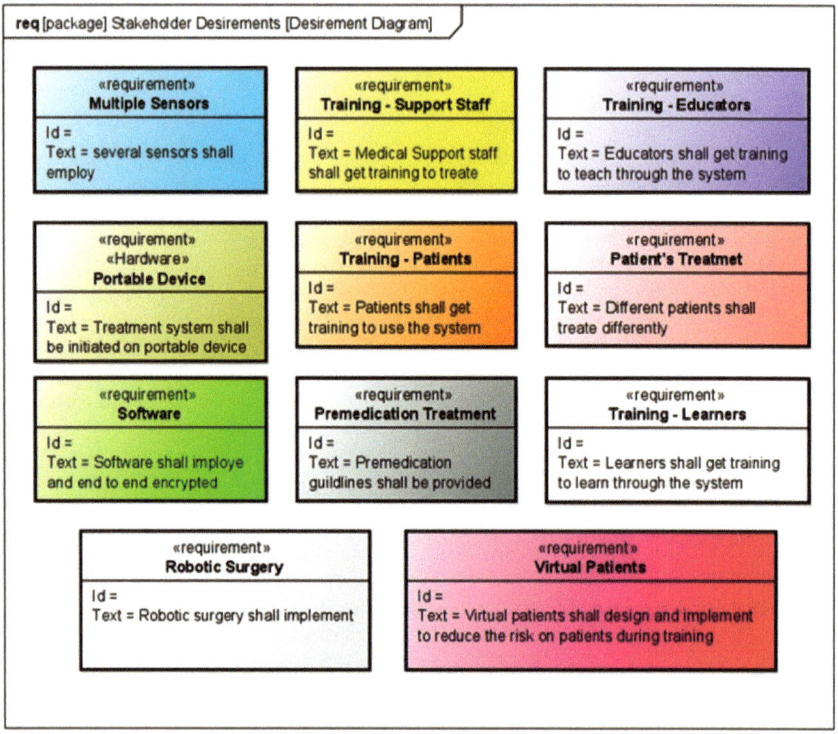


**FIGURE 4.4** The desirements diagram of the system.

## 4.4 SYSTEM PURPOSE AND CONCEPT OF OPERATIONS

### *4.4.1 CONCEPT OF OPERATIONS*

A system can be described in a variety of ways (Mostashari, McComb, Kennedy, Cloutier, & Korfiatis, 2012). Through a mind map in Figure 4.5 and the following discussion, this section describes the intention and operational concept of the system. There are several parts included in the mind map to design the system, such as the actions of the users and the system, the system's features, preservation guidelines, and user guidelines.

As shown in Figure 4.6, the activity diagram illustrates how the system operates. In the diagram, the user wears the immersive device and connects it to their smartphone, which must be registered for use. Logging into the system and selecting an identity from the available options allows users

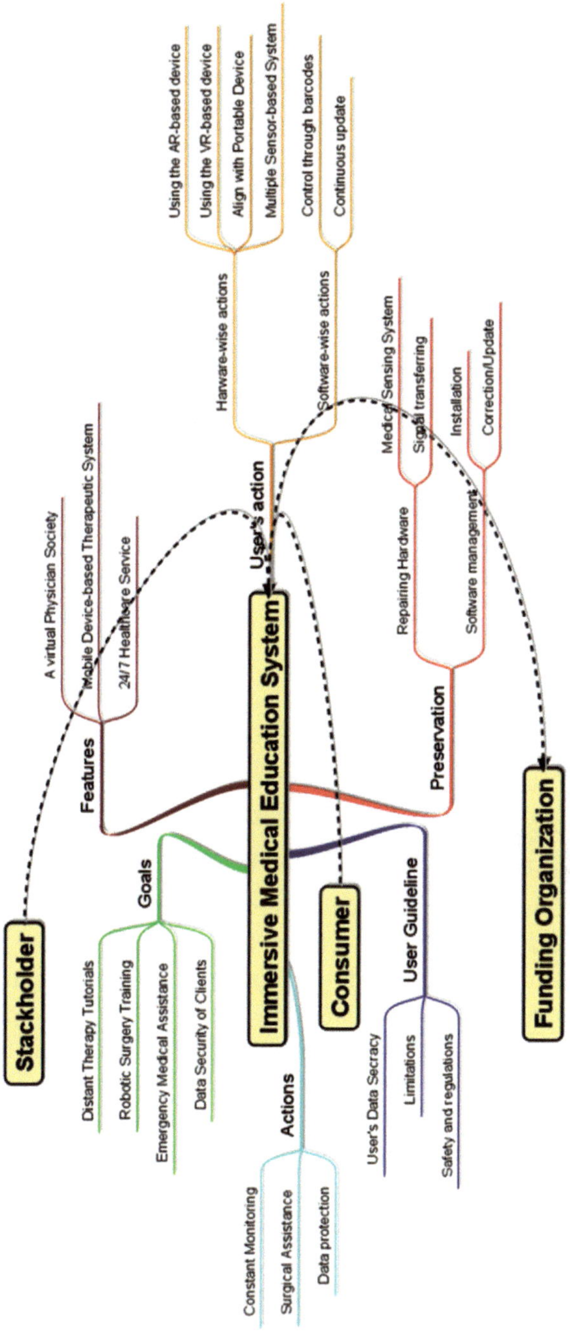


**FIGURE 4.5** A mind map of the proposed system.

to access a certain realm of medical sciences. Selecting specific options and then following the instructions allows the user to operate the system. The system gives educators and learners the option of selecting specific services.

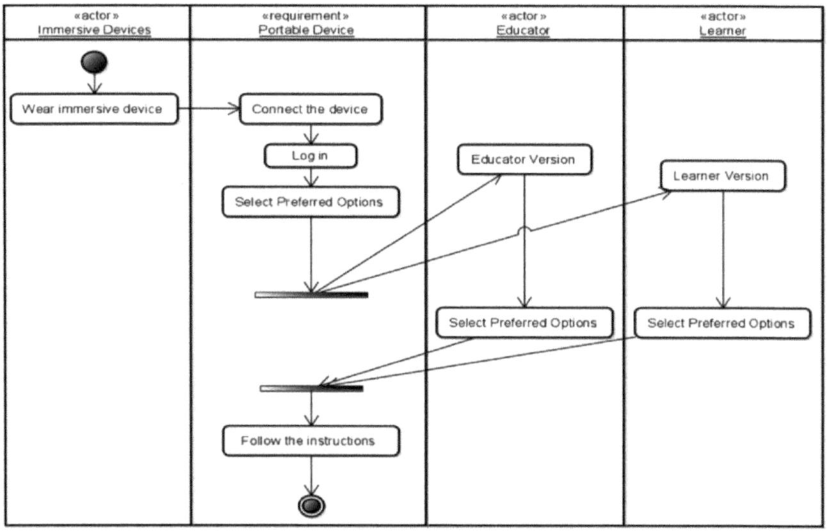


**FIGURE 4.6** Activity diagram of the proposed system.

### *4.4.1.1 SYSTEM DOMAIN*

As shown in Figure 4.7, the architecture of the proposed system is represented by the systems-domain model which specifies how the services specified by the services model are provided. Several subsystems are demonstrated in this section, such as the user, multiple sensors, the system environment, and the external support provider, as well as some requirements, like software management, devices (portables and immersive devices), and device maintenance.

There are a variety of therapeutic systems that are available in the modern world, some of them relying on intelligent frameworks. Among the best examples is ScenicSoft, a company that has spent the past 10 years developing a VR-based product for cancer trials. VR has been incorporated into their methodology for creating a healthcare worker training program.

Despite this, the paradigm is of little use to patients since it emphasizes clinical professional training over patient perspectives (Di Meglio & Estrella, 2012).

Ghost Productions, on the other hand, provides training frameworks that can help in reducing catastrophic human errors across almost all mission-critical services. The techniques of VR can be used to improve medical training and decrease medical errors, which are the third leading cause of death in the United States. As a result, they designed and developed a very successful training program based on simulations, Wraith (Highly Effective VR Medical & Surgical Training, 2020). Although this is true, our members and research team believe that no system currently offers realistic medical and surgical virtual-assisted aid that is both beneficial to medical personnel and patients.

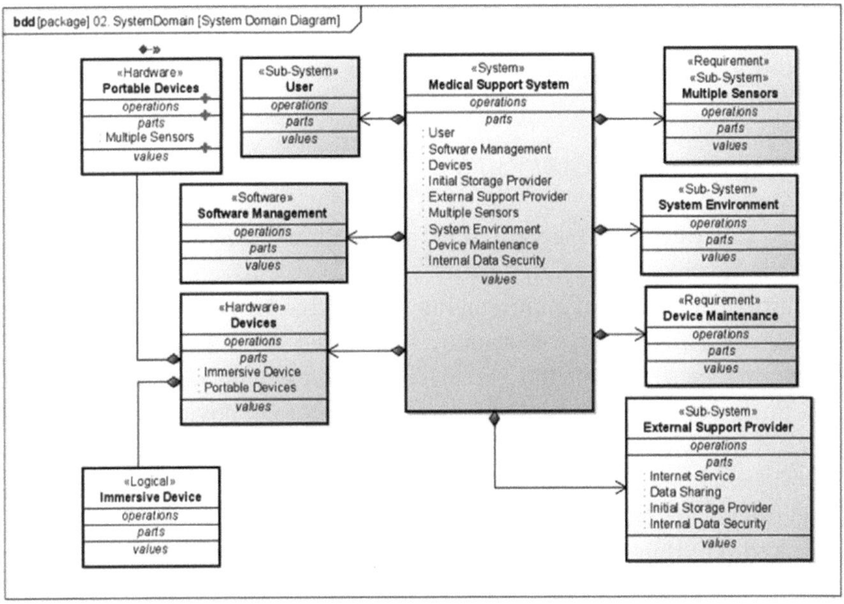


**FIGURE 4.7** Illustration of the system domain.

A diagram (Figure 4.8) is also shown of the external medical support system, which contains information about patients, caregivers, learners, and doctors.

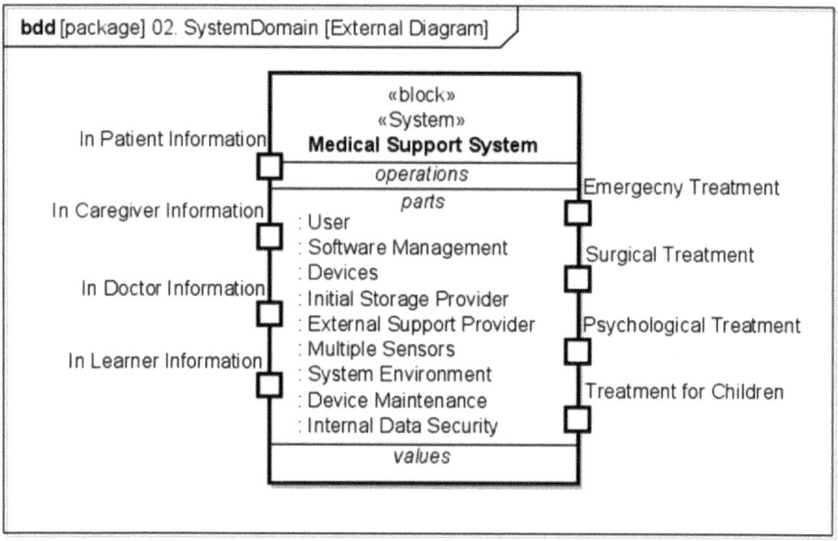


**FIGURE 4.8** External diagram of the medical support system.

### *4.4.1.2 SYSTEM REQUIREMENTS*

Three subsystems of the system are pictured in Figure 4.9, which depicts the top-level system requirements. The subsystems are the performance requirements, external requirements, and design requirements. In addition to quick response, proper training, and quick recovery, there are three performance requirements. The external requirements subsystem consists of three components: storage capacity, portable devices, and internet providers. Along with the AI-based system, the design requirements subsystem comprises four other components: data collection, data sharing, and treatment.

A discussion of stakeholder desires has already taken place. The requirements must be aligned with these desires. This section illustrates examples such as the implementation of a portable device. A portable device is a mobile device, such as a smartphone, or an immersive device, such as VR goggles. There should be multiple sensors in items such as watches. Afterward, a robotic surgery training system based on artificial intelligence (AI) will be used to perform and teach robotic surgery. Our last goal is to use AI to understand the differences in ethnicity, race, and culture, which will lead to a different type of medical student training. Figure 4.10 illustrates how requirements correspond to wishes.

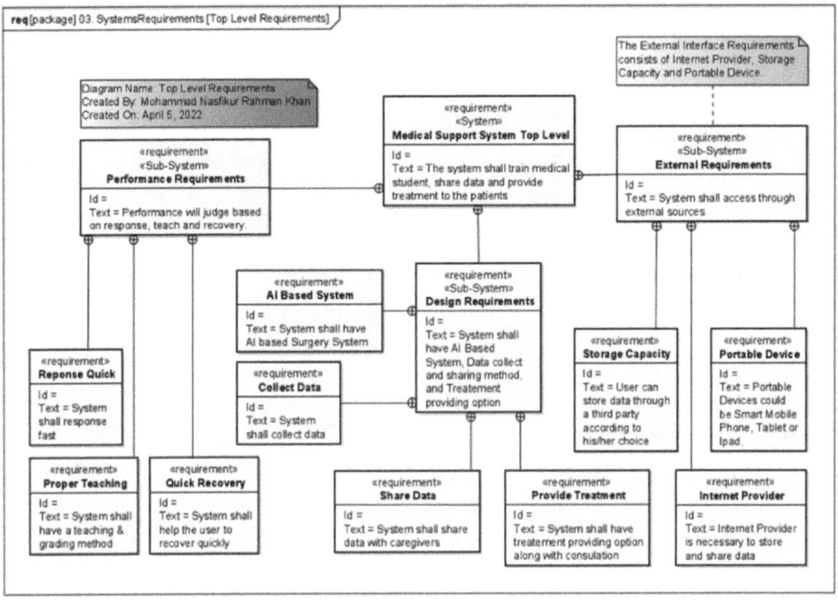


**FIGURE 4.9** Top-level system requirements.

#### *4.4.1.3 USE CASES*

User interaction with a system is visualized with a use case map. In its simplest form, a use case diagram depicts the different ways in which an application can be used, as well as the types of users. There can usually be additional diagrams added together. This section will illustrate four ways the system can be used. Using a portable device and multiple sensors and an immersive device, Figure 4.11 illustrates how a patient might receive treatment from a doctor. Furthermore, educators can use immersive and portable devices to teach a student.

Figure 4.12 illustrates an activity wherein a user can access his preferred service via a portable device by selecting from the provided options. An internet provider is required to provide Internet access to the user. The user might also store his data using an external storage system.

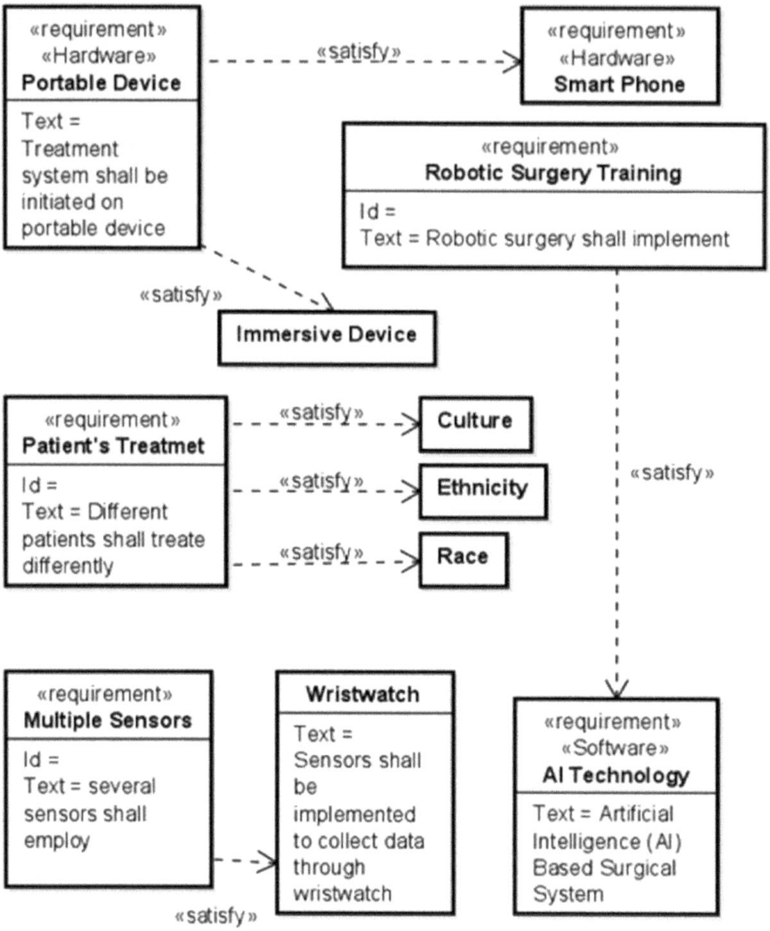


**FIGURE 4.10** Mapping of desirements to requirements.

## 4.5 SYSTEM ARCHITECTURE

### *4.5.1 LOGICAL ARCHITECTURE*

In a logical architecture, all of the subsystems, classes, layers, and layers of software together form the entire system. A logical architecture is an architecture in which the components are arranged randomly within a system. According to the diagram in Figure 4.13, the main system will be the medical training system, along with ports for the immersive device, portable device, numerous sensors, the internet, the user's data, and AI. The system will include ports for diagnosing, training on emergency services, pre-medication training, providing virtual assessments, providing virtual counseling, and performing robotic surgery training.

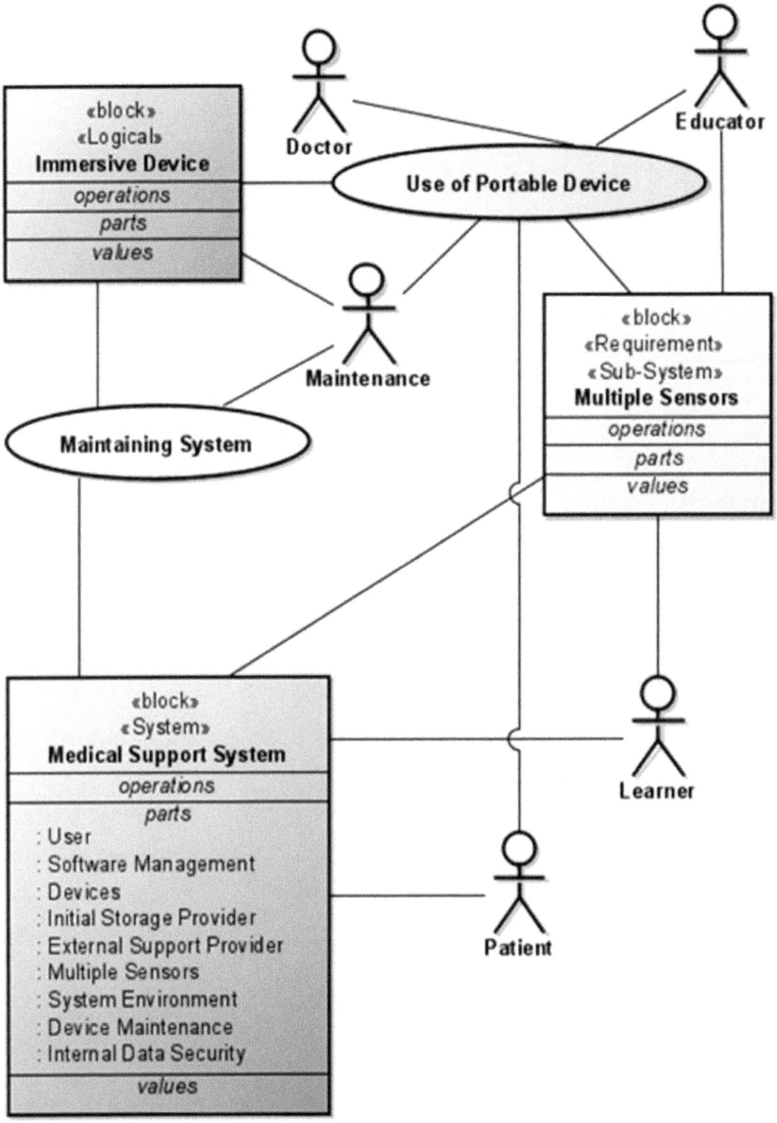


**FIGURE 4.11** A use case diagram of the proposed system.

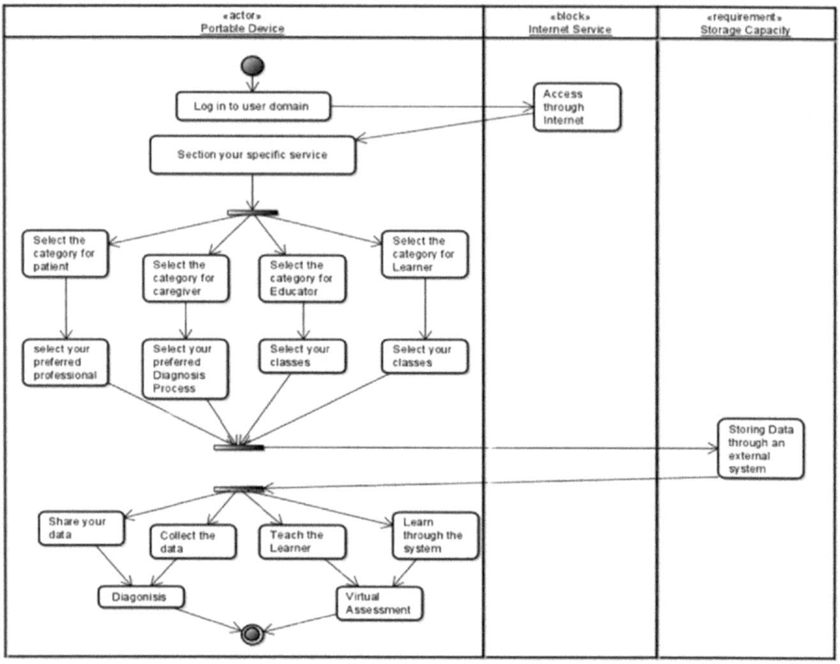


**FIGURE 4.12** An activity diagram to demonstrate the use of the system.

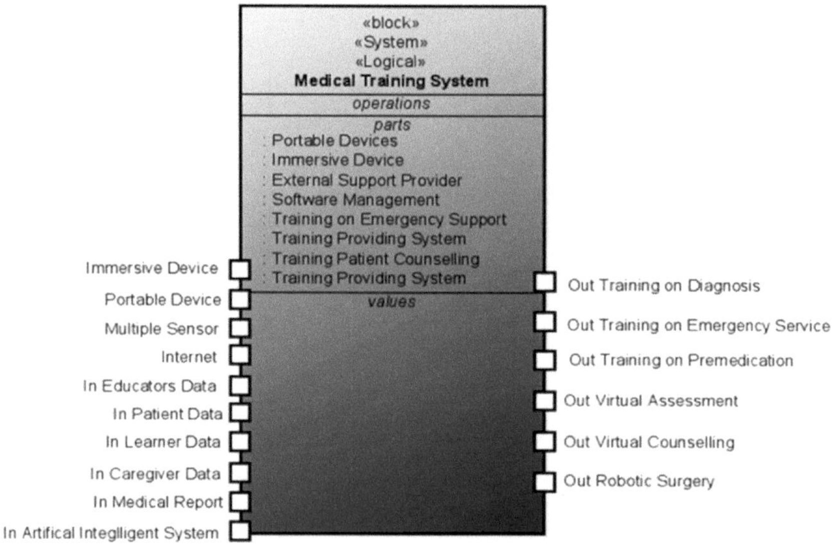


**FIGURE 4.13** A logical architecture of medical training system.

Figure 4.14 shows the overall logical architecture of the system, with the medical support system as the main system and key logical sections including immersive devices, portable devices, training on emergency support, external support, training on patient counseling, and software management. For the system to work, all these logical subsections must be aligned.

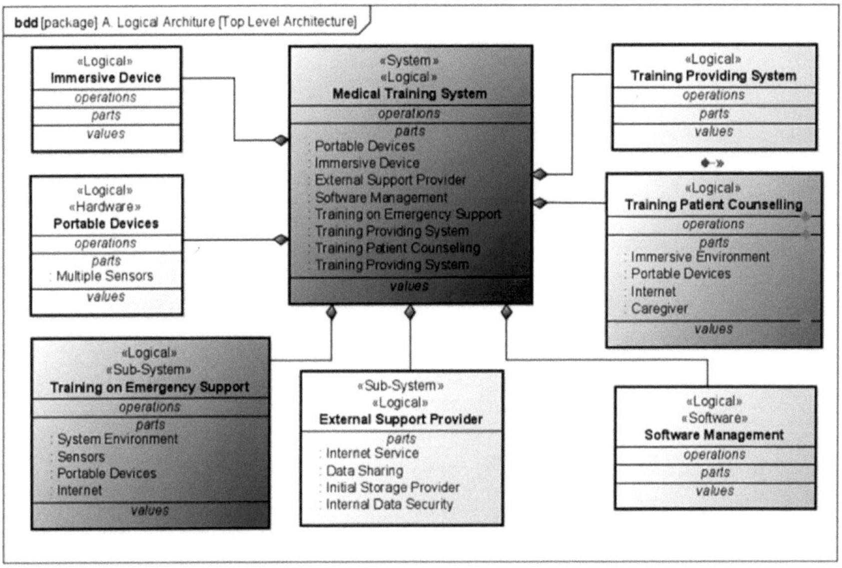


**FIGURE 4.14** A logical architecture of the system.

### *4.5.2 PHYSICAL ARCHITECTURE*

The design of the system's components is represented by a schema in physical architecture. As an organization or representation, a system diagram shows the physical elements of a system. Physical architecture must be incorporated into the allocations and product baselines. There are three subsystems in the physical architecture in Figure 4.15: the data management systems, the hardware management systems, and the software management systems. Among the components of the data management system are a processor, a storage device, a data protection system, and a device for sharing information. The hardware management system for the immersive environment includes an immersive device, a smartphone, and multiple sensors. Furthermore, the software management system consists of three parts: software development, software maintenance, and software updates.

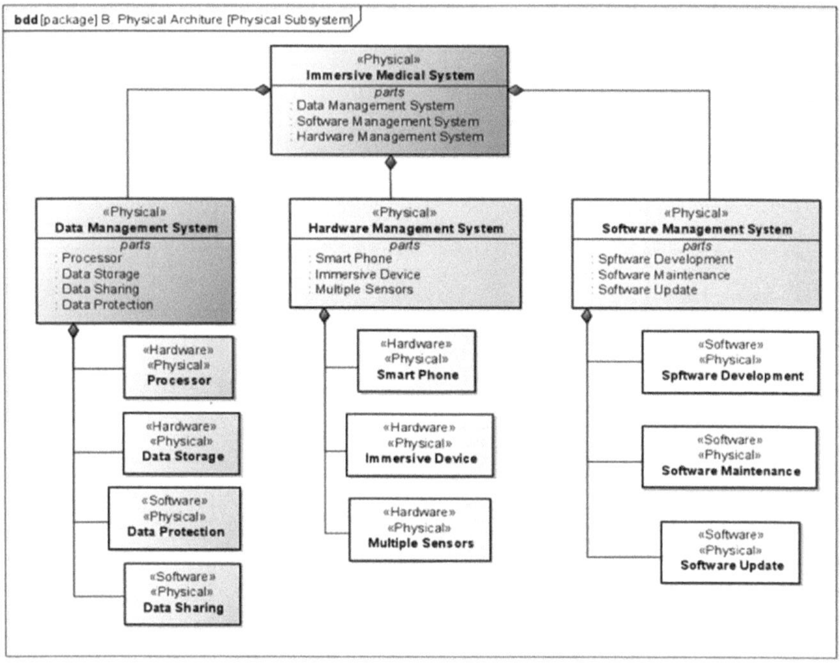


**FIGURE 4.15** A physical subsystem architecture.

In order to consider a physical architecture model for a system, it is first necessary to identify the components of the system as well as any interfaces capable of implementing input-output and control functions. Systems engineers must assign design properties, derived from requirements, to identify potential elements within a logical architecture. Functions are decomposed, gathered, or separated in partitioning and allocating to determine which elements of a system may be able to support the function. As an alternative, they may already exist and can be repurposed, redeveloped, or technology implemented.

A diagram illustrating the allocation of logical resources to physical resources has been shown in Figure 4.16. As shown in the diagram, logical architectures are allocated with physical architectures like hardware management systems. Alternatively, external support providers assign data management systems and software management systems to external support providers.

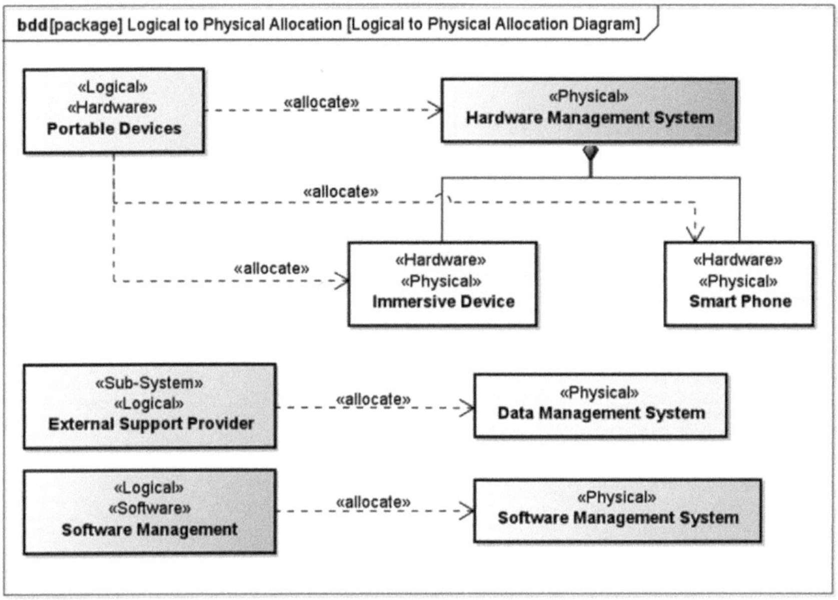


**FIGURE 4.16** Logical to physical architecture allocation.

### *4.5.3 TRACEABILITY AND PARAMETRIC DIAGRAM*

In software engineering, traceability refers to tagging architectural sections at various stages of development. This tool is intended to help keep track of the development life cycle. The requirement for traceability is common in systems engineering. The diagram in Figure 4.17 depicts a traceability map of the proposed system.

By analyzing key metrics, SysML Parametric models can help engineers evaluate key system parameters, including availability, reliability, and energy consumption. A parametric model of the proposed system is shown in Figure 4.18.

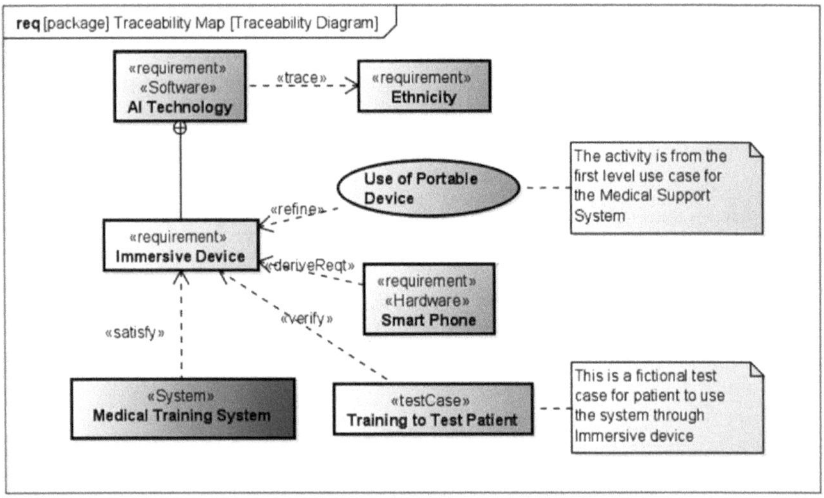


**FIGURE 4.17** A traceability map.

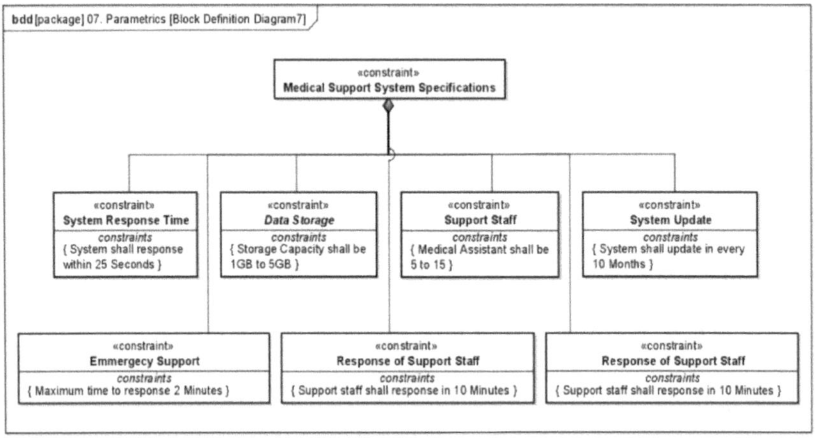


**FIGURE 4.18** A parametric diagram of the proposed system.

## 4.6 CONCLUSION

Despite its increasing popularity in the medical field for use in balance assessments, rehabilitation, and psychotherapies, some researchers point out that immersive technology is also commonly used as an educational tool in medical and dental sciences. Medical education utilizing immersive tools offers a fun, engaging, interactive, and cost-effective environment where students can acquire fun, engaging, and interactive experiences without the risks. Students can practice how to perform surgery through these situation-based learning opportunities, including specifically surgical simulations mediated by immersive technologies, and acquire knowledge and skills without experiencing the potentially life-changing consequences.

This chapter aims to design the system architecture of an immersive-technology-based educational system. As described in the opening section, it is organized around a system of interests. In order to do this, groups were created based on stakeholder types and roles, and customer needs and system requirements were outlined. This is followed by a discussion of requirements mapping. Analyzing the system included analyzing its use cases as well as the logical and physical architecture diagrams of the system and allocating logical architectures to physical architectures. Lastly, the traceability of the architecture and parametric model were demonstrated.

## KEYWORDS

- **augmented reality**
- **data sharing**
- **data transferring**
- **healthcare education**
- **healthcare training**
- **logical architecture**
- **medical education**
- **stakeholders**
- **virtual reality**

## REFERENCES

Baukal, C. E., Ausburn, F. B., & Ausburn, L. J., (2013). A proposed multimedia cone of abstraction: Updating a classic instructional design theory. *Journal of Educational Technology, 9*(4), 15–24. Retrieved from: https://www.learntechlib.org/p/194433/ (accessed on 13 December 2023).

Bloom, B. S., (1974). Time and learning. *American Psychologist, 29*(9), 682–688. doi: 10.1037/h0037632.

Di Meglio, A., & Estrella, F., (2012). *ScienceSoft: Open Software for Open Science.* 032. 10.22323/1.153.0032.

Felnhofer, A., et al., (2015). Is virtual reality emotionally arousing? Investigating five emotion-inducing virtual park scenarios. *Int. J. Hum. Comput. Stud., 82,* 48–56.

Ferrer-García, M., et al., (2017). A randomized controlled comparison of second-level treatment approaches for treatment-resistant adults with bulimia nervosa and binge eating disorder: Assessing the benefits of virtual reality cue exposure therapy. *European Eating Disorders Review: The Journal of the Eating Disorders Association, 25*(6), 479–490. doi: 10.1002/erv.2538.

Gamito, P., et al., (2017). Cognitive training on stroke patients via virtual reality-based serious games. *Disability and Rehabilitation,39*(4), 385–388. doi: 10.3109/09638288.2014.934925.

Haller, G., et al., (2009). Quality and safety indicators in anesthesia: A systematic review. *Anesthesiology, 110*(5), 1158–1175. doi: 10.1097/ALN.0b013e3181a1093b.

*Highly Effective VR Medical & Surgical Training,* (2020). Ghost Productions, https://ghostproductions.com/medical-vr-virtual-reality/surgical-training/ (accessed on 13 December 2023).

Hoffmann, T., & McKenna, K., (2006). Analysis of stroke patients' and carers' reading ability and the content and design of written materials: Recommendations for improving written stroke information. *Patient Education and Counseling, 60*(3), 286–93. doi: 10.1016/j.pec.2005.06.020.

Johnson, J. K., & Paul, B., (2009). Patient care handovers: What will it take to ensure quality and safety during times of transition. *The Medical Journal of Australia, 190*(S11), S110–112. doi: 10.5694/j.1326-5377.2009.tb02614.x.

Khan, M. N. R., & Lippert, K. J., (2022a). A framework for a virtual reality-based medical support system. In: Kishor, K. R. C., (ed.), *The Intelligent Systems and Machine Learning for Industry: Advancements, Challenges, and Applications* (pp. 8–28). CRC Press, Taylor & Francis Group.

Khan, M. N. R., & Lippert, K. J., (2022b). Immersive technologies in healthcare education. In: Kishor, K. R. C., (ed.), *The Intelligent Systems and Machine Learning for Industry: Advancements, Challenges, and Applications* (pp. 111–132). CRC Press, Taylor & Francis Group.

Khan, M. N. R., Shakir, A. K., Nadi, S. S., & Abedin, M. Z., (2022). An android application for university-based academic solution for crisis situation. In: Shakya, S., Balas, V. E., Kamolphiwong, S., & Du, K. L., (eds.), *Sentimental Analysis and Deep Learning: Advances in Intelligent Systems and Computing* (Vol. 1408). Springer, Singapore. https://doi.org/10.1007/978-981-16-5157-1_51.

King, C. L., et al., (2018). A trial of a triple-drug treatment for lymphatic filariasis. *The New England Journal of Medicine, 379*(19), 1801–1810. doi: 10.1056/NEJMoa1706854.

Kirmse, S., et al., (2021). A comprehensive commercialization framework for nanocomposites utilizing a model-based systems engineering approach. *Systems, 9*(4), 84.

Marie-Stéphanie, B., et al., (2019). Virtual reality simulation in nontechnical skills training for healthcare professionals: A systematic review. *Simulation in Healthcare:*

*Journal of the Society for Simulation in Healthcare*, *14*(3), 188–194. doi: 10.1097/SIH.0000000000000347.

Mostashari, A., McComb, S. A., Kennedy, D. M., Cloutier, R., &Korfiatis, P., (2012). Developing a stakeholder-assisted agile CONOPS development process. *Syst. Engin.*, *15*, 1–13. https://doi.org/10.1002/sys.20190.

Negro, C. E., et al., (2019). New frontiers for cognitive assessment: An exploratory study of the potentiality of 360° technologies for memory evaluation. *Cyberpsychology, Behavior and Social Networking*, *22*(1), 76–81. doi: 10.1089/cyber.2017.0720.

Norris, M. W., Spicer, K., & Traci, B., (2019). Virtual reality: The new pathway for effective safety training. *Prof. Safety,64*, 36–39.

Rafael, S., Amotz, P., & Ronen, B., (2013).Construction safety training using immersive virtual reality. *Construction Management, andEconomics,31*(9),1005–1017.doi: 10.1080/01446193.2013.828844.

Rene, G.,(2018).Revolutionizing education: The promise of virtual reality.*Childhood Education,94*(1),40–43,doi: 10.1080/00094056.2018.1420362.

Riches, S., et al., (2021). Virtual reality relaxation for the general population: A systematic review. *Social Psychiatry and Psychiatric Epidemiology*, *56*(10), 1707–1727. doi: 10.1007/s00127-021-02110-z.

Riva, G., et al., (2016). Transforming experience: The potential of augmented reality and virtual reality for enhancing personal and clinical change. *Frontiers in Psychiatry*, *7*, 164. doi: 10.3389/fpsyt.2016.00164.

Roy, A., et al., (2018). Correction: The evolution of cost-efficiency in neural networks during recovery from traumatic brain injury. *PloS One*, *13*(10), e0206005. doi: 10.1371/journal.pone.0206005.

Sánchez-Cabrero, R., et al., (2019). Improvement of body satisfaction in older people: An experimental study. *Frontiers in Psychology*, *10*, 2823. doi: 10.3389/fpsyg.2019.02823.

Thompson-Butel, A. G., et al., (2019). The role of personalized virtual reality in education for patients post stroke-a qualitative case series. *Journal of Stroke and Cerebrovascular Diseases: The Official Journal of National Stroke Association*, *28*(2), 450–457. doi: 10.1016/j.jstrokecerebrovasdis.2018.10.018.

Ustun, A. B., Yilmaz, R., & Yilmaz, F. G. K., (2020). Virtual reality in medical education. In: *Mobile Devices and Smart Gadgets in Medical Sciences* (pp. 56–73). IGI Global.

Vaughan, N., et al., (2016). A review of virtual reality-based training simulators for orthopedic surgery. *Medical Engineering & Physics*, *38*(2), 59–71. doi: 10.1016/j.medengphy.2015.11.021.

Wiederhold, B. K., & Giuseppe, R., (2012). Positive technology supports the shift to preventive, integrative health. *Cyberpsychology, Behavior and Social Networking*, *15*(2), 67–8. doi: 10.1089/cyber.2011.1533.

Zhang, J., et al., (2018). LeNup: Learning nucleosome positioning from DNA sequences with improved convolutional neural networks. *Bioinformatics (Oxford, England)*, *34*(10), 1705–1712. doi: 10.1093/bioinformatics/bty003.

## CHAPTER 5

# Modeling Interactive E-Books to Support Personalized Teaching in the Online Environment

VU MINH TRANG and NGUYEN TUNG LAM

*University of Education, Vietnam National University, VNU-UED, Hanoi, Vietnam*

## ABSTRACT

Implementing online teaching activities to adapt to the current global social context has caused learners to face many difficulties and barriers, especially in accessing appropriate learning resources. However, the changes in the online teaching process are the driving force behind the development of more diverse and influential digital learning materials. At the same time, E-books have taken on space, context, and opportunities for teaching activities. They are deployed in the form of interactive experiences that meet the flexible learning needs of learners through the construction and application of multimedia interaction models in interactive E-book design to enable the personal learning process.–One of the solutions adopted in the context of digital transformation is online teaching today. The chapter will analyze, comment, and evaluate the feasibility of interactive e-books in personalized teaching to ensure access to learning, form, and developing competencies for learners in an online environment.

Intelligent Learning Paradigms and Student Empowerment: Digital Integration and Transformation. Souvik Pal, Ton Quang Cuong, & R. S. S. Nehru (Eds.)

## 5.1 INTRODUCTION

Industry 4.0 is a combination of reality and virtual systems with many new inventions such as the internet, artificial intelligence (AI), robots, nanotechnology... all aspects and areas of social life (European Commission, 2019), especially education and training, because learners acquire not only interdisciplinary knowledge and skills but also administrative and technical skills. Ability to control machines in an ecosystem, where all elements are linked together through cyberspace and cloud computing. Therefore, the relationship between teaching and learning is also enlarged not only between teachers and students but also students with students, students with the community, and students with open sources of knowledge based on the support of digital breakthroughs, thereby contributing to building high-quality human resources to meet the requirements of the technology world (Prensky, 2001).

Therefore, the digitization and digital transfer of information data sources and input educational content according to the principles of rich content, multi-format, strong interaction, reuse, and accessibility, accessing, searching, sharing, and contributing will help increase "multi-sensory perception" for learners... so digital learning will become a compelling goal and means in educational processes. Among them is the interactive E-book – A form of digital learning that provides not only information and learning content but also creates strong interaction between those contents and learners (Nguyen Quy Thanh, 2020) through video, graphics, audio-visual, hyperlinks, quizzes, back-and-forth animations, and search features (Askar, 2014; Buzzetto, 2007). Therefore, interactive E-books will allow learners to build a learning path in their style (Yang, 2018; Zajac, 2009). In addition, the effects of interactive E-books in creating motivation for learning, research, forging reading habits, improving learning results, and having a positive impact on students' emotional and psychological well-being have been proven by many research groups from different countries (Akpokodje, 2016; Ebied, 2015; Rockinson-Szapkiw, 2013).

Research group Blossfeld & Süss has demonstrated that using technology can provide creative, enjoyable, and motivating learning environments for students (Blossfeld et al., 2018; Süss, 2013). This was confirmed when 4.0 technology created a new learning environment for students: online classrooms during the worldwide COVID-19 pandemic. Teachers bring into full play their abilities and diversify the ways of conveying lesson content. Therefore, when technology combines with personalized teaching, it will bring success in improving student learning outcomes, especially for those who are not yet interested in learning and gifted students. They face educational barriers while also helping to increase students' self-confidence (Hayes, 2013; Bousnakis, 2011; Whipp, 2014).

With the analysis of the outstanding advantages of interactive E-books and the initial successes of personalized teaching, the chapter will focus on analyzing E-book design models and providing principles and the processes of building an interactive E-book to support the teaching of personifications.

## 5.2 NEW EDUCATIONAL TECHNOLOGY TRENDS

In the first decade of the 21st century, new technologies exploded and developed strongly, which pushed educational technology to move towards "deeper for people" and "open learning opportunities in all ways, anything, any subject, all the time." Technology-based education has gone beyond traditional school campuses, opening a "lifelong" and "life-oriented" education space creating equal access to education for everyone (Nguyen Quy Thanh, 2018).

This approach has given rise to a wide range of new forms of education/teaching (formal or informal based on extensive knowledge-sharing and society) placed under a broad category of digital education. With that approach, education/teaching technology has made profound qualitative changes compared to the methods, processes, and use of technology in teaching (Nguyen Quy Thanh, 2018).

In 2014, through the final report of the Smart Schools Committee in New York, educators, students, and parents judged the need to modernize facilities and classrooms to apply the power of technology to boost educational effectiveness. The report also highlights that supporting technology for teaching and professional development is critical to ensuring every American has access to high-quality education and is ready for global competition. Educational institutions, educators, students, and families benefit when digital tools and materials are effectively integrated into the classroom and community.

Technology helps to strengthen the participation of students and academic accountability, enhance student achievement, and transform the relationship between student and teacher. Technology also helps students acquire the skills to rival for in-demand employment in the 21st-century economy.

Technology has the power to remove the distance between parents and teachers, families, and classrooms, and between schools across the state. It is possible under the condition of increasing the interaction between students, parents, and teachers and helps the expansion of learning not only within the school but also at home. Technology allows teachers to train through online methods and can add to the credibility of the most experienced teachers. Moreover, equipping all students with essential up-to-date tools guarantees students in New York State develop the necessary skills to survive and adapt flexibly in the 21st century (New York Smart Schools Commission Report, 2014).

In the 1990s, Finland was one of the leading information nations worldwide. The government supports ICTs (information and communication technologies) in education. This country has issued national strategies and policies to develop the country into an information society. This nation's program "Information Society" is of particular interest to high schools. Finland has developed an international image as an innovative and high-tech country. IT has progressed in Finnish schools through improvement projects such as distance education networks and enhanced video communication. Mobile learning has been published in some form and has become a concern of educational research.

Finland has focused its national effort on making IT an everyday driver of 21st-century skills in schools. A new national strategy for using ICT for education in schools has been initiated. ICT effectively empowers all children in the school community to learn. Practices may change from traditional Internet usage to mobile technology and the most modern social media. The main criterion is that technology should be considered a learning tool (Hannele Niemi, 2013).

Chinese author Zhi-Ting Zhu also identified a learning environment supported by technologies that allow students to use digital resources and interact with learning systems anywhere and anytime but also proactively give the essential study guides, support tools, or helpful learning tips. Different sorts of technologies are applied to support and intensify learning, including hardware and software. Hardware includes physical objects such as interactive whiteboards, smartboards, e-bags, mobile phones, wearable devices, intelligent devices, ubiquitous sensors, cloud computing, ambient intelligence, and IoT technology; the software includes learning systems, learning tools, online resources, educational games using social networks, learning analytics, visualizations, virtual reality (VR), and more.

Under the support of different technologies, the learning environment provides a personalized learning experience and precise and abundant learning facilities using learning analytics (Zhi-Ting Zhu, 2016).

In an article on standards for intelligent education, Norwegian authors Tore Hoel and Jon Mason have made a statement about an intelligent learning environment that needs to use various digital technologies to assist with learning, education, and training. At the same time, based on assessments of pioneering issues in intelligent learning, innovative education and a smart learning environment, the authors also highlighted cognitive intelligent learning models. Among them, Koper defines an innovative learning environment (SLE) as "a physical environment enriched with digital devices, contextual awareness, and adaptive devices" to foster more effective and faster learning. According to Koper, SLE is a technical system consisting of one or many digital devices supplemented with the physical locations of learners. Those are aware of learners' location, context, and culture; and add study capabilities for these elements, such as reinforcement, assessment, remote collaboration, and feedback; in addition, they also track the learner's progress and provide relevant information to the stakeholders (Tore Hoel, 2018).

## 5.3 DIGITAL EDUCATION

Digital education includes three levels of implementation:

1. **Digitization:** A "mechanical" (physical) conversion from a traditional format to a digital format. For example, publications, printed materials, pictures, and analog signals. Converted to digital form (but still used with the previous function).
2. **Digitization:** Converting to digital format is accompanied by the transformation and increase of new functions, implemented based on digital technology. For example, digitized learning materials are embedded on technology platforms, capable of interacting, simulating, and customizing according to needs.
3. **Digital Transformation:** The digital transformation process is systematic and complex, creating qualitatively new processes and

output products; For example, e-learning, environment, virtual learning space, personal learning applications (apps) on mobile platforms (mobile technology).

The process of digitization and digital transformation creating equality in online access strongly promotes the production of knowledge content, turning teaching content in previously conventional formats into metadata packages (Meta-data), "mobile content" (Mobile/portable content) by different methods (on online platforms) to meet the needs of the information society. Following the success of the trend of "Smart Schools" (Smart Schools, Computing Schools) in the early years of the last decade, the teaching process is increasingly changing in terms of quantity and quality with new capabilities application of "hand-held devices" (Mobile Devices) and touch (All in One + touch) to create a vast source of knowledge, even from a small learning community, expanding the learning space VR (classes, study groups... on the physical-cyber platform).

With many opportunities to access knowledge and the need to exchange information, learners are increasingly active in acquiring knowledge, choosing learning content according to their own needs, and being flexible in the learning process. Learning, so learning is more personalized in the context of connected teaching. In self-directing learning and selecting appropriate content according to their needs, learning styles, and personal interests, learners will create their own "learning space" by applying technology. Alongside the fresh, adaptable, and modernized approach to education and teaching, learners are progressively adopting a novel learning methodology tailored to address the diverse developmental requirements of individuals through a range of learning opportunities.

## 5.4 DIGITAL TEACHING ENVIRONMENT

One of the new features of the digital learning environment is the digital transformation of handheld devices.

Derived from Google's training practice, the trend of "bringing personal handheld devices into the classroom"–BYOD/BYOT (Bring Your Own Devices/Bring Your Own Technology/Tool) is increasingly attracting the teachers' attention. Although there are many controversies about the benefits, effectiveness, or limitations in practice, the BYOD trend is still widely applied in some advanced education systems.

According to statistics on the website https://buildfire.com/app-statistics/, currently, the average opening frequency of mobile applications for 49% of users is generally more than 11 times/day; for 21% of young people (born after 2000), more than 50 times/day; On average, each user uses up to 30 apps per month.

According to other statistics at the website https://42matters.com/stats, the number of existing applications (as of 2019) on the Apple App Store is about 1.8 million, and that of the Google Play Store is more than 3.0 million, with a total of more than 4,000 new applications for two of the operating systems updated daily on mobile devices; including over 400,000 free educational apps. Moreover, educational applications always hold the top position (Google Play Store) and second (Apple App Store) at the Top 50 of specific application groups.

This shows a need for a continuous survey, selection, and serious research to incorporate these applications into BYOD teaching processes.

This process strongly promotes interaction between learners and the digital learning environment, creating highly differentiated and personalized learning opportunities. With "handheld/wearable" and "mobile" digital devices, learners can access, operate, and manage their entire learning environment using handheld devices (tablets, iPad, Smartphone, E-reader) to interact with any content according to personal purposes and needs. For example, a digitized chemical laboratory space, chemical company environment, etc. The connection between smartphones and VR glasses will create an entirely new environment for receiving quality information for learners (Nguyen Quy Thanh, 2018).

## 5.5 DIGITAL LEARNING MATERIALS

In the current context of substantial book transformation, the field of education in general and the development of digital learning materials, in particular, face opportunities for transformation and explosive development. Information and knowledge data sources are digitized (designed, produced, published, and stored), transferred via digital tools, and used on smart devices such as laptops, iPads, and tablets to meet learners' increasing demand for experience and interaction.

Developed based on digital tools and platforms on the principle of content-rich, multi-format, intensely interactive, reusable, easy to access, lookup, share, and contribute, digital learning gradually becomes a goal. Effective means in educational processes.

Not only stopping at converting to digital format for documents or opening up learning resources so that content, knowledge, and knowledge can be circulated, recirculated, and reproduced in the digital environment as before, articles learning, learning content is "gamified" increasing opportunities for seamless, immersive experiences and embedding learners in multi-virtual-reality environments to solve problems; realistic 3D simulation (3D simulation), animation (Animation), image creation (Hologram), video creation, AI lectures, interactive E-books... this has helped the concept of digital learning It is only about providing information and knowledge content, but also in the ability, feedback, and intense interaction between learners with digital content and learners with teachers through digital content (Nguyen Quy Thanh, 2018).

## 5.6 THE MAIN IDEAS OF PERSONALIZED TEACHING APPROACH

Individualized teaching, more broadly, adaptive learning, is the organization of the teaching process in the direction of teaching "learners" rather than teaching "classes" to respond to students' needs directly and establish individual learning paths for learners.

Based on a rather massive system of theoretical foundations of teaching theories (Didactic, learning theories), the way learners perform practical learning activities, the context of impact and support is becoming more and more modern according to the trend. With the development of society, personalized teaching is becoming an advanced scientific, systematic, and widespread approach today. In today's development of non-traditional education, teaching through a network (Grid, network), the role of each connection node (i.e., learner) becomes more critical than ever.

Hence, personalized teaching is based mainly on an essential combination or linkage between systematic activities following specific principles and processes, realizing the relationship within the "common" (educational programs, learning objectives, or environment, etc.) and learner's identity (learning style, pathways, methods, capacities, qualifications, motivations, needs). The pedagogical process and teaching elements are primarily geared toward finding the "gold" dynamic balance. On the other hand, this balance may answer the essential questions in the teaching process: What is precisely personalized and contextualized learning? How do we personalize or contextualize the learning process without adverse effects on the learning community while still maintaining and ensuring the common purpose among learners?

Nowadays, learners are increasingly becoming "the center of their learning," more freely in self-direction and choosing how to learn according to their needs, interests, speed, learning style, and adaptive capacity. Therefore, learning increasingly bears the personal imprint of the learner. Educators have introduced many concepts such as differentiation, individualization, personalization, and customization to indicate the teaching trend that requires focused practice, towards the learner, for the learners themselves in general; some characteristics can be listed as follows:

- Differentiated learning is a "prism" to detect, screen, classify, and acknowledge learners as different individuals (including attributes, qualities, abilities, personality, etc.). This may prefer the concept of a specific learning relationship, "the unified diversity" (i.e., learning based on respecting learners' differences).
- Individualized learning recognizes the "individual" and uniqueness of learners in the learning process and their relationship with the learners themselves (uniqueness, individuality). For example, the choice of majors, subjects, and technological means according to individual learners' needs and interests; programs are designed to be diverse, flexible, interconnected, and highly selective to meet the unique needs of learners; learners are unique (customized learning), the program is combined, designed, and customized for themselves (tailored learning).
- Personalized learning (personalized learning) acknowledges the "diversity" of learners compared to other individuals in the classroom, collective, or learning community. For example, learners have different learning styles, so teachers must diversify teaching methods to maintain a fair opportunity in learning access.

Depending on the name and expression of these teaching approaches, they may be different in practice, but they all aim for a common goal: learning must come from the learner's context; there is no general concept of learning (one-size-fits-all) or learning by itself, which explicitly from a combination of attributes, characteristics, and abilities of learners (Nguyen Tung Lam, 2021; The model of contextualization and personalization in learning).

## 5.7 TRENDS OF TECHNOLOGY INTEGRATION IN PERSONALIZED TEACHING

In particular, in the past few years, there has been a strong trend of changing from the traditional method of experimental education to the orientation of personalized and interactive teaching. The digitization and digital transformation process are increasingly penetrating the education field with technologies that provide educational products, activities, knowledge, and skills to apply technology solutions and creative innovation. Through that, the application of technology in teaching has strongly supported and promoted learners' learning activities, becoming a regular, continuous, anytime, anywhere, lifelong learning process. At the same time, digital education is also expected to thrive with many beneficiaries across all learners' geographic regions, ages, and socioeconomic conditions.

Besides, educational technology is expected to play an essential role in creating significant changes and job opportunities. Global education is moving towards learner-centered and inclusive learning based on technology (better responsive to learners with special needs).

Personalized teaching according to technology's innovative education model (SMART Education). In which the elements are set up according to a whole system, have mutual effects, and promote quality and efficiency for the personalization process (including S: self-directed; M: motivating; A: highly adaptive; R: resources, extended learning materials; T: based on technology, technology enables a rich environment).

This model can substantially impact the personalized teaching process in the following directions: Creating a change in learners' expectations and learners' ability to respond to the continuous change in the social context development association (self-direction, lifelong learning); Orientation to diversify outputs "educational/teaching products," the process of ensuring and improving the quality of learning outcomes according to individual learning styles and learning capacities; Change management and administration models in teaching based on individual learners' learning plans and speeds; Suggestions for designing teaching programs in the direction of flexibility and adaptability (learning content and assessment), with a strong focus on learner objectivity and capacity development.

Applying the SMART Education model makes it possible to deploy non-traditional teaching methods that strongly focus on individual learners comprehensively, such as e-Learning, Blended Learning, and Flipped learning (Nguyen Tung Lam, 2021; The model of contextualization and personalization in learning).

## 5.8 DESIGN INTERACTIVE E-BOOK TO SUPPORT PERSONALIZED TEACHING

### *5.8.1 DEFINITION OF INTERACTIVE E-BOOK*

According to the website www.thuvien-ebook.com, "E-book is an acronym for electronic book. In the simplest terms, electronic books (E-books or digital books) are digital (or electronic) versions of books. Contents of digital books can be taken from paper books or be independent depending on the publisher. Some people often use this term to refer to devices used to read digital books (also called book-reading appliances or E-book readers)."

### *5.8.2 MODEL OF INTERACTIVE E-BOOK DESIGN*

#### *5.8.2.1 INTEGRATED INTERACTIVE MULTIMEDIA MODEL (INTERACT)*

The Multimedia Interactive Integration Model (INTERACT) includes six main components that make up an integrated system: learning environment, behavior, cognitive, motivational, and emotional activities, human variables studies, and mental models of humans (Domagk et al., 2010) (Figure 5.1).

#### *5.8.2.2 MODEL INTERACT-XP*

To examine the theory of multimedia learning in interactive E-books, the study adopted the interactive multimedia model (INTERACT). This can help provide research information and build learning components required to design and develop interactive E-books from which the INTERACT-XP (Multimedia Interactive Integration Model in Context/Environment of Personalized learning) model is designed (Nguyen Tung Lam, 2021).

The E-book is an effective medium to support many different purposes, primarily to support personalized learning. The interaction process when using the E-book is represented by the feedback loops connecting these components (Figure 5.2).

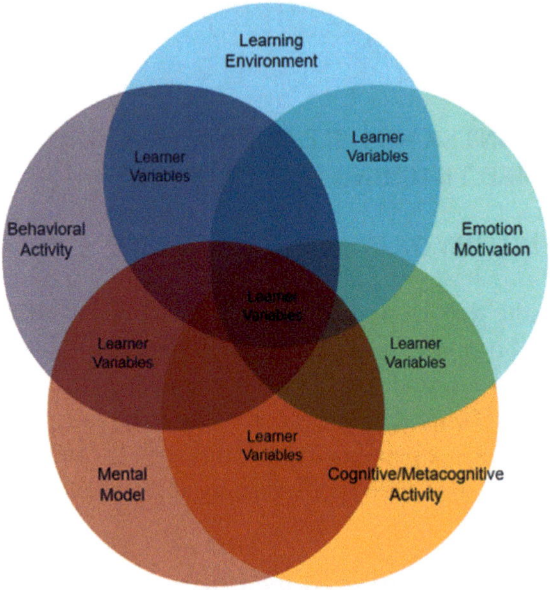


**FIGURE 5.1** The integrated model of multimedia interactivity (INTERACT).
*Source*: Adapted from Domagk et al., 2010

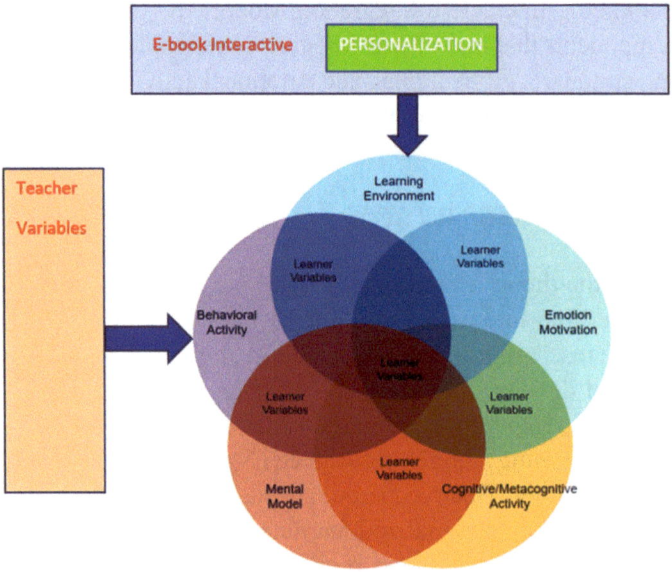


**FIGURE 5.2** Modeling impact of personalization on INTERACT.

Indeed, research suggests that E-book teachers or designers should follow the principles of interactive multimedia learning during E-book design.

From the perspective of INTERACT, learning environments that integrate feedback loops connecting learning systems, behavioral processes, and cognitive processes can activate students' learning motivation and engage them in cognitive activity. For example, an E-book can provide facilities such as video, audio, images, audio recording..., and user-controlled interactivity that improves feedback loops for learning with e-books.

### *5.8.3 DESIGNING INTERACTIVE E-BOOKS*

#### *5.8.3.1 PRINCIPLES OF INTERACTIVE E-BOOK DESIGN*

An E-book is a very effective teaching and learning support tool. However, to be able to design and use E-books effectively, it is necessary to keep a few principles in mind.

- Integrate many audio-visual multimedia applications to encourage different paths to receive different knowledge.
- Please make the most interactive activities on the E-book interface to make them more learner-friendly.
- For terms that are difficult to understand, it is necessary to provide an online explanation (in-line dictionary) or descriptive illustrations.
- Pay attention to using multimedia elements flexibly to attract student's attention but ensure the requirement of providing scientific knowledge.
- Develop test exercises, and reasonable assessment, with good difficulty and discrimination.

#### *5.8.3.2 INTERACTIVE E-BOOK DESIGN SOFTWARE*

There is much-supporting software for building e-books, such as Lectora, iBooks Author, and Kotobee Authors. These software functions generally allow the integration and arrangement of documents, images, tables, and interactive applications into one book. Interactive applications include photo galleries, audio files, video files, and short and multiple-choice tests. However, in the framework of this chapter, we choose Kotobee software. The author is the primary tool for the design. Kotobee Author is an E-book design software in EPUB format and can be read on many different devices, suitable for education, training, or publishing purposes. The software allows us to create E-books with the designer's own "colors," logos and brands; Interactive applications are prioritized thoroughly. This software has a very user-friendly interface and can work on today's popular operating system platforms, Windows and Mac OS.

#### *5.8.3.3 INTERACTIVE E-BOOK DESIGN PROCESS (Figure 5.3)*

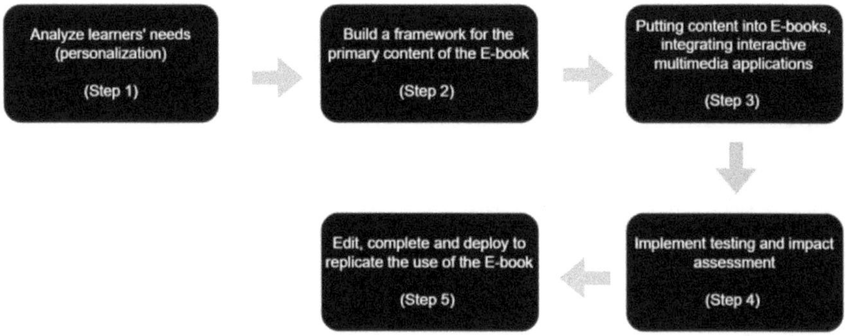


**FIGURE 5.3** Interactive e-book design process.

#### *5.8.3.4 USAGE MODES IN INTERACTIVE E-BOOK*

In our opinion, there are two primary purposes when using interactive e-books: reading and learning and research (Takev, 2020).

Suppose the user uses the interactive e-book to read. In that case, it works like a typical e-book with flipping and note-taking mode, and the user can freely read the contents designed in the e-book, deal with random requests or interact with the e-book without any barriers. If users use interactive e-books to study and research, the learning process occurs sequentially, with each chapter of content designed to help learners achieve specific learning goals. Learners must pass the mini-tests or end-of-chapter assignments because that will be the key for learners to continue with the following learning content; this process is like we are gamifying the content. E-book, learners need to complete some tasks before going next door. Alternatively, interactive e-books can prompt learners to review selected sections of specific chapters so that learners can achieve better results when completing a quick quiz or final assignment. This means that learners can customize the learning content to suit their individual needs without going through all the content available in the interactive e-book.

### *5.8.3.5 PARTICIPANT'S ROLES IN INTERACTIVE E-BOOK MODE*

We also categorize E-book user roles by features, purposes, and interactions with the E-book. (Figure 5.4):

- The role of the reader or learner, the ultimate beneficiary of the E-book;
- The role of designer, content creator or teacher is reserved for the author of the E-book.

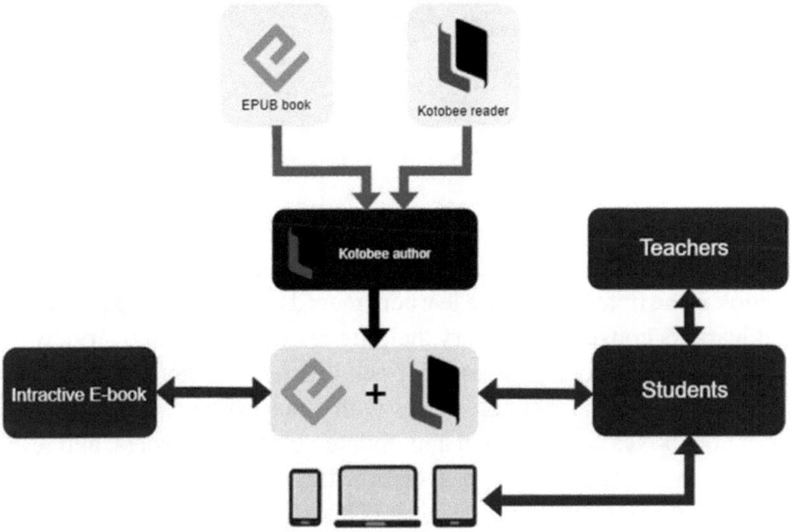


**FIGURE 5.4** User role diagram.

### *5.8.3.6 CONTENT CREATORS' ROLE OF LEARNERS*

With the original idea of creating a learning forum among E-book users through the Padlet application, learners can create a community of users around the E-book. That means they can exchange and respond to questions about learning content with teachers or classmates who are using E-books, and at the same time, they can get instant answers on different platforms that rock. This feature is not only beneficial for student users, where learning is personalized, and the E-book is contextualized like in a live classroom where there is immediate feedback from the teacher. Students and other classmates, but also help the author, who is the teacher, update, adjust, and supplement the content of the E-book in the following courses and semesters. An illustration of this process is in Figure 5.5.

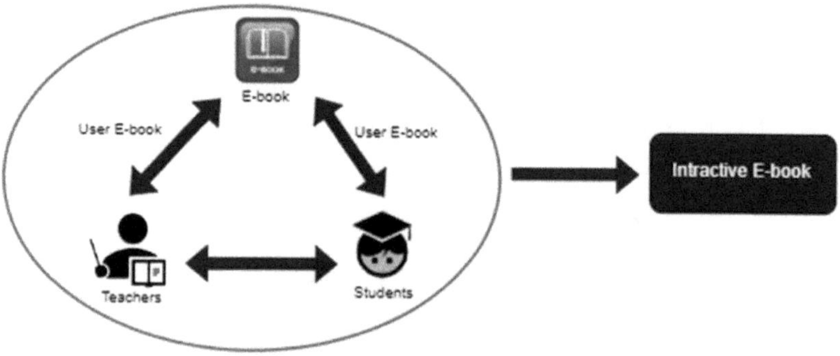


**FIGURE 5.5** Ecosystem using E-book.

The E-book must be used on devices with an Internet connection to achieve this function. Another outstanding feature of the interactive E-book is the note box, where learners record notes, keywords, and content that learners consider necessary, helping learners have an overview of the content of knowledge just gained. Each learner will have their note boxes and can share individual note boxes with other learners. At the same time, these note boxes can be added and updated by other learners, and teachers can use these note boxes as a demonstration of the student's learning process without depending on tests. This means that student assessment becomes flexible, tailored to each learner, and based on the student's entire learning process instead of summative assessments through the test.

## 5.9 INTERACTIVE E-BOOK APPLICATION IN CHEMISTRY TEACHING

### *5.9.1 STRUCTURE OF THE INTERACTIVE E-BOOK*

Our initial goal when designing interactive E-books is to use E-books for personalized teaching. This is a challenge when the E-book needs more than an electronic version with flip effects and can easily be used on mobile devices. For this reason, the E-book content and the applications used within it should provide activities or experiences for students, such as quizzes and especially with Chemistry where possible, and labs or lessons files can be processed in an interactive E-book environment.

When a user logs in to Kotobee Reader, an e-book library appears on the screen, and the system automatically loads the e-book selected by the student (Figure 5.6). A good point when using the Kotobee platform is that students can use it on computers, phones, iPods or any other portable smart device while the screen resolution is still of good quality.

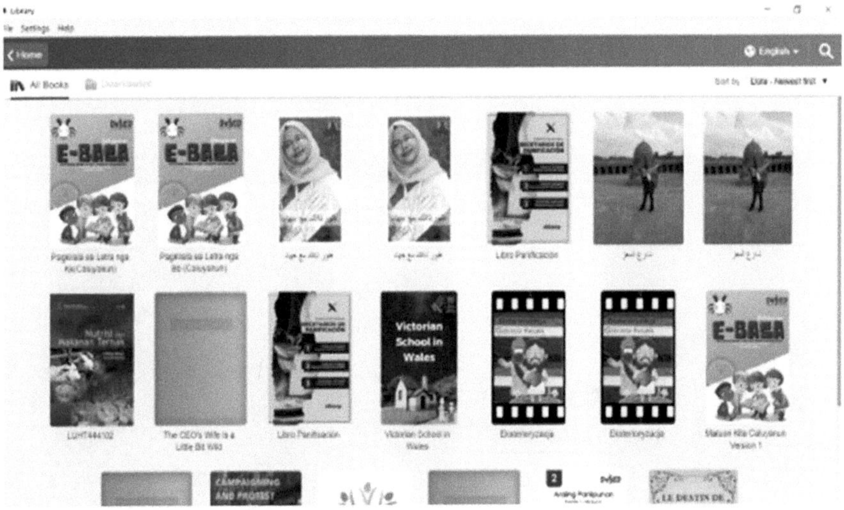


**FIGURE 5.6** The first page of Kotobee reader.

The E-book's table of contents will be built according to the textbook content framework. Students can easily follow and add other content, such as user manuals and applicable content not mentioned in the textbooks, the library of general knowledge lectures, and the test system (Figures 5.7 and 5.8). In addition, each page of the book is designed with a full range of tools such as information search, images, sounds, labels, notes, zoom in, zoom out, and return to the table of contents to help maximize improve the ability to read and use E-books according to the needs of each student.

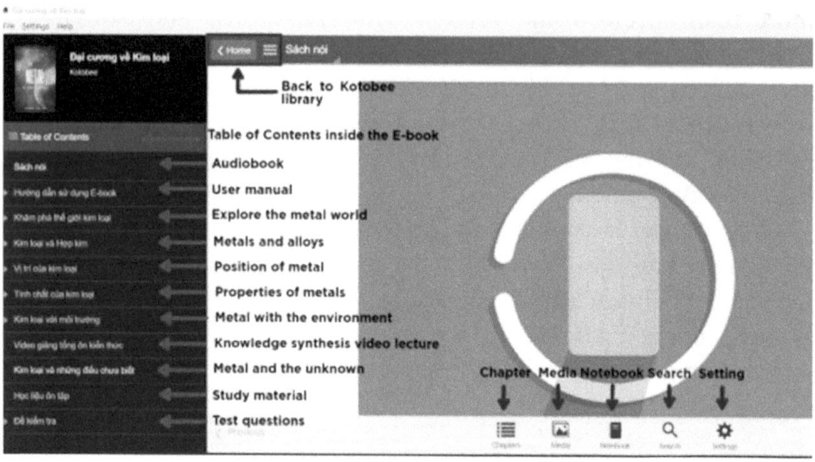


**FIGURE 5.7** The content of the interactive book.

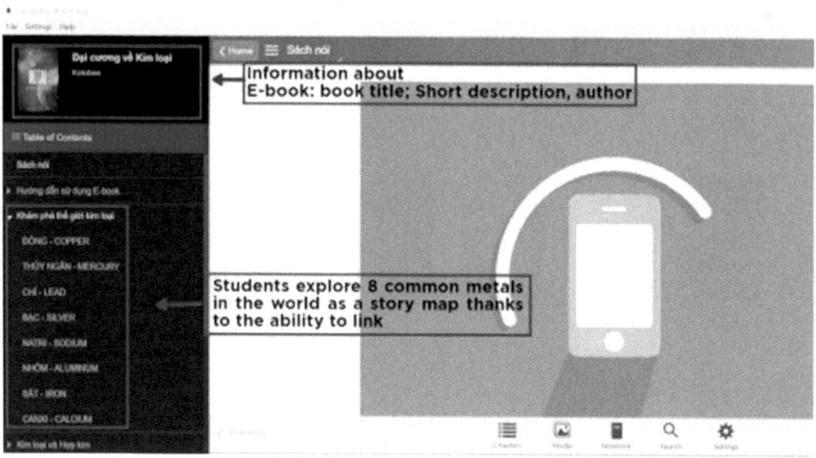


**FIGURE 5.8** Intro page of the E-book.

The e-book developed in this study includes multimedia content such as videos, audio recordings, images, PDF text, and interactive components such as user forums. The Padlet.com app is a short quiz that uses the Quizi.com app and relies on a linker feature for use on an e-book. Additionally, to attract students to read and use e-books, we have designed knowledge content pages in info graphics and built knowledge content associated with real-life examples, such as the activity design of the eight path-tied metallic elements using the StoryMap application. The e-book tracks students' learning progress automatically through direct tests on the e-book and quizzes on Quizi.com; then, the results are sent back to teachers for them to be able to timely grasp and orient students to learn.

Finally, students can share information and problems in the learning process with the e-book through the link between the e-book and the Padlet application installed on the teacher's phone and receive immediate feedback from the teacher. Students can also choose to share the book they are reading with friends or the community through the Kotobee book library.

## 5.10 CONCLUSION

The Industrial Revolution 4.0 requires education and training to create dynamic, independent people with self-study and self-research skills, especially creating conditions to maximize students' creativity. On the other hand, in education 4.0, digitized classrooms, intelligent devices, wireless devices, and virtual digital multimedia are strongly developed, causing education to change in teaching and learning methods to be suitable and asymptotic to the new educational trend with features such as learning society, split lessons, open educational resources, and personal learning devices. The chapter has mentioned the following contents:

- Digital education has three levels of implementation, which are the replacement of digital format, digitization, and digital transformation. In this process, learners create their own "learning space" on the Web platform as an open, flexible learning environment that is both competitive, socially shared, and highly interactive to develop personal capacity.
- Digital teaching is implemented according to the "lifelong learning" approach based on two e-learning models and an online teaching model, thanks to cloud computing technology.
- The digital teaching environment creates opportunities for learners to access rich and diverse information sources through AI, VR, AR, and MR technologies... to promote interaction between learners and the learning environment.
- Digital learning materials are developed in the direction of solid interaction with learners through digital applications, including "gaming," 3D simulation, animation, image creation, video creation, interactive E-books...

According to the SMART education model, an overview of personalized teaching provides a direction to integrate technology into personalized teaching.

- Overview of interactive E-books and gives five criteria along with two models, five principles and a 5-step process for interactive E-book design. The chapter also gives one example of an Interactive E-book design for teaching metal part chemistry.

## KEYWORDS

- **digital education**
- **digital learners**
- **digital teaching**
- **integrated interactive multimedia model**
- **interactive e-book**
- **online environment**
- **personalized teaching**

## REFERENCES

Akpokodje, V. N., &Ukwuoma, S. C., (2016). Evaluating the impact of e-Book on reading motivation of students of higher learning in Nigerian Universities. In: *Proceedings of IFLAWLIC in Session 189.* Ohio: Colombus.

Askar, A., (2014). Interactive e-Books as a tool of mobile learning for digital-natives in higher education: Interactivity, preferences, and ownership. *Educational Technology Research and Development, 60*, 7–13.

Blossfeld, H. P., et al., (2018). *DigitaleSouveränität und Bildung[Digital Sovereignty and Education].* Münster: Waxmann Verlag GmbH.

Bousnakis, M., Burns, T., Donnan, L., Hopper, S., Mugavero, G., & Rogers, K. B., (2011). Achievement integrated model: Interventions for gifted indigenous underachievers. *Giftedness from An Indigenous Perspective, 21*(2), 43–77.

Buzzetto, N., Sweat, R., &Elobaid, M., (2007). Reading in a digital age: E-Books are students ready for this learning object? *Interdisciplinary Journal of Knowledge and Learning Objects, 3*, 239–250.

Domagk, S., Schwartz, R. N., & Plass, J. L., (2010). Interactivity in multimedia learning: An integrated model. *Computers in Human Behavior, 26*(5), 1024–1033.

Ebied, M. M. A., &Shimaa, A. A. R., (2015). The effect of interactive e-Book on students' achievement at Najran University in computer in education course. *Journal of Education and Practice, 6*(19), 71–82.

European Commission, (2019). *Digital Education at School in Europe*. The Education, Audiovisual and Culture Executive Agency (Education and Youth Policy Analysis).

Hannele, N., Heikki, K., & Vahtivuori-Hanninen, S., (2013). Towards ICT in everyday life in Finnish schools: Seeking conditions for good practices. *Learning, Media, and Technology*, *38*(1), 57–71.

Hayes, D., (2013). Customization in schooling markets: The relationship between curriculum and pedagogy in a "pop-up" learning project, and the epistemic opportunities afforded by students' interests and backgrounds. *International Journal on School Disaffection, 10*(2), 3–22.

*New York Smart Schools Commission Report*, (2014). www.smartschoolsny.com (accessed on 13 December 2023).

Nguyen, Q. T., & Ton, Q. C., (2018). Trends of education 4.0: Application in training at the University of Education, Vietnam National University, Hanoi. *Proceedings of the National Scientific Conference on Human Resource Needs for Development in the Context of the 4th Industrial Revolution and the Responses of Higher Education in Vietnam* (pp. 327–333). Vietnam. Economic Publishing House. Ho Chi Minh.

Nguyen, Q. T., & Ton, Q. C., (2020). *New Trends in Educational Technology.* Accessed http://hvcsnd.edu.vn/nghien-cuu-trao-doi/dai-hoc-40/nhung-xu-the-moi-cua-cong-nghe-trong-giao-duc-6543 (accessed on 13 December 2023).

Nguyen, T. L., Ton, Q. C., Nguyen, H. H., & Pham, T. H. Y., (2021). The model of contextualization and personalization in learning: The case of VAR and mobile learning application. *Proceedings of 1st Hanoi International Forum on Pedagogical and Educational Sciences, Vietnam, 2021*, tr (pp. 175–186). Viet Nam National University Press Ha Noi.

Nguyen, T. L., Vu Minh, T., Nguyen, H. H., & Ton, Q. C., (2021). Modeling interactive e-Book: Computational perspective and design principles. *Proceedings of 2nd International Conference on Mathematical Modeling and Computational Science, XX*, 540. Springer Singapore.

Prensky, M., (2001). Digital natives, digital immigrants part 1. *On the Horizon, 9*(5), 1–6. https://doi.org/10.1108/10748120110424816.

Rockinson-Szapkiw, A., Courduff, J., Carter, & Bennett, D., (2013). Electronik versus traditional print textbooks: A comparison study on the influence of university students' learning. *Computers & Education, 63*, 259–266. https://doi.org/10.1016/j.compedu.2012.11.022.

Süss, D., Lampert, C., &Wijnen, C., (2013). Mediensozialisation: Aufwachsen in mediatisiertenLebenswelten [Media Socialization: Growing up in mediatized worlds] In: Süss., D., Lampert, C., & Wijnen, C., (eds.), *Medienpädagogik; Studienbücherzur Kommunikations- und Medienwissenschaft.* Wiesbaden: Springer VS.

Takev, M., Somova, E., Artacho, M. R., Castro, M., & Martín, S., (2020). Can e-book technology be enough to support e-learning? In: *2020 IEEE Global Engineering Education Conference (EDUCON)* (pp. 1915–1921). doi: 10.1109/EDUCON45650.2020.9125342.

Tore, H., & Jon, M., (2018). Standards for smart education–towards a development framework. *SmartLearning Environments, 5*(3), 1–25.

Whipp, P., Taggart, A., & Jackson, B., (2014). Differentiation in outcome-focused physical education: Pedagogical rhetoric and reality. *Physical Education and Sport Pedagogy, 19*(4), 370–382.

Yang, C., Flanagan, B., Akcapinar, G., & Ogata, H., (2018). Maintaining reading experience continuity across e-book revisions. *Research and Practice in Technology Enhanced Learning, 13*(24), 24, https://doi.org/10.1186/s41039-018-0093-9.

Zajac, M., (2009). Using learning styles to personalize online learning. *Campus-Wide Information Systems Journal, 26*(3), 256–265. https://doi.org/10.1108/10650740910967410.

Zhi-Ting, Z., Ming-Hua, Y., & Peter, R., (2016). A research framework of smart education. *Smart Learn. Environ., 3*, 4. https://doi.org/10.1186/s40561-016-0026-2.

# CHAPTER 6

# The Application of Virtual Reality and Augmented Reality (XR) Technology: Challenges and Opportunities for Preschool and Lower Secondary Education in Vietnam

TON QUANG CUONG,[1] HOANG ANH DUC,[2] NGUYEN TUNG LAM,[1] DAU THUY HA,[3] and NGUYEN THI LINH YEN[4]

[1]*University of Education, VNU-UED, Hanoi, Vietnam*

[2]*EdLab Asia Educational Research and Development Center, Hanoi, Vietnam*

[3]*The Online Management Training Company (OMT), Hanoi, Vietnam*

[4]*University of Languages and International Studies, VNU-ULIS, Hanoi, Vietnam*

## ABSTRACT

In the context of the COVID-19 pandemic (2020–2021), Vietnamese schools had to drastically change their mode of operation to continue education even when schools had to be closed during most of the school year due to the pandemic. The online learning mode mobilized over the schools supported by digital learning resources, environment, and pedagogy approaches. New educational technology, especially VR (virtual reality) and AR (augmented virtual reality) technology to education promises a new trend for education with optimistic forecasts for

Intelligent Learning Paradigms and Student Empowerment: Digital Integration and Transformation. Souvik Pal, Ton Quang Cuong, & R. S. S. Nehru (Eds.)

continued adoption in the next five years. Its application may have new prospects for both teaching and learning at the participating schools in various aspects: building digital learning materials, transferring changes in teaching methods in a digitally connected environment, integrating digital capabilities in teacher training (including pre-service and in-service). This study focuses on assessing the impacts of VR and augmented reality (AVR or XR-extended reality) technology on educators and students, using the TIM framework (technology integration matrix) to evaluate the capacity to use technology, with recommendations for policy decisions and implications for relevant units and agencies in orienting VR/AR technology in education.

## 6.1 INTRODUCTION

Currently, the education system of countries worldwide is changing strongly in the application of new technologies to teaching and learning activities. Some typical technology trends can be mentioned as Omni Channel experiences for learners (Squire, 2021) and technologies to support changing the role of teachers (Kormos, 2021). In particular, there has been a significant increase in technologies for personalizing and personalizing education, based on applying theories of integrated play-based learning (Fantozzi, 2021), gamification (Tóth et al., 2021), and adaptive learning technologies (Ghergulescu et al., 2021). Therefore, if we do not make substantial strides in applying technology to teaching and learning, especially in finding suitable Vietnamese education models, we will fall behind, depending on foreign educational models and solutions (Andersson & Grönlund, 2009; Hoang et al., 2020).

The applications of images, sounds, videos, natural specimens... in teaching have long been recognized as an effective visual channel to support multi-sensory learning. The software and solutions to simulate practical and interactive experiments to support skill training (in difficult or impossible conditions to perform for various reasons) have expanded teaching space and opportunities for both teachers and learners. On the other hand, multi-format digital learning materials displayed on digital screen devices also increase the opportunity to access, store, contribute, share, and distribute relevant information to the teaching content, supporting the students' cognitive process to be more effective and profound.

In addition, the role and meaning of bringing phenomena, things, and problems of life into the classroom is an inevitable trend in education, forming and developing the capacity and quality of people, studying, meeting the new requirements of society, and the job market. Teaching theories such as Cognitivism, Social Constructivism, Behaviorism, Interactive Pedagogy, Connectivism, Self-directed Pedagogy (Heutagogy), Experiential learning... all emphasize the role of experience (by various means) and the connection with practice obtained in the learning process of the learners themselves.

Although they are interpreted from different points of view, the starting point of these theories is that they all value the "experience," the accumulation of experience, and the mobilization of "the highly experienced" in learners (personalization/individualization/differentiation, adaptation). This process needs to be done by the laws of general perception. From concrete experience (doing), reflective observation (observation), forming abstract concepts (thinking) to experimental activities (applying learned knowledge and skills to a specific situation) in real life.

The 2020-2021 school year is the first year of implementing the 2018 General Education Program, with many significant changes in teaching and learning philosophy, shifting from the orientation of knowledge acquisition to the orientation of capacity development, quality. The policy of "one program, many textbooks," "disruptive classes, but undisruptive learning" has also changed the concept of the uniqueness of textbooks with learning activities in physic-cyber environment. This change has allowed teachers to have the freedom to choose open learning resources and materials to incorporate into their lessons and learning activities, keeping pace with the global trend of open learning materials. In 2020, with the support of the United Nations Children's Fund (UNICEF) in Vietnam, the Ministry of Education and Training (MOET) had also developed a Digital Competency Framework for Vietnamese students (MOET, 2020b), and Digital Competency Access Framework for Early Childhood Education (Ngo & Hoang, 2021). Vietnam's National Digital Transformation Program until 2025 with orientation to 2030 also emphasizes the development of technologies for education towards personalized training, including virtual/accurate reality technology augmented reality (VR/AR), enhancing learning capabilities in the digital environment (Decision 749/QD-TTG, dated June 3, 2020).

In recent times, the application of imaging technologies, especially VR/AR in education, is becoming a popular trend, creating opportunities for the present. Realize many ideas of implementing teaching activities based on pedagogical principles and theories of teaching in general. In this project, the technology above is described, abbreviated as AVR. According to many educational technology experts, AVR technology can make learners more "immersed" in reality, feel committed and motivated to act and interact with real-world entities (Ton Quang Cuong, 2019). It has promoted new research directions in applying virtual technology to education according to the approach of increasing specific learning experiences for learners.

## 6.2 APPLICATIONS OF VR/AR IN EDUCATION

To develop high-level thinking, learners not only observe and remember things and phenomena but also interact to discover them. However, it is not always, anywhere, and with any audience, that learners can do this experiential activity. VR/AR solutions applied in teaching will create opportunities for personal interaction in physical/virtual space, multi-dimensionality, increasing accessibility and information processing; expanding space, learning environment (real-virtual); developing capacity for creative thinking and problem solving; enhance adaptive learning, immersive experiences, and seamless learning for individual learners (Figure 6.1).

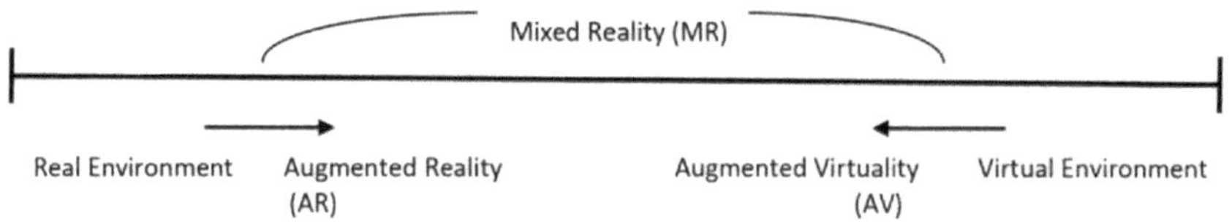


**FIGURE 6.1** The relationship between virtual reality and augmented reality.

Besides the ability to integrate multimedia and multi-format, VR/AR aims to create a highly simulated environment, contextualize the problem, and activate multi-dimensional interaction in teaching. VR/AR solutions force individual learners to face problems/situations (simulated in virtual space), self-identify, and make appropriate choices and solutions, creatively solve problems in hypothetical situations. Thereby, learners simultaneously experience the psychological states that appear when performing their decision-making tasks. By repeating over and over again the actions and experiences integrated with VR/AR technology, learners will perform learning tasks to achieve teaching goals in their way. Specifically:

1. **Remove Barriers in Content Access:** Learners interact directly with learning content, extract virtual objects from the display screen (simulation, 360° videos, 360° photos, sound, simulation…), automatically perform object navigation multi-tasks.
2. **Activate Multi-Sensory Activities, Multi-Channels of Movement:** Hearing, vision, and movement are integrated with experience activities and emotional and psychological states.
3. **Promote Creativity and Critical Thinking:** The virtual environment will create a sense of security from within, encourage taking risks, failing, learning from mistakes, and thinking clearly to find a solution. Some studies also show that learners who interact with lifelike AR/VR/MR content tend to ask higher-order questions to delve deeper into abstract concepts.
4. **Develop Independence, Self-Confidence in Learning:** Virtual learning context allows learners not to be afraid of making mistakes (freely making mistakes from which to learn from mistakes), promoting independence and self-esteem and confidence in learning, forming a belief in being ready to overcome challenges to achieve goals.
5. **Encourage Individual Efforts in Collaborative Activities:** Real-life situations and problems in project teaching are contextualized thanks to VR/AR technology. Learners are "embedded" in the virtual environment, directly participating in the project, and interacting with other learners to accomplish a common goal.

## 6.3 APPLICATION OF VR/AR AND AVR (XR) TECHNOLOGY IN PRESCHOOL AND LOWER SECONDARY EDUCATION IN VIETNAM

The project "Piloting the application of virtual reality and augmented reality (AVR or XR) technology at two levels of preschool and lower secondary education in Vietnam" took place in the context of the COVID-19 pandemic (2020-2021), when Vietnamese schools had to drastically change their mode of operation to continue education even when schools had to be closed during most of the school year due to the COVID-19 outbreak.

The online teaching method applied in most localities and provinces requires meeting shared digital learning materials, a system of electronic, online/blended/flipped lessons, simulation software, 3D, and support solutions.

Teaching methods in the digital (online) environment require fundamental transformation at all levels, as stipulated in the guidelines on online teaching by the MOET, the Government's policy on National Digital Transformation by 2025 and vision to 2030.

Applying new technologies, especially VR and AR technology, to education is a promising trend for education with optimistic forecasts for continued adoption in the next five years. In this context, the project "Piloting the application of VR and AR (AVR or XR) technology at two levels of preschool and lower secondary education in Vietnam" is timely to enable the adoption of technology in both teaching and learning at the participating schools in various aspects: building digital learning materials, transferring changes in teaching methods in a digitally connected environment, and integrating digital capabilities in teacher training (including for both pre-service and in-service teachers).

Based on choosing a platform suitable to the conditions and context of Vietnamese education (EON-XR), the project's content program provides implementation guidelines, processes, and tools for designing learning content AVR number data. The EON technology platform (https://eonreality.com/) provides AVR tools and solutions for teachers to perform the following activities (Figures 6.2-6.4):

- Selecting suitable subjects (available in the platform's Digital Library) to design teaching content and activities.
- Designing digital content according to the given functions, corresponding to the organizational roadmap of learners' activities (knowledge acquisition activities, reflection, practice, application activities, creative discovery activities, creating, interactive activities, sharing, testing, and evaluation activities).
- Integrating digital content into actual lectures: introducing lessons, organizing group work, individual, and group experiences, creative self-discovery activities, self-/peer-/co-assessment activities in physical-cyber learning environment.
- Integrating formats of information and knowledge related to the lesson (video clips, pictures, audio files, YouTube links, texts, test questions) flexibly and vividly meet the requirements of multi-sensory

**FIGURE 6.2** EON platform screenshot.

**FIGURE 6.3** Smart VR glasses combined with EON platform for lesson activities.

and interactive, personalized, and collaborative learning activities for learners.

- Adding, updating, storing, and sharing digital content on the platform: after designing digital content, it is put on the platform system, creating a shared data warehouse (Digital Library) that can be regularly updated according to the teacher's pedagogical records, etc.

**FIGURE 6.4** Learning activities using EON experience.

## 6.4 THE EFFECTIVENESS OF AVR (XR) TECHNOLOGY IN PRESCHOOL AND LOWER SECONDARY EDUCATION

### *6.4.1 TIM MATRIX (TECHNOLOGY INTEGRATION MATRIX, 2011)*

The project implementation results were analyzed and evaluated according to the TIM Matrix of the Florida Center for Instructional Technology (FCIT). The TIM matrix is used by educators as a basis for the overall assessment, locating, and optimizing the value of a technology solution, tool or platform integrated with the school educational program. The technology integration matrix (TIM) is a framework that describes the goals of the process of using and integrating digital technologies to improve learning effectiveness (Welsh et al., 2011).

The TIM matrix includes five criteria (interdependence characteristics) of the teaching strategy and the significant learning environment: active learning, collaborative learning, constructive learning, authentic learning, and goal-directed learning. Each of these criteria (features) is evaluated according to five levels of technology integration implementation: entry, adoption, adaptation, infusion, and transformation, which combined with instructional performance descriptions (face-to-face or online or blended) (Table 6.1).

Survey data collected is a combination of self-assessment reports of 17/18 school principals and survey questionnaire responses by 248 teachers from participating schools.

Due to the COVID-19 pandemic, the schools' closure during most of the project duration, the level of application of AVR implemented after the initial teachers' training are small-scale applications in several schools. Based on the analysis from the final report of 17/18 schools, the level of application of AVR technologies in the pilot framework of the project, according to the TIM matrix still poses a significant challenge to teachers. Teachers' proactive use of AVR technology is the criterion with the most satisfactory results, with 07 schools reaching level 02 (including 03 preschools, 02 primary schools, and 02 junior high schools). In other words, in implementing AVR applications at the project's pilot school sites, students could grasp how to use the tools with decent speed at all three piloted learning levels. The collaboration between students in using the tool was the second most successful aspect, with 02 elementary schools and 02 middle schools. The three aspects of Creation, Originality, and Goal-Oriented activities have not yet recorded positive results. Specifically, in addition to the only one that achieved level 03 as mentioned above, only 01 primary school initially appeared in activities of applying tools to the process of creating new knowledge, associated with learning activities have clear goals, along with measures of learning progress and outcomes (Figure 6.5).

### 6.4.2 LEVEL OF ADOPTION OF AVR TECHNOLOGY BY TEACHERS

At most of the schools participating in the pilot, the dynamism, positivity, and flexibility in accessing new technologies in general and AR technologies, notably, were recognized by a group of young, dynamic teachers. Specifically, 16% of teachers agree, and 54.5% agree that the activities are suitable for teachers' capacity and local conditions and contexts. However, older teachers still face many obstacles, including difficulties in information technology competence, difficulties in integrating technology

**TABLE 6.1** The Assessment Matrix for Integrating Technology into Teaching TIM (Welsh et al., 2011)

| | **Level of Technology Integration** | **Entry (Level 1)** | **Adoption (Level 2)** | **Adaptation (Level 3)** | **Infusion (Level 4)** | **Transformation (Level 5)** |
|---|---|---|---|---|---|---|
| | | Teachers begin to use tools to convey content. | Teachers guide students about the features and process of using the tool. | Teachers coordinate students' independent discovery and use of tools. | Teachers provide new situations for students to choose the right tools for themselves. | Teachers encourage creative use of tools. |
| Learning Strategy and Characteristics of Learning Environment | **Active Learning**<br>Students engage in using the tool instead of just receiving passive information from the tool. | Information is passively received by students. | Students understand the process and operation of using common applications. | Students initially select and explore the features of the tool. | Students self-direct the use of tools. | Students proficiently use tools and apply them to higher-order thinking activities. |
| | **Collaborative Learning**<br>Students use tools to collaborate rather than work alone. | Students use tools alone. | Students collaborate in using common features. | Students initially collaborate in the selection and discovery of tools. | Students choose tools to increase collaboration efficiency. | Students collaborate with friends, outside experts… with the help of tools. |
| | **Constructive Learning**<br>Students use tools to connect new information with known knowledge, rather than passively receiving information. | Information communicated to students. | Students are guided to find information and form knowledge on their own. | Students initially have the choice and explore the features of the tool to develop their own knowledge. | Students choose and often use tools to develop knowledge. | Students use tools thoroughly to develop knowledge. |

**TABLE 6.1** *(Continued)*

| **Level of Technology Integration** | **Entry (Level 1)** | **Adoption (Level 2)** | **Adaptation (Level 3)** | **Infusion (Level 4)** | **Transformation (Level 5)** |
|---|---|---|---|---|---|
| **Authentic Learning**<br>Students use tools to connect learning activities with the world outside the classroom. | Tools used are unrelated to the context outside the classroom. | Guided activities, tied to some meaningful context. | Students initially use tools themselves in activities connected with daily life. | Students choose different tools and use them frequently in meaningful activities. | Students creatively use tools in higher order thinking activities, connecting with the world outside the classroom. |
| **Goal-Directed Learning**<br>Students use tools to set goals, plan, monitor, and evaluate progress. | Instructions are given step-by-step under supervision. | Students practice according to the usual procedure under supervision. | Students initially plan and track tool use in purpose-specific activities. | Students use the tool flexibly and confidently in planning and tracking learning activities. | Students proficiently use tools in planning and tracking learning activities. |

into learning activities, and difficulties related to teaching and learning activities prejudices around technology and electronic devices. The pilot implementation period is still short, so teachers have not mastered the technology, cannot fully exploit, and apply it to prepare lesson plans with integrated AR technology. Specifically, 13.2% of teachers agree, and 59.3% of teachers agree that the time to implement the project is enough to ensure the implementation of the set goals. However, the number of activities that teachers participate in is limited. For example, with AR book content on the Umbalena application (https://umbalena.vn/), 134 teachers (66.3%) have used the tools less than three times, 50 teachers (24.8%) have used the tools three-to-five times, and only 18 teachers (8.9%) used AR tools more than five times.

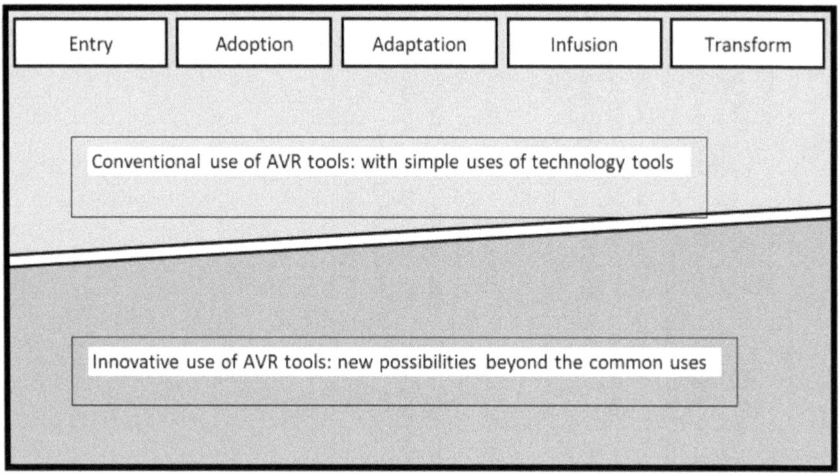


**FIGURE 6.5** The challenges of using AVR tools in a creative and innovative way of learning.

### *6.4.3 LEVEL OF ADOPTION OF AVR TECHNOLOGY BY STUDENTS*

In schools in urban areas (Hanoi), students quickly access and can effectively use AVR tools. However, in most schools in rural areas, students themselves are also new. There are still many surprises and stumbling around when manipulating, especially in facilities lacking intelligent devices. For preschool age, students are mainly interested in playing with AR images (80.4%) or taking selfies with images (13%) but are not interested in the learning contents (6.5%). In addition, the implementation time of the pilot project was not long enough, so students could not fully make use of all the features the AVR platform (EON-XR) can offer. However, interviews with school teachers and principals show that teachers who went through project training are ready to continue using EON XR after the project phases out in December 2021.

### *6.4.4 CHALLENGES OF SCHOOL INFRASTRUCTURE AND DIGITAL DEVICE AVAILABILITY*

Most school facilities lack equipment. Include the number of personal devices per student's head and projector/TV monitor for teachers. Specifically, 129/248 (52%) teachers wanted to support more equipment. Some units have the equipment, but because it has been invested for a long time, it has degraded, unable to meet the demand for configuration. In addition, Internet connection limitations also bring interruptions in the student experience, causing much downtime.

### *6.4.5 CHALLENGES OF RELEVANT AVR CONTENT FOR EDUCATION*

The data warehouse also has a limited number of resources, especially those that are suitable for the general context of Vietnam; Teachers also face technical problems when creating Vietnamese content (Vietnamese language, fonts), 360-degree image size, using VR glasses, synchronizing device connection, integrating AVR lectures in teaching online (on Zoom, MS Teams, Google Meet platform, etc.). There are limitations in content, so it has not been deployed in many classes. The new content only stops at creating excitement for students and has not yet delved into knowledge discovery and development activities.

In general, the project needs to continue to invest more to enrich the library of materials and improve user-friendliness, ensuring as much as possible the reduction of obstacles that teachers and students with a limited technical background may encounter. At the same time, it is necessary to research to develop more integrated and interactive scenarios, orienting students more deeply into the learning process, to avoid the pitfalls of having fun and exploring but not being associated with the learning process and learning goals. In addition, we also received comments from four elementary and middle schools about parents' emotional support for students' access to new technologies.

## 6.5 CONCLUSION AND RECOMMENDATIONS

### 6.5.1 CONCLUSION

Applying new technologies, especially VR (virtual reality) and AR (augmented reality) technology to education, is a promising trend for education with optimistic forecasts for continued adoption in the next five years (as stipulated in the guidelines on online teaching by the MOET, the Government's policy on National Digital Transformation by 2025, vision to 2030).

In this context, the project of Piloting the application of virtual reality and augmented reality (XR) technology at two levels of preschool and lower secondary education in Vietnam is aimed to enable the adoption of technology in both teaching and learning at the participating schools in various aspects: building digital learning materials, transferring changes in teaching methods in a digitally connected environment, integrating digital capabilities in teacher training (including future and current teachers), among others. This project also focuses on assessing the impacts of technology use for educators and students, based on the TIM Framework for determining capacity to use technology. The consultant team makes many recommendations with policy implications for relevant units and agencies in orienting the application of AVR technology in education.

### 6.5.2 RECOMMENDATIONS

#### 6.5.2.1 AT THE MACRO-LEVEL, POLICYMAKING

- It is necessary to conduct more research activities to understand better the difficulties of each specific group of teachers (by grade level, age of teachers, teaching experience, and information technology capacity). It proposes regular training and retraining methods suitable for each group.
- It is necessary to pilot the project for a more extended period, expand the pilot population, including many grades in each grade level, and expand to the upper secondary level.

- It is necessary to improve policies to shape the directions of digital transformation in schools: Indicators of eradicating digital knowledge and digital capacity.
- There should be policies to encourage and support teachers to participate in the digital transformation process, suitable for each locality and target group.

  It is necessary to mobilize private and international partners' participation to reduce barriers to investment in equipment and facilities.
- It is necessary to have specific plans to monitor and measure the readiness for digital transformation in education at the provincial and municipal levels. Ensure optimization of resources for digital transformation and ensure awareness of digital transformation gaps between regions and regions.

There should be a pre-feasibility study on building a national difference science to optimize localities' resources.

### *6.5.2.2 AT THE MESO-LEVEL*

- There should be a budget plan for infrastructure investment, including equipment for teachers, students, and a server system to serve the local digital data warehouse.
- There should be regular development plans for teachers' digital transformation capabilities, including the ability to use digital technologies and integrate digital tools into subject-specific content.
- Combine training content on AVR technology with open learning projects (MOOCs on Coursera, Co-study.edu.vn) to optimize funding.
- Implement different research topics on program design, lessons, and learning activities using AVR technology.

  Implement long-term research projects to monitor and evaluate the performance of learning activities with the application of AR technology, especially the multi-dimensional impacts on students' psychology and physiology and other effects, content, and knowledge.
- Supplementing training content for teachers on physical and mental health in digital technology application activities, data security, and safety.
- Develop tutorials on combining the use of AVR tools with other digital tools and platforms.

#### *6.5.2.3 AT THE MICRO-LEVEL*

- Deploy learning communities, learning clubs for teachers to share experiences on applying AVR technology, develop teaching content with AVR application, and contribute to building a repository of learning materials shared numbers in the school.

  In addition to the existing subjects and lessons in textbooks in the Early Childhood Education program, it is necessary to expand AVR experiential activities to experiential learning contents at primary and lower secondary levels. Such as disaster prevention training, simulated evacuation drills, etc.
- There is consistency from the school in implementing and integrating AVR tools with the school's digital tools and platforms, avoiding overlap, wasting resources and time.

## KEYWORDS

- **augmented reality**
- **digital device availability**
- **digital learning**
- **digital tools**
- **preschool and lower secondary education**
- **technology integration matrix**
- **virtual reality**

## REFERENCES

Adedoyin, O. B., & Soykan, E., (2020). COVID-19 pandemic and online learning: The challenges and opportunities. *Interactive Learning Environments*, 1–13.

Andersson, A., & Grönlund, Å., (2009). A conceptual framework for e-learning in developing countries: A critical review of research challenges. *The Electronic Journal of Information Systems in Developing Countries*, *38*(1), 1–16.

Blayone, T. J., Mykhailenko, O., Kavtaradze, M., Kokhan, M., & Barber, W., (2018). Profiling the digital readiness of higher education students for transformative online learning in the post-soviet nations of Georgia and Ukraine. *International Journal of Educational Technology in Higher Education, 15*(1), 1–22.

Clark, A. E., Nong, H., Zhu, H., & Zhu, R., (2021). Compensating for academic loss: Online learning and student performance during the COVID-19 pandemic. *China Economic Review, 68*, 101629.

Fantozzi, V. B., (2021). It's everyone's iPad": Tablet use in a play-based preschool classroom. *Journal of Early Childhood Research, 19*(2), 115–127.

Ghergulescu, I., Flynn, C., O'Sullivan, C., Van, H. I., & Slob, M., (2021). A conceptual framework for extending domain model of AI-enabled adaptive learning with sub-skills modeling. In: *CSEDU* (pp. 116–123).

Hoang, A. D., Pham, H. H., Nguyen, Y. C., Nguyen, L. K. N., Vuong, Q. H., Dam, M. Q., & Nguyen, T. T., (2020). Introducing a tool to gauge curriculum quality under sustainable development goal 4: The case of primary schools in Vietnam. *International Review of Education, 66*(4), 457–485.

Kormos, E., (2021). Technology as a facilitator in the learning process in urban high-needs schools: Challenges and opportunities. *Education and Urban Society*, 00131245211004555.

La, V. P., Pham, T. H., Ho, M. T., Nguyen, M. H., Nguyen, K. L. P., Vuong, T. T., & Vuong, Q. H., (2020). Policy response, social media, and science journalism for the sustainability of the public health system amid the COVID-19 outbreak: The Vietnam lessons. *Sustainability, 12*(7), 2931.

Lee, C. Y., & Sloan, T., (2015). A comprehensive evaluation rubric for assessing instructional apps. *Journal of Information Technology Education, 14*.

*Ministry of Education and Training*, (2020a). Directive 666/CT-BGDĐT dated August 24, 2020 on tasks and solutions for the 2020 – 2021 school year.

*Ministry of Education and Training*, (2021a). Circular 01/2021. Regulations on codes and standards for professional titles and appointment and salary ranking of teaching staff in public preschool education institutions. https://luatvietnam.vn/giao-duc/thong-tu-01-2021-tieu-chuan-bo-nhiem-xep-luong-giao-vien-mam-non-198080-d1.html (accessed on 13 December 2023).

Nguyen, M. H., Pojani, D., Nguyen, T. C., & Ha, T. T., (2021). The impact of COVID-19 on children's active travel to school in Vietnam. *Journal of Transport Geography, 96*, 103191.

Oranburg, S., (2020). *Distance Education in the Time of Coronavirus: Quick and Easy Strategies for Professors*. Duquesne University School of Law Research Paper, (2020-02).

Pham, P. T., Thi Phan, T. T., Nguyen, Y. C., & Hoang, A. D., (2021). Factor associated with teacher satisfaction and online teaching effectiveness under adversity situations: A case of Vietnamese teachers during COVID-19. *Journal of Education*, 00220574211039483.

Quaicoe, J. S., &Pata, K., (2015). Modelling factors influencing digital readiness: A case of teachers in Ghana's basic school system. In: *International Conference on Web-Based Learning* (pp. 271–277). Springer, Cham.

Squire, K. D., (2021). From virtual to participatory learning with technology during COVID-19. *E-Learning and Digital Media*, 20427530211022926.

Ton, Q. C., (2019). *Textbook of Teaching Theory and Technology*. VNU Publishing House.

Tóth, R., Zichar, M., & Hoffmann, M., (2021). Improving and measuring spatial skills with augmented reality and gamification. In: *International Conference on Geometry and Graphics* (pp. 755–764). Springer, Cham.

Tran, T., Hoang, A. D., Nguyen, Y. C., Nguyen, L. C., Ta, N. T., Pham, Q. H., & Nguyen, T. T., (2020). Toward sustainable learning during school suspension: Socioeconomic, occupational aspirations, and learning behavior of Vietnamese students during COVID-19. *Sustainability, 12*(10), 4195.

Wang, V., & Inoue, M., (2020). *When Can We Go to School? Nearly 300 Million Children are Missing Class* (Vol. 4). The New York Times.

Welsh, J., Harmes, J. C., & Winkelman, R., (2011). Florida's technology integration matrix. *Principal Leadership, 12*(2), 69–71.

Yoo, T., De Wysocki, M., & Cumberland, A., (2018). *Country Digital Readiness: Research to Determine a Country's Digital Readiness and Key Interventions.* Cisco Corporate Affairs. Available online: https://www.cisco.com/c/dam/assets/csr/pdf/Country-Digital-Readiness-White-Paper-US.pdf (accessed on 13 December 2023).

Zheng, M., Bender, D., & Lyon, C., (2021). Online learning during COVID-19 produced equivalent or better student course performance as compared with pre-pandemic: Empirical evidence from a school-wide comparative study. *BMC Medical Education, 21*(1), 1–11.

## CHAPTER 7

# Digital Competence Development for Students in Higher Education

NGUYEN TUNG LAM,[1] NGUYEN HOA HUY,[2] NGUYEN THI LINH YEN,[3] and TON QUANG CUONG[1]

[1]*University of Education, Vietnam National University, VNU-UED, Hanoi, Vietnam*

[2]*VNU-Center for Education Accreditation, Vietnam National University, Hanoi, Vietnam*

[3]*University of Languages and International Studies, Vietnam National University (VNU-ULIS), Hanoi, Vietnam*

**ABSTRACT**

The transformation process in higher education proposes digitalization skills and competence for university students in a new mode of learning. Besides academic, soft, and social skills, students of Gen-Z have to adapt to many changes in study activities, including online, blended, immersive, seamless, and personalized learning, as well as in cyber-physical learning environments nowadays in Vietnam. For university students, digital competence (DC) is not only ICT and data literacy, but also the use of digital tools and content creation. The framework of DC may refer to their abilities to adopt, adapt, infuse, and transform digital skills and attitudes in various study activities and social life. The proposed DC development for university students provides some strategic priorities in online learning, an initial framework describing digital concepts towards teaching quality and innovating education in the new era.

Intelligent Learning Paradigms and Student Empowerment: Digital Integration and Transformation.
Souvik Pal, Ton Quang Cuong, & R. S. S. Nehru (Eds.)

## 7.1 INTRODUCTION

In Vietnam, the practices of HE (Higher Education) are often understood as competencies of graduates that need to be formed and developed after completing a training program. "Outcome standards are requirements to be met in terms of the quality and competence of learners for graduation by completing a training program with minimum requirements for knowledge, skills, autonomy, and responsibility of learners" (Circular No.: 17, MOET, 2021).

The digital transformation (DX) in higher education (HE) is becoming a phenomenon with the requirements and challenges posed at different levels (policy, curricula, learning format, pedagogical approaches, learning environment, etc.). In this process, students play an essential and important role and being the key drivers, they make digital transformation (DX) a more self-directed path and self-determined learning process for themselves. In other words, the HE institutions (HEIs) focus more and more on the development of learners' complex capacity (competence, ability) and capability towards well-prepared, adaptable participants for today's labor market.

In the light of students' competence development, it may be seen as "doing, becoming, and wellbeing digitally" with demonstration of new continued models, flexibility, creativity, innovation, and disruption in the HE context of online education, educational approaches with new ways of interactions in changing learning digital environment (physical-cyber, augmented reality (AR), personalization, human-machine interaction, deep learning, etc.). Digital platforms, solutions emerging technologies affordances may serve as a new framework for digital learning in HE today.

Moreover, online mode of learning in HE is becoming an official alternative learning format, and making HE process inside more mass and universal. As an active learner (self-directed/determined/regulated and autonomous) students become continuing players in digital learning process, and they move from the role of user to producer, influencer, and transformer in their own development of competence. Thus, online teaching mode is a certain push to promote students' DC development in HE is following new tendency of "re-configure," "re-set" and "re-boot" all institutions inside HE system.

Furthermore, there is a call for rethinking the competence concept (especially during the COVID-19 pandemic, digital age, and society today), supported learning institutions and learner agency, and constituents that facilitate the development of digital capability and capacity to learn and work for learners rather than using or enforcing ICT skills.

## 7.2 DIGITAL COMPETENCE (DC): CRITICAL CALL FOR HIGHER EDUCATION STUDENTS

Traditionally, scholars recognized and studied the relationship between digital competence (DC) and digital transformation, which happens when processes and products are digitized to improve the teaching and learning experience, make teaching and learning more flexible and accessible, use cutting-edge digital technologies in organizations, and equip students with DCs and agency as part of their HE experience to empower their "agency and identity in digital spaces" (Castañeda & Selwyn, 2018; Kühn Hildebrandt, 2019; Hung, 2021; EDUCAUSE, 2018). The understanding of "digital transformation" reflects bias "digital moving or transition" rather than "transformation" in full meaning. In fact, digital transformation occurs by continuing digitization, digitalization, and digital transformation process that make organization "transformed" in all aspects.

In another aspect, DX can also be implemented by changing from within the organization based on technology but emphasizing the organization's own transformation process in people, organizational structure, culture, and values as well as the products that the organization contributes to other processes in society. The DX may include (Table 7.1):

1. **Doing Digitalization:** The overall application of digital technology and ICT to all aspects of the training process: the whole design of the curricula, applying technologies in teaching, assessment, learner management, administrative procedures, implementation of Blended/Flipped learning models, LMS, MOOCs, SPOCs, etc., towards training efficiency and quality improvement, professional skills enhancement and capacity to the labor market for graduates.
2. **Becoming Digitalization:** Forming digital skills, digitizing activities inside the institutions, building a digital learning environment, connecting campus, changing university governance model, applying big data, blockchain, AI technologies, AI, re-designing learning process and outcomes, rethinking educational approaches.
3. **Being Digitalization:** Changing the complex of skills of actors in institutions, designing Digital, Smart, and Innovative models

of universities, changing learning culture, pedagogical paradigm, and approach (andragogy, heutagogy, HyFlex learning–hybrid and flexible...) towards a new model in a digital society, focusing on new values of the HE rather than just training and scientific research.

**TABLE 7.1** The Concepts of DX in HE

| Technology Stages | Digital Transformation Characteristics | | |
|---|---|---|---|
| | **Digitization** | **Digitalization** | **Transformation** |
| Core process. | Doing digital (adaptation, sensing). | Becoming digital (inferring, self-learning). | Being digital (anticipating, self-optimizing). |
| Technology skill. | Application (entry, adoption, adaptation). | Infusion | Transformation |
| Organization culture. | Adaptation. | Specified. | Cultivation/ popularization. |
| Learning curve. | Enforcing ICT skills. | Digitalizing activities and procedures. | Shifting learning paradigm and model. |

### *7.2.1 THE CONCEPT OF DIGITAL COMPETENCE (DC) FOR HE STUDENTS*

According to a DigComp research study, there are 21 competences necessary for digital literacy, which are divided into eight competency levels (OECD, 2018), ranging from the most fundamental (foundation) to advanced (highly specialized). DC is a critical transversal, transformational skill that refers to the ability to use digital technology in meaningful, collaborative, and creative ways. In five categories, the DigComp model (Version 2.2, 2018) determines the fundamental components of DC:

1. **Data and Information Literacy:** The ability to express information needs and locate and obtain digital data, information, and content.
2. **Communication and Collaboration:** The ability to use digital technology for interacting, communicating, and collaborating while taking into account cultural and generational diversities.
3. **Digital Content Creation:** The ability to produce and edit digital content, to improve and integrate information and content into an existing body of knowledge by awareness of copyright and licensing.

4. **Security:** The ability to secure devices, content, personal data, and privacy while protecting physical and mental health, as well as being aware of the benefits of modern technologies for social well-being and inclusion; and
5. **Problem-Solving:** The ability to recognize, identify, certify digital requirements and obstacles, as well as resolving conceptual issues and problem situations, to select and use digital tools, develop methods and products in the digital circumstance.

The DigComp framework's basic value suggests a model of prospective performance, which gives high-level descriptions of digital abilities and related learning outcomes predicted at various proficiency levels, as well as instructive examples in two application areas. The framework may be classified as "adapted" (basic) or "specified" (more specific) according to DigComp into Action Guide (Kluzer et al., 2018).

"Adapting" refers to adjustments made to the DigComp framework that resulted in a model that is more or less comparable to it. Specific areas of competence (criteria, descriptions, indicators, or proof of performance) or competences themselves might be included if they are deemed necessary by the context's target learners. Examples: The learner can...; At a basic level and with autonomy and proper coaching when needed, the learner can...; On my own and addressing simple difficulties, the learner can...; I should work independently, according to my own demands, and solve well-defined and non-routine challenges... (OECD, DigComp 2.2, 2018).

Framework "specialized or highly-specialized" usually occurs from the point of view of next implementation steps in the level of HEIs or higher, i.e., the policy or strategy of digital competency education and training programs design (curriculum, learning, assessment, outcomes, etc.) for a specific audience or purpose of certain competencies and proficiency levels in complex. Examples: As well as guiding others, I can...; At the advanced level, according to my own needs and those of others, and in complex contexts, I can...; At a highly technical level, I can...; At the most advanced and specialized level, I can... (DigComp 2.2, OECD, 2018).

On the other hand, the DeSeCo project of Definition and Selection of Competencies (OECD Education 2030) states and recommends "Transformation Capabilities" with other types of competencies to encourage young people to innovation, responsibility, and a sense of "create new value, reconciling stress and dilemmas, responsible."

Although Vietnam has not yet proposed to build its own digital competency framework, in fact, many universities integrated some components of the digital competency framework developed by UNESCO in their survey (UNESCO, 2018; Hoa, Hung, 2021). The goal of the digital literacy global framework (DLGF) project is to create a methodology that can really serve as the foundation for thematic Indicator 4.4.2 of the sustainable development goals (SDGs): "Percentage of youth/adults who have achieved at least a minimum level of proficiency in digital literacy skills."

The digital competency framework is primarily mentioned in policy documents such as Prime Minister's Decisions "Introducing program for national digital transformation by 2025 with orientations towards 2030" (No. 749/QD-TTG, June 2020); "Approval for the national strategy for the development of digital economy and digital society by 2025 with orientations towards 2030" (No. 411/QD-TTG, March 2022); and "Approval for the project increase the application of information technology."

Furthermore, based on references to the European Commission's Digital Competence Framework for Citizens (DigComp 2.0, 2.2) and DLGF (UNESCO), as well as training open short courses of Google Applied Digital Skills and Microsoft Digital Skills, many HE institutions in Vietnam have designed their programs to achieve the goal in the following perspectives: hardware and software operation (physical operations of digital devices), information and data literacy (focus on Man and Machine), and Information and data literacy (focus on Man and Machine).

### *7.2.2 THE CONCEPT OF "DIGITAL LEARNER" IN HE*

The current generation of learners in HE traditionally identified as "i-Generation," "Digital natives," "Gen Z" (Rosen, Carrier, & Cheever, 2010; Prensky, 2012; Thompson, 2012; Deloitte, 2018; Falloon, 2020). Along with the opportunities to access new technology in education, the current learners are increasingly becoming "the center of their own learning" (self-regulated, self-directed, and self-determined), with more freedom in orienting and choosing content knowledge according to their needs, motivations, and styles of learning.

Hence, in the digital practice of HEIs learning is becoming more and more contextualized: it must come from the learner's own context without the concept of "one-size-fits-all" learning, and self-learning must be viewed as a phenomenon, specifically based on a complex of personal attributes and characteristics and the capacity of learners. On the other hand, digital technology in all prospectuses also supports, affects, and changes the methods of communication, living, learning, etc.

According to Deloitte's Analysis Report (2018), the general trend shows that digital learners today are "very busy, curious, and eager to learn" (https://bit.ly/2KzqxFz). These overarching features of them can be identified in the following:

- Always overwhelmed and easily distracted before too many new things appear;
- Tend to be interested in learning and absorbing new things;
- With a penchant for access to quality, timely response and personalized content;
- Consider learning as a necessity anytime, anywhere;
- Use smartphone or portable mobile device as an inseparable object;
- Want to integrate what is learned into practical experience that may be relevant and useful for future work;
- Most emphasize the quality, ease of use and suitability of technology solutions in online learning;
- Always eager to learn and improve soft skills;
- Motivated to learn because always want to do better and be more productive.

In fact, with today's digital technology solutions and tools, any learner can search, contribute, share, and process data, turning them into "co-producers/creators of knowledge," rethinking the ways of contributing "intelligence of the masses."

Therefore, to be able to develop DC capacity for students, HEIs need to change the mindset for both academic and teaching staff, restructure current training programs, and ensure the requirements of digital infrastructure and digital learning environment towards "moving" their own students' contingent from "campus-based" learner to self-efficacy, autonomous, responsible, adaptable, and transformed digitally.

### *7.2.3 THE WAYS OF DC DEVELOPMENT FOR HE STUDENTS*

The current teaching and learning process in HE has been faced with many challenges from a technology perspective (high requirements for digital literacy for teachers and a new generation of learners–"digital citizens/natives") to drastic changes in the nature, approaches, and models of learning, outcomes of training programs, and "new value chains" of learners. Moreover, the expansion and flexibility in space and time, hybrid digital-based learning environments provide new solutions and opportunities to optimize collaborative learning, enhance informal and non-formal learning, and focus on individual learners more effectively.

Hence, digital transformation in HE learning may be applied according to the smart education model (SMART Education) based on technology. In which the elements are set up according to a whole system, have mutual effects promoting quality and efficiency for the personalization and transformation process, including S (self-directed), M (motivated), A (adaptive), R (resources) and T (technology) (Uskov, 2019).

In the meso- and micro-level HEIs practice suggests the curriculum, pedagogy approaches as well as teachers' confidence and competence play an important role in students' digital experiences or competence development. Moreover, there is also the challenge of ensuring a consistent student experience when using technology, by providing support for all users, the relevant digital solutions and tools, and flexible digital learning environments.

Hence, it maybe the outline of key challenges and service provider solutions, training services as well as more comprehensive directions towards students' DC development in all prospectives such thinking digitally, acting digitally and wellbeing digitally (Figure 7.1):

- The policy and practice to develop digital skills; creating value by "tailored" frameworks, whole-institution approach to developing the students' DC to certain learning contexts;
- Mobilizing interest, motivation, and cognition in self-determined/directed/regulated learning and inspiring learning activities, flexible, hybrid, seamless, and immersive environment;
- Designing relevant programs and learning opportunities (digital technology enabled, integrated, transformed) toward digital skill development for students;
- Assessing, recognizing, and certifying levels of digital competence towards both teachers and students' digital experience and empowerment;
- Supporting continuing professional development for teachers to deliver digital skills for students;

- Implementing digital transformation ideas and projects with academic and Edtech enterprises (co-teaching, embedded apprenticeship, entrepreneurship, etc.) to universalize and socialize students' DC.

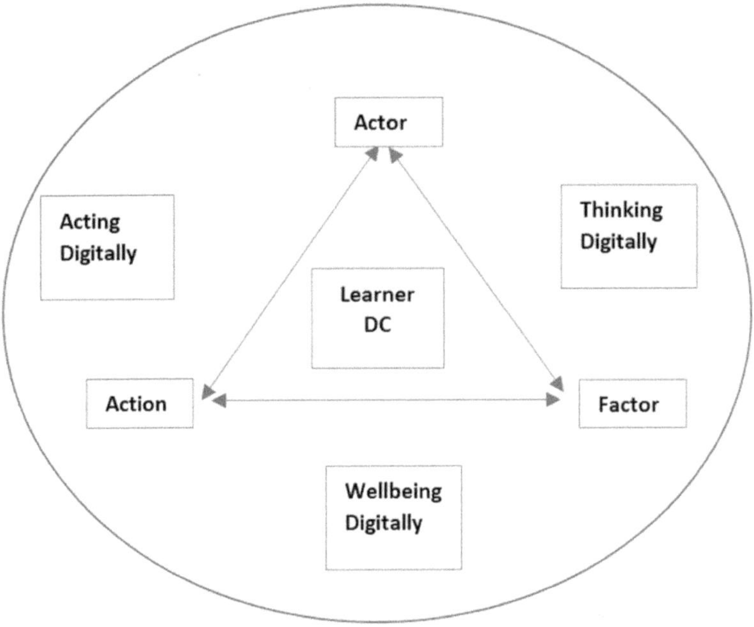


**FIGURE 7.1** Digital transformation in HEIs students' DC development.

## 7.3 PROPOSED HE STUDENTS DC MAPPING

This mapping has been proposed based on an approach combining elements of digital literacy and its classification requirements (from "adoption" to "specialized or highly specialized" through interim stages such as adaptation, sensing, inferring, and optimizing) with the concept of digital transformation (thinking digitally, acting digitally with digital tools, and well-being digitally) in the context of HEIs.

The main idea for both integrated concepts is that over time they have transformed from a daily operational and digital focus on teaching-learning process of academic staff as well as students towards critical and responsible perspectives of digital transformation in the HEIs (Table 7.2).

**TABLE 7.2** Students' Digital Competence Mapping

| Competence Area | Competence Description | Criteria | Performance Indicators |
|---|---|---|---|
| | | **1. Basic Competence** | |
| Using digital devices. | – | • Operate digital equipment.<br>• Operating software on digital devices. | • Use office automation tools to process information (word editor, digital presentation editor, spreadsheet, database, etc.).<br>• Proficient in digital image, audio, and video processing tools (Gimp, Photoshop, Audacity, CDex, Moviemaker, etc.).<br>• Use existing and emerging digital tools effectively to locate, analyze, and evaluate information sources.<br>• Use communication tools based on webmail and client-style email services (Eudora, Thunderbird, Gmail, Outlook, etc.).<br>• Master the web tools for sharing and publishing online resources (Google Video, YouTube, Flickr, SlideShare, Scribd, etc.)<br>• Manage computer's resources through different operating systems (Windows, Linux, Mac).<br>• Create a database through specific software (access, FileMaker) that allows to organize and manage information.<br>• Develop online chats through synchronous web communication tools (chat, instant messaging services, Skype, video conferencing tools, etc.).<br>• Develop online conversations through web-based asynchronous communication tools, both traditional and emerging (forums, distribution lists, discussion groups, tweets, etc.). |

**TABLE 7.2** *(Continued)*

| Competence Area | Competence Description | Criteria | Performance Indicators |
|---|---|---|---|
| | | | • Performing collaborative work through online tools of the groupware category (Kolab, Google Docs, etc.).<br>• Effective use of e-learning/b-learning platforms for online training and collaboration (Dokeos, Moodle, BSCW, WebCT, Ilias, etc.). |
| Information and data capacity. | Determine information requirements, then seek and access data, knowledge, and digital materials.; Evaluate the substance and sources of news; Store, manage, and organize and share data, information, digital content. | • Identify needs and solve problems.<br>• Look for information.<br>• Evaluate information and think critically.<br>• Store and organize information.<br>• Use and distribution of information. | • Information identification in different contexts.<br>• Use web sources to find digital content relevant for academic studies.<br>• Using scholarly sources to find digital content relevant for academic studies.<br>• Collecting digital information in novel ways using online collection tools.<br>• Determining if digital information is reliable and timely.<br>• Use folders, bookmarks, reference management software, and labeling to organize the digital content for learning.<br>• Following a referencing style with digital information sources cited.<br>• Recognizing and respecting the intellectual/property copyrights how to share material publicly online.<br>• Identify problems to be solved with the use of ICT.<br>• Design a research project based on a problem to be solved, identifying the most appropriate ICT resources. |

**TABLE 7.2** *(Continued)*

| Competence Area | Competence Description | Criteria | Performance Indicators |
|---|---|---|---|
| | | | • Make a plan to find information to solve the problem.<br>• Perform the retrieval, organization, and management of information using technology tools and services.<br>• Identify relevant information evaluating different sources and their origins.<br>• Synthesize selected information, logically organize for building and absorbing new knowledge.<br>• Demonstrate the usefulness of acquired knowledge for decision-making to solve a problem.<br>• Return the solution of a problem to the community in the form of digital resources. |
| **2. Specific Competence** | | | |
| Digital communication skills. | Use digital technology to interact, communicate, and collaborate while keeping cultural and generational diversity in perspective; Social interaction through public and private digital services, as well as civic practice, facilitate social connection. Take control of your online identity and reputation. | • Digital technology facilitates interaction.<br>• Using digital technologies to share.<br>• Using digital technology to practice citizenship (digital citizenship) (public rights and services in the digital environment). | • Collaborate and publish electronic materials with peers through sharing digital media and settings.<br>• Interact with experts or others using social networks and ICT-based communication channels.<br>• Use a range of mediums, formats, and platforms to effectively communicate information and ideas to a large audience.<br>• Connect with experts from other cultures to improve cultural comprehension and global awareness.<br>• Communicate with experts from other fields through ICT-based communication channels. |

**TABLE 7.2** *(Continued)*

| Competence Area | Competence Description | Criteria | Performance Indicators |
|---|---|---|---|
| | | • Collaborate at work through digital technology.<br>• Communicating over the internet.<br>• Digital identity management. | • Form interdisciplinary and multidisciplinary working groups to develop projects or solve problems.<br>• Create and stimulate professional knowledge networks and communities for collaborative work in virtual environments.<br>• Share experiences on social networks.<br>• Participating in several digital networks related to your interests, profession, and/or academic field.<br>• Recognizing acceptable methods to connect in specific digital situations.<br>• Recognizing the potential for digital media to be used to abuse, embarrass, and harass others and speaking in a respectful and inclusive manner.<br>• Identifying misleading or harmful digital interactions – exchanging any expert ideas.<br>• Creating digital communications for a variety of uses.<br>• Ascertain an ethical commitment to the use of digital information and ICT, including copyright, intellectual property, and adequate source documentation.<br>• Encourage the appropriate, safe, and legal use of information and technology.<br>• Use technology to facilitate collaboration, learning, and productivity with a positive attitude use IT to demonstrate personal responsibility for lifetime learning. |

**TABLE 7.2** *(Continued)*

| Competence Area | Competence Description | Criteria | Performance Indicators |
|---|---|---|---|
| | | | • Assume a leading role in the area of digital citizenship.<br>• Appropriate use of digital tools and resources.<br>• Understand digital etiquette (netiquette) when building acceptable social interactions with information and technology.<br>• Interacting with experts from other cultures using digital communication and collaboration tools to develop cross-cultural knowledge and global awareness.<br>• Using multiple digital media to manage your online presence for personal, business, and academic objectives. |
| Digital content creation. | Create and edit digital content. Enhance and integrate information and digital content into current knowledge and be aware of any applicable licenses and copyrights; know how to give easy-to-understand commands to a computer system. | • Development of digital content.<br>• Combine and recreate digital content.<br>• License and digital copyright.<br>• Use programming languages. | • Recognize how various systems collect and use your personal information online and adjust your security settings accordingly.<br>• Recognizing the positive and negative effects of your online communications on your digital reputation.<br>• Designing learning outcomes and other accomplishments available in digital format.<br>• Testing/examining the digital influence, footprint, and reputation using analytics or other digital features.<br>• Adapt to new circumstances and technology settings.<br>• Using ICT to develop new ideas, products, or processes based on current knowledge.<br>• As part of their regular learning and reflection process, they create creative works as solo or group methods of expression using ICTs. |

**TABLE 7.2** *(Continued)*

| Competence Area | Competence Description | Criteria | Performance Indicators |
|---|---|---|---|
| | | | • Using ICT, use models and simulations to investigate complicated systems and challenges.<br>• Identify trends by predicting ICT usage possibilities.<br>• Explore different solutions to an issue using a range of approaches and viewpoints.<br>• Identify the conditions and contexts that require the use of ICT (where, when, how).<br>• Join professional knowledge communities using ICT.<br>• Develop experiences that stimulate creative thinking and innovation.<br>• To promote learning and creativity, incorporate digital tools and resources.<br>• Creating fresh digital content.<br>• Digital media capture, editing, and production.<br>• Creating, distributing, and displaying digital artifacts with an eye toward audience and purpose.<br>• Using coding and design to create apps, digital games, virtual environments, and user interfaces.<br>• Using digital tools to develop new ideas and projects.<br>• Educating others about new digital tools and opportunities. |

**TABLE 7.2** *(Continued)*

| Competence Area | Competence Description | Criteria | Performance Indicators |
|---|---|---|---|
| Security and safety in cyber environment. | Protect devices, content, personal data, and privacy in the digital environment; safeguard health and spirit; and be aware of the impact of digital technology on social well-being and inclusion; Environmental awareness of the impact of digital technologies and their application. | • Maintain equipment.<br>• Personal data and privacy protection – protecting your health and well-being.<br>• Environmental protection. | • While employing current technologies, feeling at ease, in control, and secure.<br>• Recognizing that digital media and information may cause distraction, overburden, and worry, and disconnecting when needed.<br>• Considering the rights and wrongs of your online activity, as well as the potential consequences.<br>• Proactively combating cyberbullying and other harmful online behaviors.<br>• Using digital media to access services, monitor health issues, participate in community activities, and regulate online and real-world interactions in ways that promote healthy relationships. |
| Learning and developing digital skills. | Willingness to learn for life, self-direction, self-criticism, adaptability, confidence. | • Seize the tendency of online training.<br>• Using teaching and learning tools and methods in a digital context.<br>• Planning, controlling the learning progress in the digital environment.<br>• Assessing the learning process in the digital environment. | • Taking use of online learning opportunities and resources.<br>• Using innovative online learning methods.<br>• Taking notes, annotating, compiling, and curating learning materials, as well as reviewing and revising learning materials using digital tools.<br>• Using digital tools to record learning events/outcomes and use them for self-analysis, reflection, and achievement display.<br>• Managing your participation and involvement in digital learning environments, including receiving and responding to digital feedback on your academic work.<br>• Sharing your digital skills and digitally mentoring others. |

**TABLE 7.2** *(Continued)*

| Competence Area | Competence Description | Criteria | Performance Indicators |
|---|---|---|---|
| Related skills to careers. | Operate specific digital technologies; understand, analyze, and evaluate data, information, and digital content that are specific to a particular industry. | • Operate specific digital technologies.<br>• Understand, analyze, and evaluate information data and digital content. | • Aim for efficiency and renewal of professions by incorporating ICT in the context of their work.<br>• Demonstrate the integration of ICT knowledge in professional practice. |

## 7.4 CONCLUSION

Students' DC is a complex domain integrating motivational value, operation, and personal-reflective components in all cognitive skills between knowledge and their practice in certain modes of contextualized conditions. Because students' digital competency development is still not at the center of the educational process, digital experience, procrastination, and resilience in their learning are critical issues. The digital transformation challenges HEIs to rethink, reset, and reboot the system, embracing students' DC development as a core fundamental literacy, increasing the significance of digital technology-enabled curriculum and management without confusion of DCs as "being enhancing ICT skills."

Moreover, existing digital disparities may be exacerbated when new teaching and learning models begin to challenge the traditional paradigm (from Know-Do-Be to Do-Know-Be) with increasing emphasis on blended, HyFlex, adaptive, flipped classrooms, personalized learning, online seamless, immersive, and global connectivity, etc. This environment necessitates new approaches to DC development for both students and instructors who are expected to lead this new path in digital educational transformation.

## KEYWORDS

- **digital competence**
- **digital competence mapping**
- **digital learner**
- **digital transformation**
- **global connectivity**
- **higher education**
- **online learning**

## REFERENCES

Altukhova, E. V., Nikeryasova, V. V., Ivanova, Y. Y., Markov, M. A., & Romanchenko, O. V., (2022). Transformation of educational space in the system of digitalization of the economy. In: Trifonov, P. V., & Charaeva, M. V., (eds.), *Strategies and Trends in Organizational and Project Management: DITEM 2021;Lecture Notes in Networks and Systems* (Vol. 380). Springer, Cham. https://doi.org/10.1007/978-3-030-94245-8_22.

Castañeda, L., & Selwyn, N., (2018). More than tools? Making sense of the ongoing digitizations of higher education. *International Journal of Educational Technology in Higher Education, 15*(22), 1–10. https://doi.org/10.1186/s41239-018-0109-y.

EDUCAUSE, (2018). *Report from the 2018 EDUCAUSE Task Force on Digital Transformation.* Retrieved from: https://library.educause.edu/~/media/files/library/2018/11/dxtaskforcereport.pdf (accessed on 13 December 2023).

EU Science Hub – European Commission, (2021). *DigComp* – EU Science Hub – European Commission. [online] Available at: https://ec.europa.eu/jrc/en/digcomp (accessed on 13 December 2023).

Falloon, G., (2020). From digital literacy to digital competence: The teacher digital competency (TDC) framework. *Educational Technology Research and Development, 68*(5), 2449–2472.

Kluzer, S., & Pujol, P. L., (2018). In: Carretero, S., Punie, Y., Vuorikari, R., Cabrera, M., & O'Keefe, W., (eds.), *DigComp into Action–Get Inspired, Make it Happen.* JRC Science for Policy Report, EUR 29115 EN, Publications Office of the European Union, Luxembourg, 2018. ISBN 978-92-79-79901-3, doi: 10.2760/112945.

Pham, L., Limbu, Y. B., Bui, T. K., Nguyen, H. T., & Pham, H. T., (2019). Does e-learning service quality influence e-learning student satisfaction and loyalty? Evidence from Vietnam. *International Journal of Educational Technology in Higher Education, 16*(7). https://doi.org/10.1186/s41239-019-0136-3.

Pham, T. V. A., & Ho Thi, T. N., (2020). Teaching fundamental courses in Vietnam: Transitioning from blended learning approach to online learning approach. *International Conference on Distance Education and Learning 2020.* Beijing, China. DOI: https://doi.org/10.1145/3402569.3402592.

Prensky, M., (2012). *From Digital Natives to Digital Wisdom: Hopeful Essays for 21st Century Learning.* California: Corwin - A SAGE company.

Rosen, L. D., Carrier, M. L., & Cheever, N. A., (2010). In: Rosen, L. D., (ed.), *Rewired Understanding the IGeneration and the Way They Learn.* New York: Palgrave Macmillan.

Stephen, R., (n.d.). Covey. *The 7 Habits of Highly Effective People: Powerful Lessons in Personal Change.* New York: Simon & Schuster.

Thompson, P. M., (2012). *The Popular Profile of the Digital Learner: Technology Use Patterns and Approaches to Learning.* Michigan State University. Educational Psychology and Educational Technology.

Tran, D. H., & Do Van, H., (2021). Digital literacy framework for Vietnam students in the digital transformation. *Journal of Information and Documentation.* ISSN 1859-2929.

UNESCO, (2018). *A Global Framework of Reference on Digital Literacy Skills for Indicator 4.4.2.* Information Paper No. 51. UIS/2018/ICT/IP/51.

# CHAPTER 8

# Online Proctoring Issues in Online Learning Assessment: The Case of University of Education Students' Study

NGUYEN TUNG LAM,[1] TRAN NGUYEN THANH BINH,[1] NGUYEN NGOC MINH PHUONG,[1] NGUYEN THI LINH YEN,[2] and TON QUANG CUONG[1]

[1]*University of Education, Vietnam National University, VNU-UED, Hanoi, Vietnam*

[2]*University of Languages and International Studies, Vietnam National University (VNU-ULIS), Hanoi, Vietnam*

## ABSTRACT

The COVID-19 pandemic has spurred a powerful digital transformation in education in Vietnam. Under the circumstances, almost all higher education institutions (HEIs) use online examination (OE) as an "ad-hoc" solution to make learning undisruptive. In OE application as an education technology solution, there are main focuses on the student readiness, adoption experience at a large, multi-subject, and multi-campus approaches as well as proctoring tools or software. For the University of Education, VNU Hanoi, the most challenge is how teachers ensure academic quality and integrity of students when an examination is being taken online without the presence of a live proctor. The study conducted to examine some attempts to analyze, evaluate the functions, selection of online proctoring (OP) tools (as a complex of digital virtual tools for monitoring, checking

Intelligent Learning Paradigms and Student Empowerment: Digital Integration and Transformation. Souvik Pal, Ton Quang Cuong, & R. S. S. Nehru (Eds.)

student activities during OE) and suggest recommendations for their using during OE in universities.

## 8.1 INTRODUCTION

The COVID-19 pandemic has been radically changing the global higher education picture. Online education is used by most higher education institutions (HEIs) in the world as a temporary solution for uninterrupted learning but opens opportunities to accelerate the process of digital transformation in higher education. In Vietnam, most schools have implemented "online" teaching during the COVID-19 pandemic, in which the number of lecturers and students participating in online learning accounts for a high proportion and training institutions use a variety of tools to support online teaching. However, the online learning time accounts for a low proportion compared to the original training plan of the training program.

In Vietnam, according to a survey report about online training at HEIs during the COVID-19 pandemic, the most crucial issue is how students and lecturers are adapting in online mode of learning process with various forms of testing and assessment towards the quality of online teaching (MOET Report, June 2021). This fact is also focused on the most challenging problems of online cheating in online exams within learners.

## 8.2 LITERATURE REVIEW

The publications on online learning are increasing from 2009 to 2018 (Martin et al., 2020) with one of the most investigated issues focused on the online learning process itself and the quality of online testing. The assessment process is becoming more complex and complicated in the online testing environment because there are no direct interactive and control activities between students and educators that have made it easier for students to cheat in online exams (Turner & Uludag, 2013). For example, the use of remote desktop and screen sharing, searching for answers on the Internet or social media, asking for external support by using mobile devices or additional smartphones behind the examining screen, etc. While recognizing and avoiding online fraud is a critical issue in online testing for various exams for students, the identification of student's behavior and activities, keyboard operation recognition, and camera surveillance technologies have all been extended in recent years to serve online testing (Xiong & Suen, 2018). Hence, traditional fraud detection mechanisms have been integrated with new technologies, monitoring techniques, and digital identification to ensure assessment integrity in online tests (Fluck, 2019). These services provide a way to validate students' identities remotely before an examination, as well as techniques to ensure that students taking the assessment are not cheating or receiving illegal assistance. Online proctoring (OP) solutions do this by granting access to a proctor through a camera, or by combining technical methods such as browser lockout, voiceprint, keystroke or other biometrics, or video analysis generated during an exam.

Today in the classroom, many students feel more comfortable learning with the help of smart devices such as computers, tablets... and know well how to use them to cheat in an online testing environment. Just like when taking traditional face-to-face exams, students taking online exams prefer to cheat for several reasons: easy access to cheating materials, less control and stress, improved scores on their average, wanting a higher score for various reasons, etc. However, regardless of online or face-to-face courses/exams, students responded that proctors and monitoring tools and technology are important factors in preventing fraud (Harmon et al., 2010).

When studying in an online learning environment, students feel that the proctors or monitoring tools are subject to change their behavior during the exam (Dendir & Maxwell, 2020). The presence of various proctoring tools is considered a serious alert of cheating to them, which creates necessary psychological effects in the online testing environment. Owens (2015) states that cheating is more likely to occur in teacher-less exams than in supervised tests, and there are no significant differences between online and in-person courses when the exams are monitored. Cheating is more common in undocumented online exams (and less so in supervised online exams), and students will be more likely to engage in dishonest behavior during learning in online contexts (Dyer et al., 2020).

Alessio et al. (2017); Daffin & Jones (2018); Fask et al. (2014) are convinced that cheating becomes a serious problem when online exams are not supervised (effectively) or supported by tools, surveillance technology. These authors demonstrated that the average online test scores were substantially higher than the scores on the face-to-face and teacher-supervised tests. A recent study also found that students performed better on verbatim questions than on paraphrase questions (80.4% vs 69.1%), even after we controlled for the use of honor statements and online test-taking technology. The results of the study are consistent with the view that when faced with an interpreted bank of test questions, students cannot easily find the answers on the Internet because the questions do not exist in a verbatim direct form line. This research is important for educational institutions and professors looking to combat academic dishonesty, and for faculty who want to avoid the pitfalls of using subject banks (Golden & Kohlbeck, 2020).

On the other hand, Kellaghan & Greaney (2019) listed security challenges and gaps in administering exams and offered solutions to prevent cheating in exams. The biggest challenge with online assessment and teaching is ensuring a fair exam, free of cheating. Chase (2018) has shown that no solution is perfect. And all the research on this is just trying to keep fraud to a minimum.

The first OP software platform appeared in 2008 (ProctorU, 2020b) and is now gradually growing strongly, by 2020, there will be 54% of HEIs learning to use this software (Grajek, 2020), which is caused by the decrease in in-person school attendance due to COVID-19, which has dramatically increased the OP's appeal to universities and some students (according to Chin, 2021b). OP technology is expected to become a standard technology, frequently used in online assessment tests around the world (Selwyn et al., 2021). But currently, the use of software has not been widespread in many educational institutions and the popular alternative to virtual proctors is the form of remote monitoring of candidates, watching live videos via Zoom.

Another study by Atoumet et al. (2017) used technology in the assessment process and introduced a multimedia analysis system. The system includes a camera and a WearCam as physical components. The camera is either mounted on the head or attached to a computer screen to monitor the candidate's gaze, while the WearCam study uses a second camera to monitor the testing process and provide the examiner with a view of the candidate's area. Additionally, a microphone is used to monitor the ambient acoustics of the test site. The study presents an inexpensive and easy-to-use multimedia analysis system that only requires two inexpensive cameras and a microphone. Based on data collected from 24 test-takers representing real-life behaviors in an online exam, the research project has demonstrated the system's ability to detect almost 87% of all types of fraud based on the test segment, with a False Alarm Rate (FAR) level of 2%.

In addition to studies focusing on the assessment process, there are also studies on the risks of applying technology, social, and psychological issues. Research by Aditya Nigam et al. (2021) suggests that there are many concerns about psychology, culture, and technology, including risks of inequality in learning and assessment needs that must be considered in the development of AI-based proctoring systems (AIPS). These concerns have led to worries that AI-based systems contribute to increased levels of surveillance and mass exploitation of personal data, with a significant impact on freedom and privacy. The adoption of AIPS is also challenging when the cost of the software is too high for many universities and institutions to afford, especially those in underdeveloped and developing countries (Coghlan et al., 2020).

Virtual proctoring involves using online tools to monitor student activities in online testing and assessment activities. These tools support online exams and help students take the test at remote locations while still ensuring the security rules and regulations of the online exam. This includes authenticating students and their identities for security and maintaining exam integrity and administration (Foster & Layman, 2013). University of the South Pacific (Fiji).

A web camera on the student's computer equipment captures footage of the physical learning room and everything the student performs throughout the test session, and the virtual proctor has two primary components. The examiner or proctor can remotely monitor the video recording to see potential cheating, suspicious motions, and postures like conversing with someone in the room or looking for the answer in books, mobile devices, or other printed media. The remainder is available on a single platform, preventing the learner from accessing other computing applications, such as browsing the Internet. Copying, pasting, and printing are examples of computer processes that could lead to exam cheating. During the exam, the virtual proctor system logs all of the students' Internet actions, including the websites they attempted to access. The instructor or examiner can study a video recording of the full test in real time or later.

The virtual surveillance system serves four primary functions: (i) authentication: this is the process of confirming that a registered student is a valid student for an online supervised exam; (ii) surfing ability: this is the process of limiting students' capacity to use their computers for other purposes; (iii) remote control and authorization: allow the proctor to start, pause, and end an online supervised exam, as well as flag any suspect student activity; and (iv) report generation: the creation of a report on a supervised examination's student actions.

The exact form of the virtual surveillance system varies between providers according to Sietses (2016). It is possible to identify three main types: direct supervision, in which monitoring takes place during periods; the tests will be completed a few days later based on pictures and exam logs, and automated monitoring in which the system of tools will assist in detecting frauds.

Han et al. (2020) defined and conceptualized digital (e-proctoring, online, virtual, remote) proctoring in aspects of system development, emergency response to COVID-19 pandemic, new challenges for educators, students' authentication and authorship, comparison between un-proctored and proctored exam in students' performance, MOOC integration, and other issues such as privacy, legal, ethics, safety, security, etc. Hence, the research findings proposed technical features of OP systems have improved with both the innovations of education technology of "AI technologies for detecting misconduct and malpractice in online examinations (OEs)." From this discussion, there is the challenge of how to digitize assessment of learners' academic performance in HEIs.

By using keywords of TITLE-ABS-KEY ("ONLINE ASSESSMENTS" OR "online test" OR "online exam" OR "online examination" or "assessment quality management") AND ("online proctor" OR "online supervisor" OR "virtual supervisor" OR "virtual proctor") the concept of OP was found by the following relations: activity characteristics (academic integrity, dishonesty, cheating), area of proctoring (detection, online assessment, examination), and field of application (engineering, e-learning, education, distance education, COVID-19). Thus, the proposed main functions of proctoring in an online learning environment focus on detection, alert, report, and intelligent navigation or direction for students in testing (SCOUPUS database). The diagram of the search literature review process is shown in Figures 8.1 and 8.2.

The OP can be classified into three categories.

1. **Standalone Proctors:** Supervision occurs throughout students' proctored examination, directly directing/supervising the online, virtual examination. However, unlike regular proctors, online proctors will require expertise in using technology and training to ensure student authenticity and look for any signs of movement of

suspicious eyes or faces or the presence of any untested equipment that could signal potential fraud.

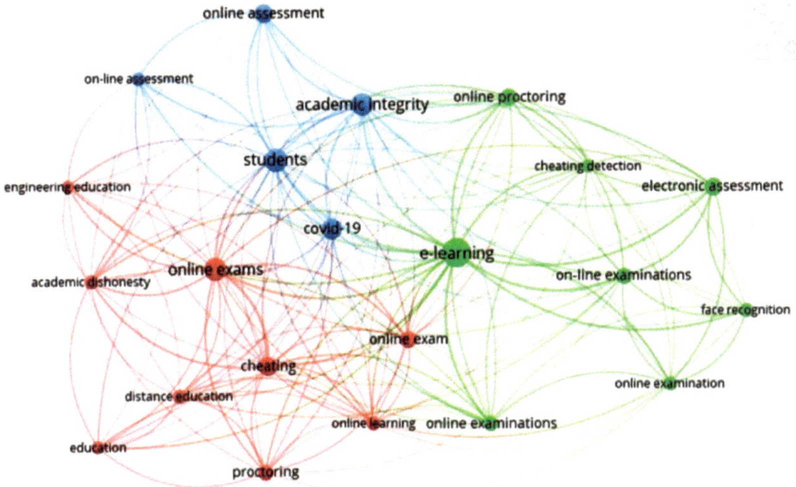


**FIGURE 8.1** Interactive map of relationships within online proctoring concepts in publications.

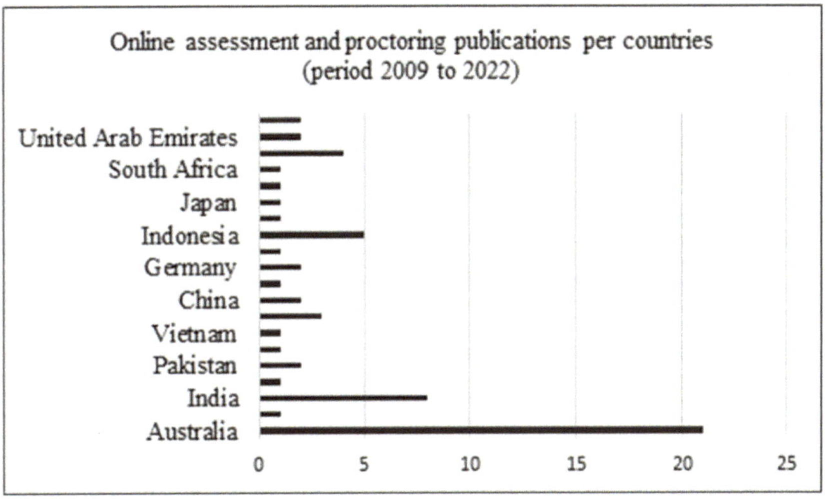


**FIGURE 8.2** The number of publications on online assessment and proctoring topics per country from 2009 to 2022.

2. **Proctoring by Recordings and Exam Logs:** The proctor checks the camera recording (audio, screenshot) and diaries of students taking the online test thereafter and judges the integrity of the exam (i.e., no cheating/cheating) committed by the candidate during the exam. This type of supervision allows students to take an exam at any time and from any location, allowing many tests to be given at the same time.
3. **Automated Proctors:** This form of automatic proctoring is more convenient for candidates because it is not mandatory to arrange an in-person supervisor for tests and exams; there is no time constraint. Time, location, personnel. At the same time, it is possible to expand the scope and scale of the exam, the human factor can be replaced by artificial intelligence (AI) or algorithms, thus solving the cost problems. The disadvantage of this form is students' familiarity with the established exam system, detecting vulnerabilities in the system and planning for cheating behaviors.

Many virtual proctoring systems offer three types of online exam monitoring, as outlined above. However, in order to choose and deploy a virtual supervision system, it is necessary to consider several factors first, which include: the ability to quickly and flexibly integrate technical performance and capacity of the virtual surveillance system (often due to insufficient internet connection, weak hardware capabilities), task automation efficiency, and reporting and feedback capabilities with the existing learning management system (LMS). Other significant factors to consider when choosing a virtual surveillance system include privacy, security, and anti-fraud management and protection measures, as well as their associated expenses (Sietses, 2016).

Moreover, the OS system may work with a complex of designed elements of both technical and functional requirements (*see*Table 8.1).

Currently, most of the tools or software has been supported by integration into various MOOC, LMS or LCMS platforms for school and university online testing practice (built-in with learner database, analytic learning system, AI, web-conferencing, and other technology tools).

On the other hand, the consideration of compatibility of existing online testing software, supported platforms, computer system requirements, the need for an internet connection during the exam, and the testing structure for the online testing environment play a significant role (Table 8.2).

**TABLE 8.1** The Components of a Typical Online Proctoring System

| | |
|---|---|
| **Application** | Assessment context awareness and learning adaptability, assessment activities, and assessment content in accordance with the present (accessible) online testing environment, and so on. |
| **Monitoring Dashboard** | Monitoring numerous scenarios and providing metrics in general; specifically, monitoring learning quality, learner achievement, student academic performance, and so forth. |
| **Face Recognition and Identification** | Detect the faces of different learners in a variety of settings, including testing (in the classroom, in the real world), etc. |
| **Recognition and Detection of Motion** | In a testing setting, sense or detect the movements of various persons and things. |
| **Recognition of Gestures** | To recognize and proctor the learner's motions in a testing setting. |
| **Intelligent Surveillance** | Using various forms of smart devices, monitor, and proctor activities or behavioral patterns, as well as any changes in the testing environment. |
| **Recording** | Various activities (situations) in the testing environment are automatically recorded in high-quality audio and video. |
| **Analytical Forecasting** | Data analyzed from numerous sensors is processed to produce predictions about the next steps/actions in the testing process; learner report. |
| **Quick Video Processing and Analytics** | Processing of huge data from recorded videos (for example, surveillance video cameras) in a quick and relatively simple manner (getting analytics). |
| **Quick and Simple Remote Access** | Easy access to the real-time or recorded video/audio/information by the instructor (or, most likely, the safety officer) from practically anyplace, but at the very least via a central context awareness unit (system). |
| **Notifications** | Send an email, text message, or phone call notifications on a regular basis. |
| **Alerts** | Send learners real-time safety and security alerts, as well as notifications in the event of illegal action or cheating. |
| **Intelligent Navigation** | Provide the learner with highly accurate information concerning unexpected actions or cheating as well as completed report. |

*Source:* Adapted from: Vladimir et al. (2018).

**TABLE 8.2** The Comparison Within Online (Virtual) Proctoring Software

| Software | Core Technology | Advantage | Disadvantage |
|---|---|---|---|
| ExamOnline | • Secure data hosting on Amazon Cloud Services.<br>• Using artificial intelligence to provide a secure and confidential environment in which to conduct online exams. | • Highly customizable exam platform.<br>• For a continuous 360° view, use two cameras.<br>• AI-powered facial recognition and detection.<br>• Highly scalable cloud-based solution. | • Commercial version available.<br>• Use only by Google Chrome browser.<br>• Mobile responsive UI but mobile app not available. |
| SpeedExam | Secured by SSL<br>AI | • Easy to use for everyone.<br>• API integration.<br>• Automatic grading and reporting. | • The interface could look a bit better.<br>• The image inclusion process could be improved.<br>• Scope for improvement in proctoring. |
| Mercer Mettl | • Proctoring technology AI.<br>• Mettl secure exam browser. | • Proctoring options include AI-based and manual remote proctoring.<br>• Deployments on the cloud, SaaS, the web, and on mobile devices are all possible (iOS and Android).<br>• Quickly integrate proctoring services to your platform through APIs. | • Free version.<br>• Not provide a free trial period. |
| Examus | • Proctor AI – online exam monitoring technology with AI.<br>• Examus EQ – a tool to monitor learners' attention and interaction during online learning in e-learning courses. | • Patented AI technology.<br>• Open API for integration with LMS.<br>• Cost-effective and highly scalable.<br>• Low demand for bandwidth. | • Supports a small number of mobile platforms.<br>• Not suitable for small businesses, freelancers, or agencies. |

**TABLE 8.2** *(Continued)*

| Software | Core Technology | Advantage | Disadvantage |
|---|---|---|---|
| ProctorU | AI-based behavioral analysis. | • Offer API and custom integrations.<br>• Quickly verifies the environment.<br>• Convenient to utilize for tests done from the comfort of one's own home.<br>• It safeguards your reputation. | • There is a noticeable delay in initiating a test.<br>• Too sensitive to enable even a small amount of background noise, such as mumbling. |

In Vietnam, the shift from traditional face-to-face classroom proctored testing environment to remote (online, digital) testing has been stated in the legal documents of MOET as well as local authorities' revised guidelines for schools, institutions, and universities themselves. "The summative assessment of students' online learning achievement can be organized by the institutions or schools according to the regulations on planning examination and evaluation of the MOET. In case, a student cannot go to a general education institution at the time of periodic assessment and evaluation due to force majeure, the organization of periodical examination and evaluation shall be carried out online by the head of the institution" (Circular No. 9/2021/TT-BGDDT, March 2021). "Relating to the shifting into online training mode, the institutions can organize the final semester exam by online mode, as well as blended or traditional method format. The organization of online exam (if any) must have a question bank large enough to build multiple-choice questions and make sure to create at least four independent and non-duplicate test questions. The head of the unit promulgates a document guiding the process of organizing the online exam; ensure that exam questions, answers, and marking instructions are kept confidential (before, during, and after the exam)" (Decision No. 4391/QD-DHQGHN, VNU).

Thus, in the country, there is a crucial issue of online testing practice in both legal documents and research works. For Vietnam context, in particular, that can be deployed in the near future are proposing an online learning and testing system suitable to the characteristics and characteristics of the students' conditions of learners in Vietnam, the awareness of online learning, online testing, students' online activities during exams in online digital environment.

## 8.3 ONLINE PROCTORING (OP): A CASE OF VNU-UED

Faced with the context of interrupted learning due to the COVID-19 pandemic, learners and teachers are forced to adapt to online learning. A big problem that needs to be solved when learning online is the online assessment and exam to ensure fairness, transparency, and accurate results.

Besides, using a new online exam system also poses another problem of cost and security. To promptly respond to the online exam at the University of Education, Vietnam National University, Hanoi (VNU-UED) has come up with a situational solution that is appropriate to the context, taking advantage of the school's existing learning platform as a result combining the Moodle system and the Zoom application to create the complex of online exam - MZ (Moodle LMS and Zoom web-conferencing).

This system is used in the final exam for all students, with various exam forms, including essay exams, multiple-choice exams, and essays combined with multiple choice. From the features available on the Moodle system, design essay tests with complete test-taking tools such as adding images, fonts, font sizes, linking…; Multiple-choice tests with the questions in the test will be mixed, and students cannot copy the question to look up information, the report will be available instantly by test completion.

The MZ online exam system of UED mobilizes two actors in the online exam process: the proctors (admin, teacher-proctor, and technician) and the test-takers (students), with integrated digital platforms as Moodle (LMS) and Zoom (web-conferencing). In other words, to take the online test (in both synchronous and asynchronous modes) candidates need to access Moodle and Zoom tools simultaneously.

By entering the LMS Moodle (which stores and manages item banks, test structures, and delivers testing reports, etc.):

- Before participating in the exam, candidates must log in to the system to update personal information, complete exam records as required, and participate in mock exams.
- In taking the exam, students enter the correct exam subject, their exam room, and start taking the test. Students are allowed to submit work before it ends, but the system will immediately lock it when the time expires. With multiple-choice tests, students receive their results immediately after taking the exam, while with essays, they are sent to the teacher and get their results back a few days later.
- Students, after fully logging in/registering before the exam, will be given a technical supervisor to handle problems with the exam system and control the candidate's activities on this system, including testing. Students control the number of exams and the number of candidates who participate and submit successfully.

By entering Zoom (with the function supported of using web-conferencing, extended exam monitoring, surveillance of students' behaviors, prohibited action alert, recording, etc.):

- Before participating in the exam, candidates must log in to the virtual exam room on Zoom software, then follow the regulations of the exam room, such as checking the candidate's identity, turning on the camera, turning on the microphone during the exam, the test location must meet the conditions of light, sound.

- During the test, candidates can interact with the proctor through the software to respond to questions and get technical help from the proctor.
- Competitors will be observed and when there is a problem of cheating, they will be required to be tested. Tasks performed by virtual exam room proctors on Zoom are similar to actual exam rooms.

To prevent cheating in exams, all tests in different formats are given in an open format, which means that students are entitled to use hardcopy materials such as textbooks. However, candidates absolutely must not use web browsers to look up results or use intelligent devices during the test or receive help from others while taking the test. The proctor is divided into two roles to supervise closely and timely support the candidates: the main proctor (monitoring through audio and images acquired on Zoom application) and the technology supervisor (supervising) assist in monitoring test takers' performance on the Moodle system), such division is also intended to reduce cheating on each platform. In case of detecting a candidate's cheating behavior, the main proctor will take a screenshot of the candidate's cheating behavior and ask the candidate to stop taking the test; at the same time, the technology supervisor will cancel the ability to take the test—contestant's exam on the Moodle platform. The exam process is similar to when a candidate participates in a live exam, all cheating will be recorded, and the exam will be suspended.

The MZ online exam system of UED is an instant, effective, and suitable solution for the changing context of online learning as well as online testing, exams. The Moodle system supports candidates based on taking the test and manages the number of entries following the list of candidates provided by the training department and storing the candidates' test results. Zoom software helps open an online exam room with the same function as the live exam room to monitor and detect cheating behaviors from candidates.

Thus, it can be said that the MZ online exam system has helped ensure the regulations and regulations of a traditional exam room, organize the exam to ensure quality, and prevent cheating during the online exam (see Figure 8.3).

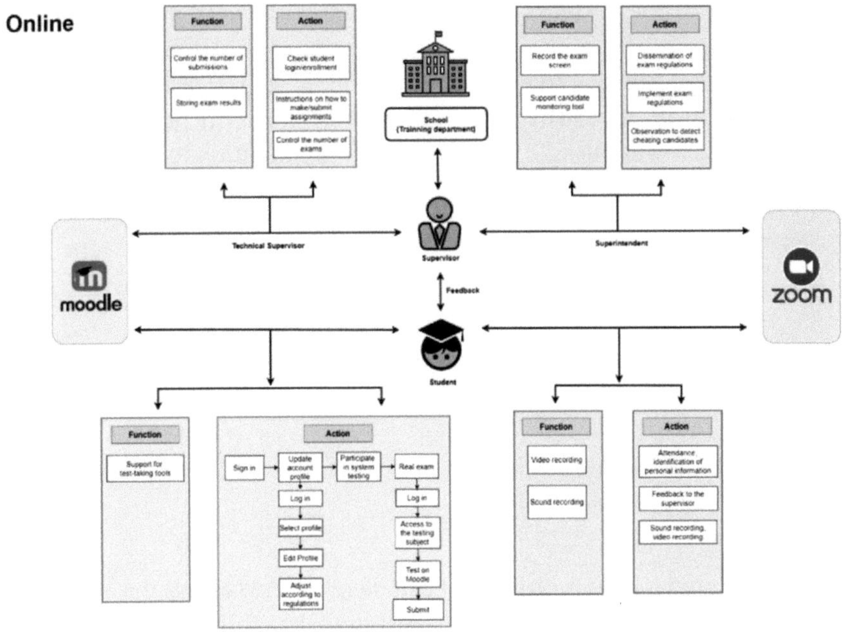


**FIGURE 8.3** Online proctoring system MZ of UED.

## 8.4 METHODS

According to research by Sukarno, Nur Laila Meilani, Yuli Karyanti, and Handoko Subawi, in determining users' perceptions and attitudes towards applying new technology is the open data kit (ODK) in the Survey. The PMA 2020 Survey in Indonesia has shown that one of the methods to determine the extent to which users accept the application of new technology is to use the technology acceptance model (TAM). The study shows that TAM has two problems. Specifically, the first problem is trust, including usefulness and ease of use. The second includes attitudes towards use, intended use behavior, and user behavior (Straub, Limayen, Evaristo, 1995 in Petra, 2005). The authors have proposed six research hypotheses (easiness hypothesis, perceived ease of use hypothesis, perceived usefulness hypothesis, utility hypothesis, attitude hypothesis towards use, hypothesis) behavioral intention to use). Then, an assessment of the adoption of new technology can be made by looking at the likes and dislikes of people with attitudes about the usefulness of the system. The analysis results also prove that only one is rejected out of the above six hypotheses. The relationships between variables that are positively significant include: (i) ease of use versus perceived usefulness; (ii) perceived ease of use; (iii) perceived utility; (iv) attitude toward usage; and (v) behavioral intention to use throughout the system (*see* Figure 8.4).

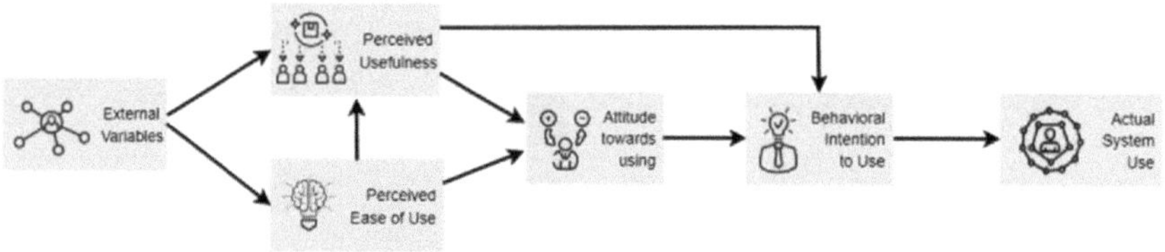


**FIGURE 8.4** Technology acceptance model.

*Source*: Adapted from Davis, 1985

In this study, hypotheses have been developed to assess the acceptance of MZOP system according to the TAM model as follows:

- **$H_1$:** Is understanding MZ technology positively related to the intent to use this technology?
- **$H_2$:** Is perceived ease of use positively related to Intent to Use this technology?
- **$H_3$:** Is the utility of MZ technology positively related to the intent to use this technology?
- **$H_4$:** Is the intention to use MZ positively related to the ease of use and usefulness of this technology?

The Likert scale has been used in the survey to investigate and receive feedback from students at the University of Education, Hanoi National University, regarding the use of MZ online exam technology. The questionnaire has been divided into two parts. The first part consists of questions related to demographics such as age, field of study, and frequency of using the MZ model. The second part focuses on testing and technology aspects, such as the assessment of assistive technology: usefulness, ease of use, and intentions and possibilities of using the MZ system in the testing process.

Each question has four answer options that indicate the satisfaction level of students who have used the technology: (i) strongly disagree; (ii) disagree; (iii) neutral; (iv) agree; and (v) strongly agree. The survey aims to assess the understanding and acceptance of the online exam technology that combines Moodle and Zoom technology, as well as evaluate the ease of use and usefulness of these two software and their intended use in the future. The survey results were obtained from 243 answer sheets from students at the University of Education, with 59.7% first-year students, 15.6% second-year students, 24.7% third-year students, and 2.1% fourth-year students.

## 8.5 FINDINGS

Research findings represented the result of statistically significant variation in various evaluation contents between the groups of people with different disciplines in HEIs training programs.

Table 8.3 shows that the more users rate the usefulness, ease of use, and support of MZ, the more likely they are to continue using MZ. The level of influence of factors on usability, from high to low, is the usefulness, ease of use and support of MZ, respectively (r is 0.661, 0.399, and 0.283, respectively), all p (2-tailed) = 0.000 < 0.01. An 'r' value of 0.20 or 0.20 is the minimum that the correlation is statistically significant and large enough to be of interest. The correlation coefficient r = 0.10 is considered a "little" effect; r = 0.30 is considered a "medium" effect; and r = 0.50 is considered a "large" effect (Cohen, 1988). The above results show that the usefulness of MZ has a large influence on the user's ability to continue using the MZ application, and the supportability of the MZ has little influence on their intention to continue using the MZ. The user evaluation results also show that: the ease of use of MZ is highly appreciated, the usefulness is also highly appreciated by users (r = 0.482), and the supportability of MZ also has a medium influence. Average (r = 0.338) to the usefulness of this application.

Moreover, according to the received descriptive statistics, there is a statistically significant difference in some assessment contents between the third and fourth-year learners (at a much higher level) and the learners in the third and fourth years the first year, second year. Levene's test of equality of variance was used to determine whether there is a significant difference in the assessment results between the first and second-year students (Group 1) and the third and fourth-year students (Group 2) or not. The results show that the variances of these two groups of subjects in some content HD1, DD2, DD5, and KN5 are not different (significant level > 0.05), so the test for balanced variance is used for these contents. For the KN2 content, the results show that the variances of the two groups of subjects are different (significant level 0.039 < 0.05), the test for unbalanced variance is used for this content.

The comments on the ease of use of the MZ: the third- and fourth-year groups of learners (mean = 3.85, standard deviation = 1.215) easily handle problems arising when using MZ in testing, assessment, and participation online test than the group of first year and second-year learners (t = -3.353; df = 325; sig. (two-tailed) = 0.001 < 0.05); however, the first- and second-year groups (TB = 3.54, standard deviation = 0.920) agreed to a higher degree than the third- and fourth-year groups that MZ allowed many users to participate in the assessment price, take the online test (t = 2.423; df = 235; sig. (two-tailed) = 0.016 < 0.05).

With the statements about the usefulness of MZ participants (the third- and fourth-year group of learners) showing a higher degree of agreement that MZ technology effectively supports the requirements of the control online assessment and test for first- and second-year students (t = –1.978; df = 235; sig. (two-tailed) = 0.049 < 0.05).

By comments on the intention and possibility of using the next MZ group of third- and fourth-year students has a higher level of agreement than the sophomores and second-year one towards their intention of use, willingness to share their use experience. MZ in checking other people's online reviews (t = –2.616; df = 1,54,777; sig. (two-tailed) = 0.010 < 0.05), they also believe that using MZ will continue to motivate, interested in assessment, taking the online exam (t = –1.991; df = 235; sig. (two-tailed) = 0.048 < 0.05) at a higher level.

Besides, descriptive statistics show statistically significant differences between learners of training disciplines in some evaluation contents. Levene's test of equality to see if there was a significant difference in assessment outcomes between the group of students majoring in teacher mathematics and natural sciences education (Group 1), teacher literature, history, and geography education (Group 2), and the Group 3 of students from Education majors overall such as Primary Education, Early Childhood Education, Educational Sciences, and Education Technology Management.

The survey results showed that students of Group 2 (TB = 3.74, standard deviation = 1.215) are easier to deal with problems arising when using MZ in testing and assessment, taking online exams more Group 1 (t = -2.343; df = 145; sig. (two-tailed) = 0.020 < 0.05). Moreover, they are also more willing to share their experiences of using MZ in checking online assessments for others (t = -2.142; df = 145; sig. (two-tailed) = 0.034 < 0.05).

The group of learners (Group 3) agreed at a higher level than others (mean = 3.93, standard deviation = 0.790). While the students of Group 1 are more suitable with the conditions of technical infrastructure, connectivity, ensuring stable online exam deployment (t = –2.088; df = 189; sig. (two-tailed) = 0.038 < 0.05), the Group 3 considers the highest level of flexibility of use MZ on different connected devices such as computers, phones, etc., in comparison with Group 1 (t = –2.023; df = 189; sig. (two-tailed) = 0.045 < 0.05) (TB = 3.64, standard deviation = 0.903).

**TABLE 8.3** The Correlation of Significance of MZ

| Correlations | | | | | |
|---|---|---|---|---|---|
| | | **KNM** | **HTM** | **HDM** | **DDM** |
| **KNM (Intentions to Use)** | Pearson correlation | 1 | 0.283** | 0.661** | 0.399** |
| | Sig. (2-tailed) | – | 0.000 | 0.000 | 0.000 |
| | N | 237 | 237 | 237 | 237 |
| **HTM (Perception of OP)** | Pearson correlation | 0.283** | 1 | 0.338** | 0.250** |
| | Sig. (2-tailed) | 0.000 | – | 0.000 | 0.000 |
| | N | 237 | 237 | 237 | 237 |
| **HDM (Usefulness)** | Pearson correlation | 0.661** | 0.338** | 1 | 0.482** |
| | Sig. (2-tailed) | 0.000 | 0.000 | – | 0.000 |
| | N | 237 | 237 | 237 | 237 |
| **DDM (Easy to Use)** | Pearson correlation | 0.399** | 0.250** | 0.482** | 1 |
| | Sig. (2-tailed) | 0.000 | 0.000 | 0.000 | – |
| | N | 237 | 237 | 237 | 237 |

***Correlation is significant at the 0.01 level (2-tailed).*

## 8.6 CONCLUSION AND RECOMMENDATIONS

Using the MZ online exam system is a flexible, efficient, and adaptive solution for the University of Education (VNU-UED) in the very first period of COVID-19, realizing the motto "disruptive classes but undisruptive learning" at HEIs. Teachers and students give positive feedback and willingness of MZ system use in the next online exams.

The application of OP in online testing process also shows a positive potential for digital transformation in HEIs while changing thinking, educational approaches, and culture associated with online assessment and testing by technologies. This process requires systematic implementation of procedures such as research on new approaches and assessment changes in the online testing model, user characteristics of the online testing environment, development of both educational and technological procedures, and institutional administration and policy. Technical training manuals on online testing for learners, administration guidelines, digitizing items bank, upgrading more intelligent OP support systems based on big data, AI, and block chain, learning analytic and adaptive testing conceptions, etc. The arguments and recommendations for enhancing implementation and MZ system use for online testing may be as follows: (i) increase adaptability, interactivity, and meet diversity, simplicity in access and use of learners: Fully exploit different functions in the same tool to minimize presentation; Integrate learning analysis tools and solutions (analyze learning progress, achievements, progress, task tracking, recognition, reward…); (ii) Increase flexibility in using integrated tools for instructors in online exams: Combine using Moodle synchronously (before and after the exam) with groups of technology solutions to support during the online exam (QR Code), VR/AR for various activities such as attendance, answering questions, participating in online discussions…); integrated recording support tools; record right on LMS (create working space); and (iii) create a virtual learning environment, seamlessly switch between learning activities: install the online learning application API or web-conferencing as Zoom, MS Teams, Google Meet, Jitsi Meet…

In fact, HEIs can continue to work on integrating APIs into MZ, to design, reconstruct, and "refresh" test items bank, learners' visualization and operation adapted to online testing mode with providing necessary training for both academic staff and students in terms of MZ use. Furthermore, the HEIs may develop cooperation with EdTech enterprises towards advancing digital technology features, especially AI, big data, learning analytic features to make MZ system more friendly, secure, and reliable.

## KEYWORDS

- **big data**
- **COVID-19**
- **digital education**
- **higher education institutions**
- **online examination**
- **online proctoring**
- **web-conferencing**


## REFERENCES


Alessio, H. M., Malay, N., Maurer, K., Bailer, A. J., & Rubin, B., (2017). Examining the effect of proctoring on online test scores. *Online Learning, 21*(1), 146–161 https://doi.org/10.24059/olj. v21i1.885.

Atoum, Y., Chen, L., Liu, A. X., Hsu, S. D., & Liu, X., (2017). Automated online exam proctoring. *IEEE Transactions on Multimedia, 19*(7), 1609–1624.

Brown, M., McCormack, M., Reeves, J., Brook, D. C., Grajek, S., Alexander, B., & Weber, N., (2020). 2020 Educause horizon report teaching and learning edition. *Educause* (pp. 2–58).

Chase-Dunn, C., & Hall, T. D., (2018). *Rise and Demise: Comparing World-Systems.* Routledge.

Coghlan, S., Miller, T., & Paterson, J., (2020). *"Good Proctor or Big Brother"? AI Ethics and Online Exam Supervision Technologies.*arXiv preprint arXiv:2011.07647, https://doi.org/10.48550/arXiv.2011.07647.

Daffin, L. W. Jr., & Jones, A., (2018). A. Comparing student performance on proctored and non-proctored exams in online psychology courses. *Online Learning Journal, 22*(1), 131–145.

Dendir, S., & Maxwell, R. S., (2020). Cheating in online courses: Evidence from online proctoring. *Computers in Human Behavior Reports, 2*, 1–10. https://doi.org/10.1016/j.chbr.2020.100033.

Dyer, J. M., Pettyjohn, H. C., & Saladin, S., (2020). Academic dishonesty and testing: How student beliefs and test settings impact decisions to cheat. *Journal of the National College Testing Association, 4*(1), 1–30.

Fask, A., Englander, F., & Wang, Z., (2014). Do online exams facilitate cheating? An experiment designed to separate possible cheating from the effect of the online test taking environment. *Journal of Academic Ethics, 12*(2), 101–112. https://doi.org/10.1007/s10805-014-9207-1.

Fluck, A. E., (2019). An international review of eExam technologies and impact. *Computers & Education, 132*, 1–15. https://doi.org/10.1016/j.compedu.2018.12.008.

Foster, D., & Layman, H., (2013). *Online Proctoring Systems Compared.* https://caveon.com/wp-content/uploads/2013/03/Online-Proctoring-Systems-Compared-Mar-13-2013.pdf *(accessed on 12 December 2023).*

Golden, J., & Kohlbeck, M., (2020). Addressing cheating when using test bank questions in online classes. *Journal of Accounting Education, 52*, 1–14. *https://doi.org/10.1016/j.jaccedu.2020.100671.*

Han, S., Nikou, S., Ayele, W. Y., Balasuriya, B. L. P., & Eric-Oluf, S., (2022). *Digital Proctoring in Higher Education: A Systematic Literature Review.*ECIS 2022 Research Papers. 57. https://aisel.aisnet.org/ecis2022_rp/57 (accessed on 12 December 2023).

Harmon, O. R., Lambrinos, J., & Buffolino, J., (2010). Assessment design and cheating risk in online instruction. *Online Journal of Distance Learning Administration, 13*(3), https://www.surf.nl/binaries/content/assets/surf/en/knowledgebase/2016/whitepaper-online-proctoring_en.pdf (accessed on 12 December 2023).

Kellaghan, T., & Greaney, V., (2019). *Public Examinations Examined.* World Bank Publications.

Lương, D. H., (2021). *Research Trends in Online Testing and Assessment in the Period of 1989–2021: Data from Scopus.*The Vietnam National Institute of Educational Sciences.

Martin, A., (2020). *How to Optimize Online Learning in the Age of Coronavirus (COVID-19): A 5-Point Guide for Educators* (Vol. 53, No. 9, pp. 1–30). UNSW Newsroo*m*. https://newsroom.unsw.edu.au/news/social-affairs/how-optimise-online-learning-age-coronavirus (accessed on 12 December 2023).

Nigam, A., Pasricha, R., Singh, T., &Churi, P., (2021). A systematic review on AI-based proctoring systems: Past, present, and future. *Education and Information Technologies, 26*(5), 6421–6445.

Owens, H. S., (2015). *Cheating Within Online Assessments: A Comparison of Cheating Behaviors in Proctored and Unproctored Environments.*Mississippi State University.

Reddy, S., Allan, S., Coghlan, S., & Cooper, P., (2020). A governance model for the application of AI in health care. *Journal of the American Medical Informatics Association, 27*(3), 491–497.

Selwyn, B., & Leyden, D., (2021). Oligopoly-driven development: The World Bank's trading for development in the age of global value chains in perspective. *Competition & Change.* 1024529421995351.

Sietses, L., (2016). *White Paper Online Proctoring: Questions and Answers About Remote Proctoring.* Utrecht.

Srikanth, M., &Asmatulu, R., (2014). Modern cheating techniques, their adverse effects on engineering education and preventions. *International Journal of Mechanical Engineering Education, 42*(2), 129–140. https://doi.org/10.7227/IJMEE.0005.

Straub, Limayen, Evaristo, 1995 in Petra, (2005). Analisis proses penerimaansistemin-formasi icons denganmenggunakan technology acceptance model pada karyawanpt. bank negara indonesia (persero) tbk. *Valid JurnalIlmiah*, doi: https://doi.org/10.35748/valid.v14i2.38.

Turner, S. W., &Uludag, S., (2013). Student perceptions of cheating in online and traditional classes. In: *2013 IEEE Frontiers in Education Conference (FIE), US,* (pp. 1131–1137). *IEEE.*

Vladimir, L. U., Jeffrey, P. B., Robert, J. H., & Lakhmi, C. J., (2018). *Smart Universities: Concepts, Systems, and Technologies.* Springer International Publishing AG.

Xiong, Y., & Suen, H. K., (2018). Assessment approaches in massive open online courses: Possibilities, challenges, and future directions. *International Review of Education, 64*(2), 241–263. https://doi.org/10.1007/s11159-018-9710-5.

## CHAPTER 9

# Learning Management System and Its Impact on Academic Achievement Among College Students of Darjeeling District, India

RANITA CHAKRABORTTY

*Faculty of Education, Salesian College Siliguri Campus, Siliguri, West Bengal, India*

## ABSTRACT

With the onset of the global pandemic and educational institutions going under lockdown since March 2020 in India, the process of higher education has greatly been hampered. Although different states of the country resorted to various online technologies to cope with this issue, there has still been a deficiency in an organized system for the efficient and smooth transaction of the educational process. The use of learning management systems (LMS) has already been promoted extensively in India under the project named e-Kranti, a government initiative as a part of the Digital India Program initiated by the Government of India in 2015. However, there has been a sudden impetus recently due to higher educational institutions' lockdown. In this context, the present study provides an insight into the use of the LMS in order to manage learning on a regular basis by Salesian College, the only institution in Darjeeling District in this post-pandemic scenario with respect to their gender, locality, academic streams, and annual family income.

Intelligent Learning Paradigms and Student Empowerment: Digital Integration and Transformation. Souvik Pal, Ton Quang Cuong, & R. S. S. Nehru (Eds.)

## 9.1 INTRODUCTION

With the rapid advancement in the field of education, there has been an increasing need for educators to constantly keep themselves abreast with the modern techniques for the effective transaction of knowledge. One of the most recent advancements seen in this regard is the integration of information and communication technology (ICT) for the dissemination of education. This idea of using ICT in the field of education is commonly referred to as e-learning. E-learning can be referred to as the use of technology in imparting teaching and learning without the aid of any paper-based instructional materials. E-Learning can be interchangeably used as online learning, virtual learning, network-based learning, and web-based learning (Goyal, 2012). It is dependent on several factors such as the motivation and attitude of the learners, availability of proper equipment (hardware and software) and teaching-learning materials, the readiness of the teachers and the learners, and finally the learning context. This form of learning creates a sense of responsibility and accountability on the part of the learners. Not only the learners but also the teachers become responsible for their teaching and also promote proper communication with students at all times. Using ICT e-learning strategies is found to promote critical thinking among the learners thereby improving their reasoning and empirical abilities. As such, it is imperative to understand the underlying psychological concept while devising a lesson plan based on e-learning strategies. First and foremost, the teacher should understand which learning style favors the most while utilizing this form of learning. According to the Behaviorist school, the learning environment should focus on only making the learners aware of the outcomes of the learning process. As such, learning should involve the demonstration of skills and procedures for breaking down the complex content into simpler elements and providing the required information to the learners about it beforehand. The learners should also be able to determine their progress by constantly reviewing themselves through an appropriate feedback mechanism. With regard to the cognitivist perspective, the individual differences of the learners are to be taken into consideration. As such, the e-learning experience should include different activities catering to the varied cognitive requirements of the learners. The teachers are also required to bring about a change in their teaching strategy through the aid of appropriate sensors, logical and appropriate instructions, and the introduction of suitable activities focusing on the diverse cognitive needs of the learners. Proper cognitive structures are to be created by linking the new information with the already existing ideas and information. This can be done through mapping strategies. Constructivism is considered to be one of the most dominant psychological paradigms influencing e-learning. This principle focuses on the idea that the construction of knowledge is done by the learners themselves and is based on their previous experience. It propagates the idea of a learner-centric environment where the role of the teacher is that of the facilitator or guide. Therefore, in the constructivist scenario, e-learning should be based on interactive ideas, where the learners are to be given the freedom to develop their own knowledge based on the online resources being provided by the teachers. The focus should be more on a cooperative and collaborative learning environment (Borboa, Joseph, Spake, & Yazdanparast, 2017).

E-learning has brought about a huge shift in the field of education by promoting the concept of remote learning which has been highly effective, especially during the pandemic period. Even before the onset of the pandemic, many higher educational institutions were adopting ICT-based technologies for imparting education to their students. Some of the most common digital platforms that have been widely accepted by the student community include BYJU'S, Unacademy, Alibaba Cloud, etc. The different types of e-learning include:

- Computer-managed learning (CML);
- Computer-assisted instruction (CAI);
- Synchronous and asynchronous online learning;
- Fixed E-learning;
- Adaptive E-learning;
- Linear E-learning;
- Interactive online learning;
- Individual online learning;
- Collaborative online learning.

However, with the global pandemic affecting the entire world and with educational institutions in India forced to be shut down from March 2020 to November 2021, serious attention is to be given to e-learning. Even after the lockdown was removed and institutions functioning normally, the new concept that has emerged is 'blended learning.' This form of learning involves the systematic and strategic blending of ICT-based technology with the traditional face-to-face learning situation. It is also referred to as hybrid technology. This form of a hybrid classroom is becoming the new normal in a post-COVID scenario with higher educational institutions opting for the use of online-based learning along with traditional face-to-face teaching-learning.

A learning management system (LMS) is one of the most effective ways for promoting e-learning through the use of software or web-based technologies for planning, performing, and evaluating learning processes based on specific objectives.

### 9.1.1 CONCEPT OF LEARNING MANAGEMENT SYSTEM (LMS)

Learning management systems (LMS) are web-based applications that serve to provide an important platform for learning and communication for students (Coates, James, & Baldwin, 2005; Kraleva, Sabani, & Kralev, 2019). It was first developed by Sidney L. Pressey in the 1920s and was referred to as the teaching machine, which could perform various types of practical activities and solve objective questions, especially multiple-choice questions. Since then, it has undergone several modifications over the years. The first LMS software was founded in 1990 by Soft Arc, and it was a client-based software known as FirstClass.

The basic criteria for determining the effectiveness of any LMS include learning skill tools, communication tools, and productivity tools. The learning skill tools refer to the skills involved in imparting learning to the students through various student involvement strategies such as group work, community networking, and student portfolios. Communication tools focus on the use of discussion forums, file exchange tools, internal email, online notes/journals, real-time chat, and whiteboard tools for access by the users. Finally, the productivity tools in any LMS highlight features such as bookmarks, calendar/progress review, search engines within a course, synchronization tools, and orientation/help tools (Kraleva, Sabani, & Kralev, 2019). Apart from the above learner tools, a learning management software should also include various support tools such as administration tools, course delivery tools, and content development tools.

Some of the basic features of LMS include:

- It promotes remote learning by making learning accessible to students from any location, even if they belong to the same or a different campus. Such a facility promotes improved levels of interaction and feedback sharing.

- Another important feature of LMS is the use of an attractive environment for promoting effective learning. Moodle (Open-Source Learning Version) used in Salesian College Sonada and Siliguri, for instance, uses features such as Games, Interactive Content, Quizzes, Video Conferencing, and Virtual Programming to make online classes attractive and interesting for students.
- Some of the LMSs can also incorporate various laboratory-based experiences, especially for science-based subjects which proved to be quite effective for the students, particularly during the lockdown phase.
- All LMSs have the feature of constantly updating and improving the software, which provides the option of adding in the missing feature to cater to the needs of every user.

LMSs can be of various types. These are:

1. **Installed LMS:** These are the most basic forms of LMS which are installed into the system on-premises. It is highly time-consuming, expensive, and requires expertise in handling.
2. **Web-based LMS:** This form of LMS is installed in the cloud and is made available to the user through the internet. It is economical and can be easily accessed by users from any location.
3. **Hosted LMS:** In this form of LMS, the institution is responsible for hosting the LMS. In other words, the entire functioning of the LMS including its updates and upgrades will be managed by the institution themselves.
4. **Software as a Service LMS:** This form of LMS is maintained exclusively by the LMS service vendors and the institution has to pay a package which can be either annually or monthly for using the LMS. All functioning of the LMS will be managed by the vendors themselves.
5. **Open Source LMS:** This type of LMS allows any user to use the source code and utilize as well as redistribute the software to other users without paying any amount. Additionally, the source code can be downloaded and modified by any developer as needed.
6. **Closed Source LMS:** This form of LMS is created by the developer and is proprietary to the owner and therefore cannot be used or distributed freely by any other user.

Some of the most common educational LMS include:

- Moodle;
- Blackboard learn;
- Schoology;
- Adobe Captivate Prime;
- Docebo LMS;
- Talent LMS;
- iSPringlearn;
- eFront.

### *9.1.2 MOODLE IS A LEARNING MANAGEMENT SYSTEM (LMS)*

Moodle is a free and open-source LMS that was developed by Martin Dougiamas from Moodle HQ, an Australian company to promote online teaching and learning through interactive and collaborative construction of instructional materials. Moodle was initially released on 20th August 2002. As open-source software, the source code for Moodle is made available free of cost and customizations can be made as per requirements. It is also comparatively cheaper with easier licensing agreements and promotes effective project management. The Moodle Course Management System helps instructors as well as students to experience teaching and learning interactively and collaboratively.

To access the LMS, the developer has to first download the package from the website available on moodle.org. The front page of the Moodle is the page that can be reached from the browser and reflects the basic institutional information. Logging into the Moodle can be done either through institutionally generated access ids or created by the users themselves. The most basic feature of the Moodle is courses which are pages or areas where the teacher can upload and present information to the students in the form of resources and activities. Moodle also allows the teachers or the developers to change its layout to make it more systematic and appealing for the students. Each user has their own customizable dashboard and the features that are available for viewing are based on the roles that have been granted to them by the administrator. The next most striking feature of Moodle is its plugins which provide flexibility to the organization to customize its basic features as per individual requirements. This creates a highly collaborative environment in the teaching and learning scenario. As of March 2022, Moodle offers 1,967 plugins, with over 388,800 recent downloads. Some of the notable plugins available in the Moodle used in Salesian College catering to the specified needs of the learners as well as the teachers are assignments, games, H5P, quiz packages, Hot Pot, Interactive content, SCORM Package, video conferencing tools (Big Blue Button, Google Meet, Jitsi, and Zoom) and virtual programming lab in addition to the various commonly used plugins.

As an LMS, Moodle is highly effective owing to its flexibility in use for its users. It provides the opportunity for the institution to track the progress of classes along with the scope of preparing courses as per the need of the user. It not only helps to monitor progress but can also be used for maintaining academic audits by the institutional heads. This function of Moodle served to be very instrumental, especially during the pandemic when real-time monitoring was becoming increasingly difficult owing to the lockdown of educational institutions. This LMS can be easily availed by the users and only requires a laptop/desktop/mobile phone with headphones and more or less reasonable internet bandwidth.

#### *9.1.2.1 IMPACT OF LEARNING MANAGEMENT SYSTEM (LMS) ON ACADEMIC ACHIEVEMENT*

The Digital India Campaign was launched by the Prime Minister on 1st July, 2015, and the LMS is a unique project which was initiated with a vision to promote flexibility in learning, the scope for hybrid learning by including virtual classrooms in traditional classroom setup (blended learning), providing e-Learning as a Service (eLAS) and utilization of various emerging technologies in this regard. Many institutions have long been following the use of LMS across the country, however, the onset of the pandemic created a scenario where it became imperative to continue teaching-learning in the virtual mode, especially through the use of an LMS. NEP 2020 also emphasized promoting digital learning at all levels. In this regard, UGC recommended the mandatory implementation of teaching in all universities with 25% of the syllabus being completed in online mode and 75% of the syllabus being completed in offline mode. This led to the concept of a hybrid or blended learning scenario.

It has been observed that the use of LMS has improved academic performance by bringing about continuity in education without compromising the health of the students and the teachers. It also created a simulated learning environment similar to that of the traditional classroom which helped in contributing to the achievement of the students. However, it goes beyond the traditional setup as it provides a multimedia exposure to the learning context thereby promoting the creativity and interest of the students. Digital learning is found to have an impact on academic achievement. This is primarily because of the easy accessibility of course materials to the users and the interactive learning environment that is provided by the LMS. The constant feedback that is generated also serves to be an effective factor in achieving the learning objectives. This can also be attributed to a radical shift from the teacher-centric traditional classroom to a more flexible learner-centric environment thereby paving the way for constructivism. LMS promotes increased engagement by making learning highly personalized. As a result, more time could be invested in gaining new knowledge by the students. In other words, the inclusion of e-learning through the use of appropriate LMS can promote the idea of 'meaningful learning' by bringing about an improvement in the students' academic performance as well as their motivation and learning effectiveness.

#### *9.1.2.2 USE OF LMS IN SALESIAN COLLEGE, INDIA DURING THE PANDEMIC*

The Salesian College was established in Shillong in 1933 and was later shifted to Sonada in 1938. In 2009, the college expanded its campus to Siliguri which is located around 30 miles from the main campus. It is considered one of the most prestigious institutions catering to the requirements of students from not only India but also from neighboring countries such as Nepal, Bangladesh, and Bhutan. Undergraduate courses in science, commerce, and humanities as well as postgraduate courses in humanities (English, Education, and Psychology) are offered in this college. Salesian College is a minority institution and is known to provide quality education to learners from different socioeconomic statuses (Thadathil et al., 2020). On 26th February 2010, the college was given the status of a 'College with Potential for Excellence (CPE) by UGC and reaccredited with an 'A' Grade by NAAC consecutively in its second and third cycle. The college seeks to produce students who will become noble citizens possessing the qualities of social sensitivity, high moral standards, and intellectual competency.

With the onset of the pandemic in March 2020, and with the lockdown of educational institutions as per the Government order, the college was forced to continue its regular teaching and learning in virtual mode. In this regard, the college used Moodle which is an open-source software of LMS. Initially, classes would be conducted through the Big Blue Button feature available in the LMS. However, owing to connectivity issues, the institution shifted to other videoconferencing platforms such as G-suite through Google Meet as well as Zoom and Jitsi. Login credentials were generated by the college IT team for all users. Apart from conducting classes, the LMS platform provided an opportunity for its users to conduct a myriad of other activities such as creating and updating courses, conducting evaluations through assignments and quizzes, and also including games (Crossword, hangman, Snake and Ladder, Sudoku) for the entertainment of the students. For the ease of students, keeping in mind the University Examination, there was the provision of not only recording the virtual lectures but also conducting the semester-end examination as per the University regulations. Even after the lockdown has been taken up by the Government, the college is still conducting classes in blended mode by using Moodle for offering virtual learning experiences to the students (Figures 9.1–9.5).

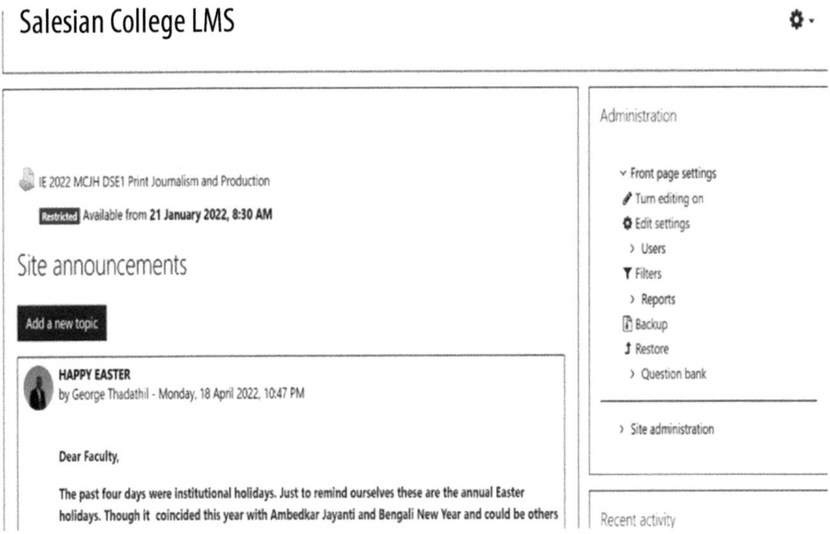


**FIGURE 9.1** Homepage showing the Moodle screen of the author from Salesian College, India.

*Source:* Salesian College. https://salesiancollege.org/moodle/.

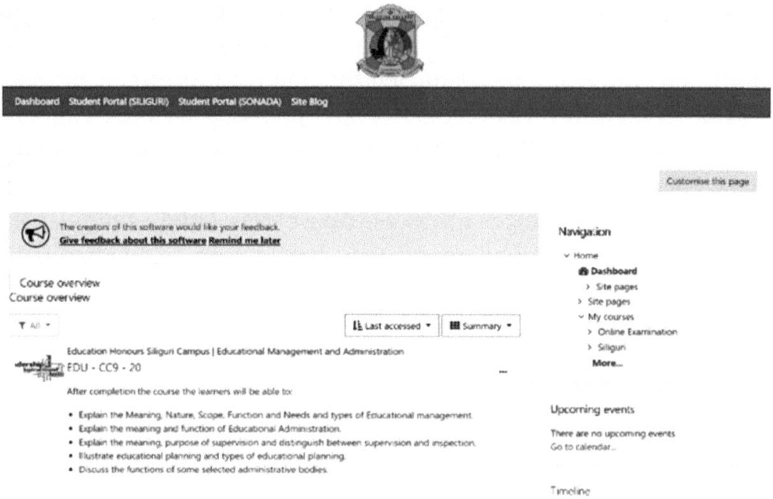


**FIGURE 9.2** Moodle screen dashboard containing a course created by the author.

*Source:* Salesian College. https://salesiancollege.org/moodle/.

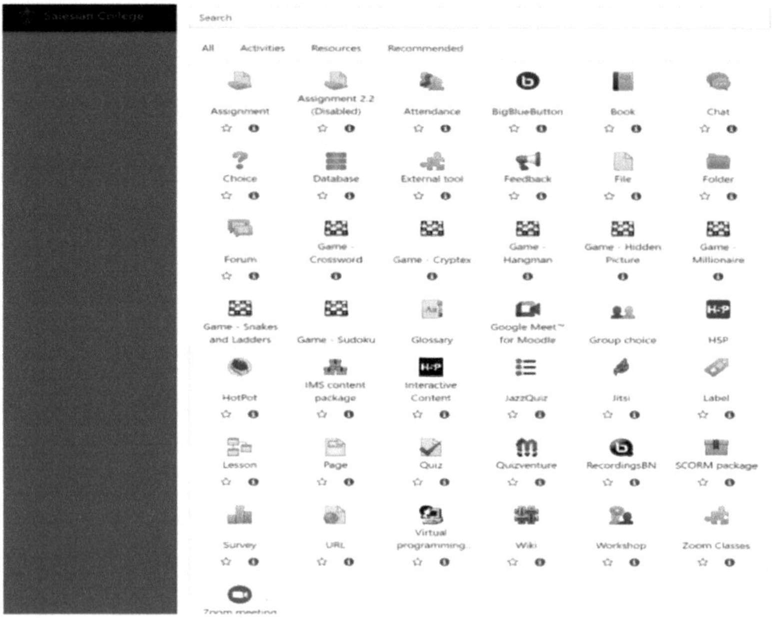


**FIGURE 9.3** Plugins in the form of activities and resources are available in Moodle used at Salesian College, India.

*Source:* Salesian College. https://salesiancollege.org/moodle/.

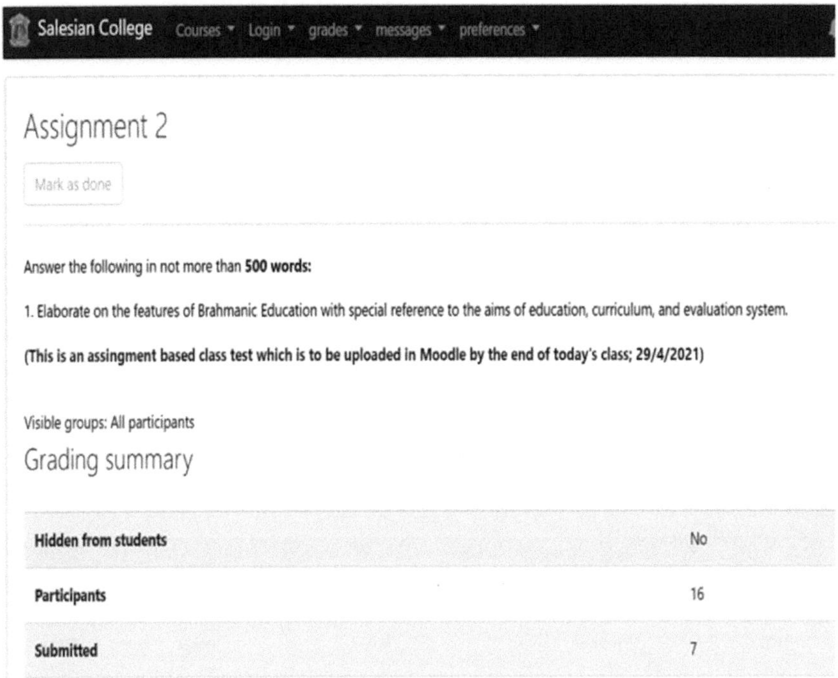


**FIGURE 9.4** Assignment submission status of students tracked through Moodle by the author.

*Source:* Salesian College. https://salesiancollege.org/moodle/.

## 9.1.3 REVIEW OF RELATED LITERATURE

Several studies have been conducted which indicate a gradual rise in the use of LMSs across the globe, especially during this pandemic. The findings have revealed that the need for students to use LMS was highly advantageous, especially during the pandemic, thereby promoting learning to be sustainably engaging (Alturki & Aldraiweesh, 2021). In this regard, e-learning policies are to be set up in various universities and higher educational institutions. The policy should address various issues about administration, training, plans for accomplishment, and other benefits. For effective management, it is therefore important to organize training and workshops (Sharma & Srivastav, 2020) along with proper optimization of the software to fully serve students, faculty, and the institutions. Although there are different types of LMS available, at present there are no proper resources available in LMS to cater to the needs of various laboratory-based/practical dimensions of the curriculum. Studies have shown that gender affects the use of LMS in undergraduate students, with male students exhibiting more usage patterns (Lim et al., 2020; Alshehri, Rutter, & Smith, 2020; Tinmaz & Lee, 2020). Analysis of different research conducted has also revealed that the use of LMS influences the academic achievement of college students (Akay & Gumusoglu, 2020). However, studies are yet to be conducted to determine the effect of locality, academic streams, and annual family income of college students. On the basis of this research gap, the investigator tried to conceptualize the research problem by taking into consideration the following problem: LMS and its impact on academic achievement among college students of Darjeeling district with regard to the categorical variables of gender, locality, academic stream, and socioeconomic status.

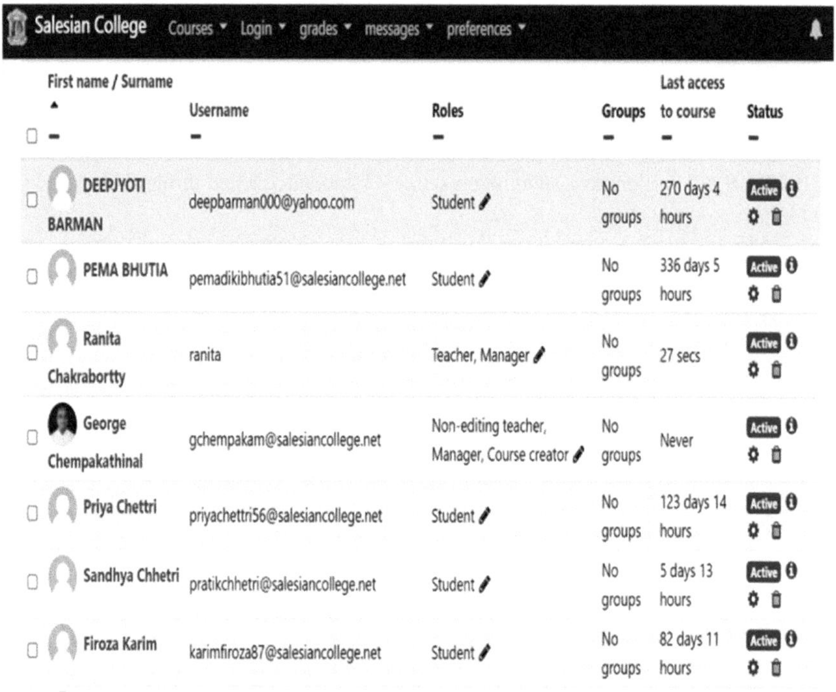

Salesian College Courses Login grades messages preferences

| First name / Surname | Username | Roles | Groups | Last access to course | Status |
|---|---|---|---|---|---|
| DEEPJYOTI BARMAN | deepbarman000@yahoo.com | Student | No groups | 270 days 4 hours | Active |
| PEMA BHUTIA | pemadikibhutia51@salesiancollege.net | Student | No groups | 336 days 5 hours | Active |
| Ranita Chakrabortty | ranita | Teacher, Manager | No groups | 27 secs | Active |
| George Chempakathinal | gchempakam@salesiancollege.net | Non-editing teacher, Manager, Course creator | No groups | Never | Active |
| Priya Chettri | priyachettri56@salesiancollege.net | Student | No groups | 123 days 14 hours | Active |
| Sandhya Chhetri | pratikchhetri@salesiancollege.net | Student | No groups | 5 days 13 hours | Active |
| Firoza Karim | karimfiroza87@salesiancollege.net | Student | No groups | 82 days 11 hours | Active |

**FIGURE 9.5** Enrolled user details along with their roles for a particular semester as reflected in the Moodle account of the author.

*Source:* https://salesiancollege.org/moodle/.

### *9.1.4 OPERATIONAL DEFINITIONS*

1. **Learning Management System (LMS):** It refers to a web-based application that serves to provide an important application for learning and communication for students by promoting e-learning for planning, performing, and evaluating learning processes based on specific objectives. In this study, the open-source LMS of Moodle was used on both campuses. It was based on the values obtained by the participants from the scale on Use of Learning Management (Moodle) that was developed by the researcher.
2. **Academic Achievement:** In this study, Academic Achievement was operationally defined as the marks obtained by the students in their end-term examination of the third semester.
3. **College Students:** It referred to the students studying in the 3rd semester in Arts and Commerce streams in Salesian Colleges of Sonada and Siliguri.

### *9.1.5 OBJECTIVES OF THE STUDY*

- To determine the nature of the distribution of scores of the learning management system (Moodle) use among students at Salesian College (Sonada and Siliguri).
- To study the difference in the level of learning management system (Moodle) use among Salesian College (Sonada and Siliguri) students with respect to gender, locality, academic streams, and annual family income.
- To identify the relationship between the scores on the variables of learning management system (Moodle) use and academic achievement among students at Salesian College (Sonada and Siliguri).

### *9.1.6 HYPOTHESES OF THE STUDY*

- ➢ **$H_{01}$:** The nature of the distribution of scores for learning management system (Moodle) use is not the same for all students at Salesian College (Sonada and Siliguri).

- **$H_{02}$:** There is no significant difference in the learning management system (Moodle) use among students at Salesian College (Sonada and Siliguri) with regard to gender.
- **$H_{03}$:** There is no significant difference in the learning management system (Moodle) use among students at Salesian College (Sonada and Siliguri) with regard to locality.
- **$H_{04}$:** There is no significant difference in the learning management system (Moodle) use among students at Salesian College (Sonada and Siliguri) with respect to their academic streams.
- **$H_{05}$:** There is no significant difference in the level of learning management system (Moodle) use among students at Salesian College (Sonada and Siliguri) with respect to their annual family income.
- **$H_{06}$:** There is no significant relationship between the level of learning management system (Moodle) use among and Academic Achievement among students at Salesian College (Sonada and Siliguri).

### *9.1.7 DELIMITATIONS OF THE STUDY*

The study was conducted on only 200 Salesian College students from Sonada and Siliguri campuses studying in Arts and Commerce streams.

## 9.2 RESEARCH METHOD

As the focus of the present study was to determine the impact of the LMS (Moodle) on the Academic Achievement of the Salesian College (Sonada and Siliguri), hence, Causal Comparative method was used in the present research taking into consideration the objectives of the study.

In this regard, the variables of the study include:

1. **Independent Variable:** Learning management system.
2. **Dependent Variable:** Academic achievement.
3. **Categorical Variables:** Gender, locality, academic streams, and annual family income.

### *9.2.1 SAMPLE*

The sample for the present study consisted of 200 students from Salesian College (Sonada and Siliguri) and stratified random sampling technique was used. The detailed description of the sample is represented in Table 9.1.

**TABLE 9.1** Distribution of Samples, Based on Gender, Locality, Academic Streams, and Annual Family Income

| Variation | Sub-Samples | Number of Samples |
|---|---|---|
| Gender | Male | 100 |
| | Female | 100 |
| Locality | Urban | 100 |
| | Rural | 100 |
| Academic streams | Arts | 100 |
| | Commerce | 100 |
| Annual family income | Less than/equal to 3 lakhs | 100 |
| | More than 3 lakhs | 100 |

### *9.2.2 TOOLS USED*

The researcher used the following tools:

- The use of the LMS was determined using the tool LMS (Moodle) use. The scale was constructed by the researcher, and it was based on the research questionnaire that is available on the official Moodle website. The scale comprised 20 items which were marked on a 5-point Likert Scale and primarily focused on factors influencing the use of Moodle, facilities/training provided for the use of the LMS, and challenges faced while using Moodle.
- Academic achievement was determined based on the marks obtained by the students in their end-term examination of the third semester.

## 9.3 RESULT AND DISCUSSION

On the basis of the above study, the researcher identified the following findings (Figures 9.6 and 9.7):

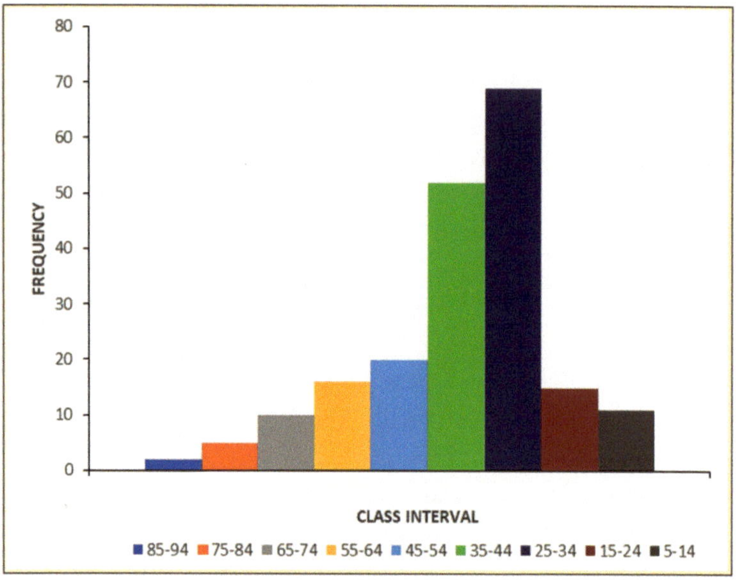


**FIGURE 9.6** Bar diagram based upon frequency distributions for total college students (Sonada and Siliguri campuses) on the variable learning management system (Moodle) use.

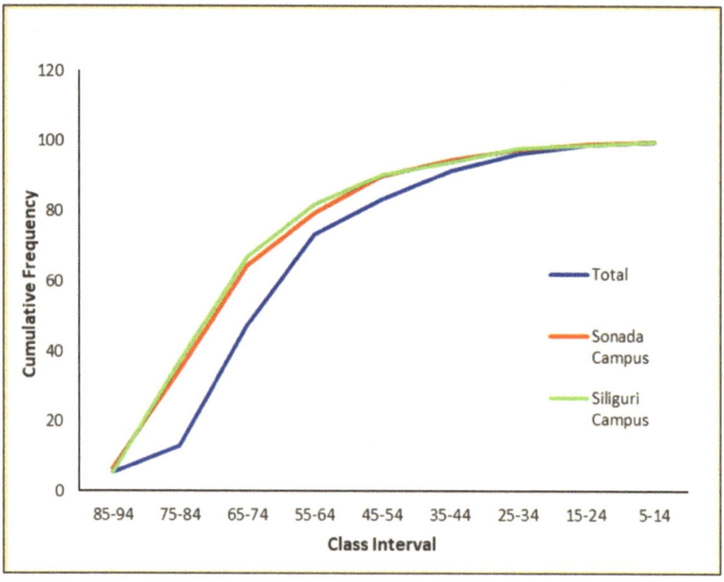


**FIGURE 9.7** Line diagram based upon frequency distributions for total students and students from Sonada and Siliguri campuses on the variable learning management system (Moodle) use.

1. The distribution of scores for total college students on the variable learning management system (Moodle) use is shown in Table 9.2.

**TABLE 9.2** Distribution of Scores for Total College Students (Sonada and Siliguri Campuses) on the Variable Learning Management System (Moodle) Use

| Class Interval | Frequency | Percent | Cumulative Frequency |
|---|---|---|---|
| 85–94 | 2 | 1.0 | 100.0 |
| 75–84 | 5 | 2.5 | 99.0 |
| 65–74 | 10 | 5.0 | 96.5 |
| 55–64 | 16 | 8.0 | 91.5 |
| 45–54 | 20 | 10.0 | 83.5 |
| 35–44 | 52 | 26.0 | 73.5 |
| 25–34 | 69 | 34.5 | 47.5 |
| 15–24 | 15 | 7.5 | 13 |
| 5–14 | 11 | 5.5 | 5.5 |
| **Total** | **200** | **100** | **610** |

It was revealed from the above tables and figures that the scores for the LMS (Moodle) Use differed among the students of both campuses. This was primarily because of the digital divide that was seen among the students accessing the LMS. The Salesian College located in Sonada, owing to its mountainous terrain, has poor network connectivity and faces regular power cuts as well. Most of the faculty from the area around were therefore compelled to come to the campus and conduct classes even during the lockdown. Although because of strict government regulations, the students of this campus had to attend classes from their homes. Even with regard to students from Siliguri Campus who were staying in the hills, were instructed by the College administration to relocate to areas where there was good internet connectivity available.

2. Testing of $H_{02}$ revealed that there were no significant differences in the LMS (Moodle) use among students at Salesian College (Sonada and Siliguri) with respect to gender.

   From Table 9.3, the t-value was calculated to be 0.21, which is not significant, thereby indicating that gender has no influence on the use of LMS. However, on the basis of a comparison of mean scores, it is found that the mean scores of male students were slightly higher than that of female students. The reason for this slight variation was owing to the use of screen time more in the case of male students as the LMS had many game features which attracted the attention of the students. The students were, however, in general highly interested in LMS which gave them the opportunity to explore many new technological aspects (Figure 9.8).

**TABLE 9.3** t-Value for Male and Female Salesian College (Sonada and Siliguri Campuses) Students with Respect to the Variable Learning Management System (Moodle) Use

| Variable | Gender | N | Mean | SD | SEM | df | t-Value |
|---|---|---|---|---|---|---|---|
| Learning management system (Moodle) use | Male | 100 | 16.65 | 7.89 | 0.79 | 198 | 0.21 |
| | Female | 100 | 16.26 | 7.94 | 0.79 | | **N.S.** |

*N.S.*: Not significant.

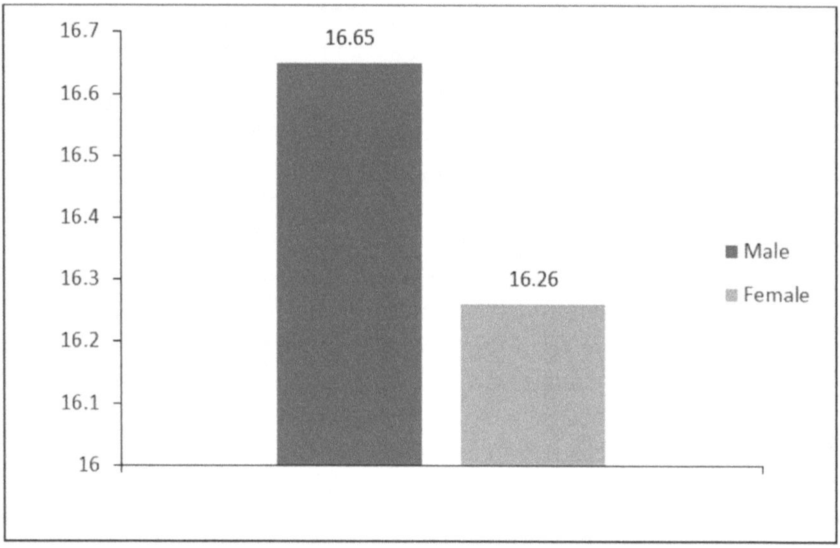


**FIGURE 9.8** Bar diagram depicting mean scores on the variable learning management system (Moodle) use with respect to gender.

3. Testing of $H_{03}$ showed that there was a significant difference in the LMS (Moodle) Use among students at Salesian College (Sonada and Siliguri) with respect to locality.

   From Table 9.4, the t-value was estimated to be 6.69. The findings revealed that students residing in urban areas showed higher

LMS use compared to rural students. Based on a comparison of mean scores, it was found that the mean scores of urban college students are higher than those of rural students. No prior studies have been conducted by other researchers in this regard. This difference was due to the digital divide caused by the mountainous terrain. It was found that students residing in rural hilly areas suffered severe network connectivity issues. The most common network providers used by the students were Jio, Vodafone, and Airtel. The network speed was 4G. Due to the existing lockdown, many students were unable to come to town regularly where the network facility was good. Another reason for the students from the villages to suffer was rampant power supply failures due to heavy rainfall and hailstorms (Figure 9.9).

**TABLE 9.4** t-Value for Rural and Urban Salesian College (Sonada and Siliguri Campuses) Students with Respect to the Variable Learning Management System (Moodle) Use

| Variable | Locality | N | Mean | SD | $SE_M$ | df | t-Value |
|---|---|---|---|---|---|---|---|
| Learning management system (Moodle) use | Rural | 100 | 13.08 | 5.79 | 0.58 | 198 | 6.69** |
| | Urban | 100 | 19.85 | 8.29 | 0.83 | | |

*******Significant at 0.01 level of confidence.*

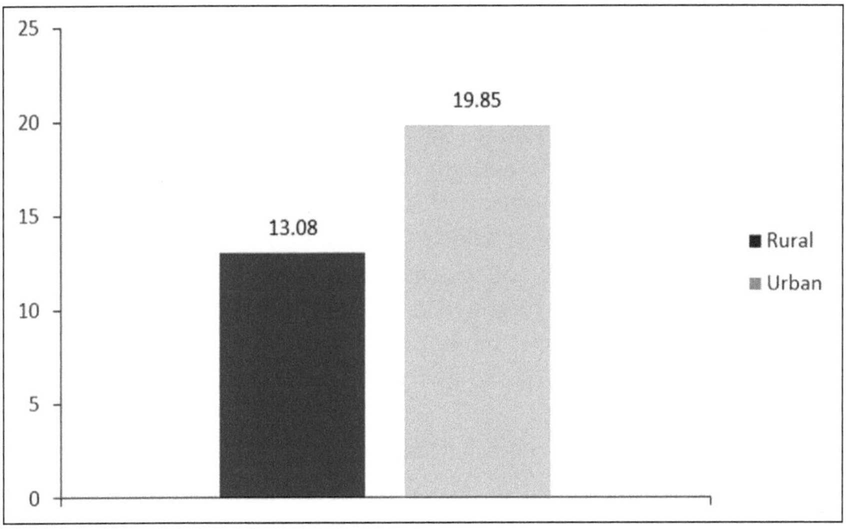


**FIGURE 9.9** Bar diagram depicting mean scores on the variable learning management system (Moodle) use with respect to locality.

4. Testing of $H_{04}$ revealed that there existed a significant difference in the level of LMS (Moodle) use among students at Salesian College (Sonada and Siliguri) with respect to academic streams (Table 9.5).

**TABLE 9.5** t-Value for Arts and Commerce Salesian College (Sonada and Siliguri Campuses) Students with Respect to the Variable Learning Management System (Moodle) Use

| Variable | Academic Streams | N | Mean | SD | SEM | df | t-Value |
|---|---|---|---|---|---|---|---|
| Learning management system (Moodle) use | Arts | 100 | 21.18 | 9.04 | 0.91 | 198 | 3.12** |
| | Commerce | 100 | 15.55 | 6.85 | 0.69 | | |

*****Significant at 0.01 level of confidence.*

The t-value obtained was 3.12. The findings revealed that students residing in Arts showed higher LMS use in comparison to Commerce students. On the basis of a comparison of mean scores, it is found that the mean scores of Arts students are higher than that of Commerce students. No prior studies have been conducted by other researchers in this regard. This was primarily due to the curricular structure of both disciplines. Although the Moodle which was being used on both the campuses of Salesian College proved to be quite an effective substitute for offline classes, however, one of the major drawbacks of the LMS was the lack of proper resources to cater to the requirements of practical based courses. The Commerce stream included various subjects which were becoming increasingly difficult for the faculty to teach owing to their practical aspects. Also, as per the curriculum, there were separate field-based courses, evaluation of which required the students to attend colleges in face-to-face mode. It was primarily because of this reason that the college authorities decided to shift to the blended mode of instruction in order to cater to the curricular diversities of different disciplines being offered in the college (Figure 9.10).

5. The testing of $H_{05}$ indicated that there were no significant differences in the level of LMS (Moodle) use among students at Salesian College (Sonada and Siliguri) with respect to annual family income (Table 9.6).

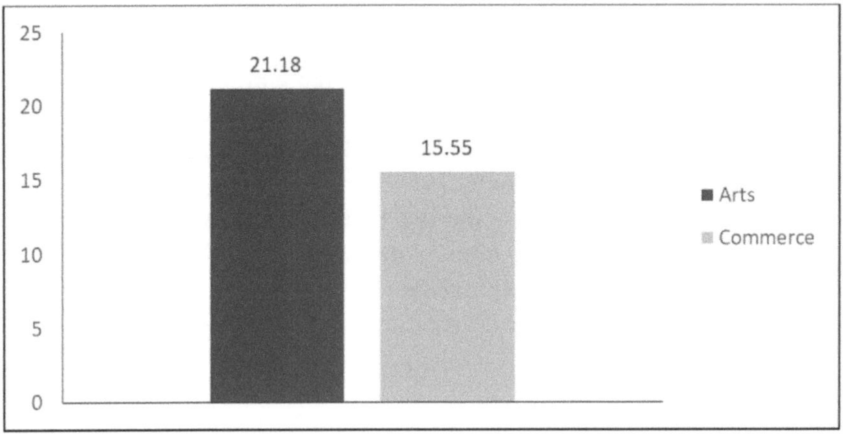


**FIGURE 9.10** Bar diagram depicting mean scores on the variable learning management system (Moodle) use with respect to academic streams.

**TABLE 9.6** t-Value for Students of Salesian College (Sonada and Siliguri Campuses) Belonging to Differing Annual Family Income with Respect to the Variable Learning Management System (Moodle) Use

| Variable | Annual Family Income | N | Mean | SD | SEM | df | t-Value |
|---|---|---|---|---|---|---|---|
| Learning management system (Moodle) use | Less than/equal to 3 lakhs | 100 | 30.62 | 5.80 | 0.58 | 198 | 0.61 |
| | More than 3 lakhs | 100 | 31.14 | 6.25 | 0.63 | | N.S. |

**N.S.:** Not significant.

It was found that the calculated t-value was 0.61, which is not significant, thereby indicating that annual has no influence on the use of LMS. However, on the basis of a comparison of mean scores, it is found that the mean scores of students coming from families with an annual family income of more than 3 lakhs are slightly higher than that of the students belonging to families with less than or equal to 3 lakhs. Salesian College is a private minority institution. Apart from admitting students from average to above-average socioeconomic status, the college is also well known for offering financial aid in the form of scholarships to students belonging to low socioeconomic status. Moreover, during the lockdown, as many families were grappling with financial constraints, the college took steps to reduce the burden on the students by decreasing the tuition fee and also providing extensions in the submission of the fees. More or less all students had their own personal mobile phones through which they could attend classes through Moodle. However, it was found that some of the features in Moodle could not be easily accessed through mobile phones and required either a desktop/laptop which was not found with many students (Figure 9.11).

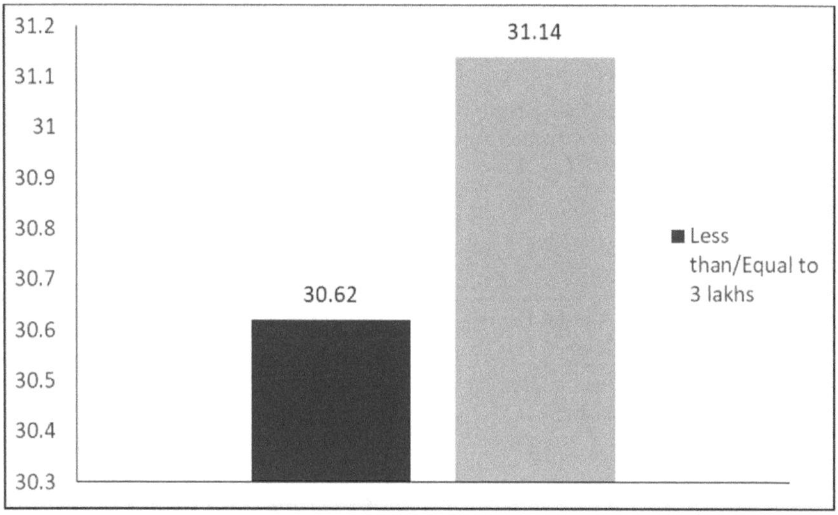


**FIGURE 9.11** Bar diagram depicting mean scores on the variable learning management system (Moodle) use with respect to annual family income.

6. Analysis of $H_{06}$ showed that there existed a significant relationship between LMS (Moodle) use among students at Salesian College (Sonada and Siliguri) and their academic achievement. The Product Moment Correlation was calculated to be 0.66, and it was found to be significant at the 0.01 level of confidence. The use of Moodle as an LMS positively affected the academic achievement of the students. Salesian College was the only college in the entire Darjeeling district that continued with its teaching-learning process through the use of LMS. With the lockdown of educational institutions, the college ensured that regular classes and other curricular activities were not

hampered. Classes commenced from 8.40 am and continued till 2 pm with regular internal assessments being conducted. Apart from that, as per the university regulations, the college also conducted selection examinations and semester-end examinations through Moodle. All the course content in the form of e-materials was uploaded in Moodle and was not only accessible to the students but also to their guardians for future reference. Constant feedback was also taken from the students to ensure that their academic needs were being fulfilled. As a result of this constant monitoring, it was found that there was not much difference in the academic performance of the students in comparison to the pre-COVID situation. This form of a structured e-learning environment helped the students to easily transition into the online mode and continue with their learning acquisition process.

## 9.4 CONCLUSION

With the advent of modern technology, learners have started focusing more on digital learning, thereby creating a rich and highly networked world. Higher education in the post-pandemic world is now no longer limited to traditional face-to-face learning but is rapidly picking up on the hybrid/blended model of education. ICT is playing an integral role in this blended system, and the concept of e-learning is the need of the hour. E-learning has enabled students as well as teachers to move beyond the restriction of time and physical location in their quest to access and disseminate knowledge. Blended learning through the use of LMS, VLE, and local area network (LAN) is being adopted by different higher educational institutions in order to widen the scope for achieving the various learning objectives. It is therefore imperative for different higher educational institutions in India to also provide their students with this digital experience in the field of learning. Although the digital divide is a serious concern in our country owing to different factors such as poor connectivity, geographical barriers, lack of awareness, and financial constraints, it is necessary for the Government to not only lay down policies with respect to the incorporation of e-learning but also allocate resources as well as create suitable follow-up procedures in this regard. The onset of the pandemic and the closing down of educational institutions have made us realize that remote learning is to be prioritized in all sectors of education, and a suitable interface is to be provided for carrying out the learning process. Apart from this, proper orientation is to be imparted to all faculty members to keep them abreast with the modern methodologies of teaching as well as familiarizing them with ICT-based teaching-learning. It is through this collaborative effort that improved learning experiences can be provided to the learners.

## KEYWORDS


- **academic achievement**
- **blended learning**
- **college students**
- **financial constraints**
- **learning management system**
- **Moodle**
- **Salesian College**


## REFERENCES


Akay, E., &Gumusoglu, E. K., (2020). The impact of learning management systems on students' achievement in language exams. *Turkish Online Journal of Distance Education-TOJDE.*, *21*(4), 206–222.https://doi.org/10.17718/tojde.803410.

Alshehri, A., Rutter, M., & Smith, S., (2020). The effects of gender and age on students' use of a learning management system in Saudi Arabia. *International Journal of Learning and Teaching*, *6*(3), 135–145. https://doi.org/ 10.18178/ijlt.6.3.135-145.

Alturki, U., & Aldraiweesh, A., (2021). Application of learning management system (LMS) during the COVID-19 pandemic: A sustainable acceptance model of the expansion technology approach. *Sustainability*, *13*(10991), 1–16. https://doi.org/10.3390/su1319 10991.

Borboa, D., Joseph, M., Spake, D., & Yazdanparast, A., (2017). Perceptions and use of learning management system tools and other technologies in higher education: A preliminary analysis. *Journal of Learning in Higher Education*, *10*(2), 17–23. https://doi.org/10.1177/1469787415616721.

Coates, H., James, R., & Baldwin, G., (2005). A critical examination of the effects of learning management systems on university teaching and learning. *Tertiary Education, and Management*, *11*, 19–36, Published online: 20 Jan 2010. https://doi.org/10.1080/13583883.2005.9967137.

Goyal, S., (2012). E-learning: Future of education. *Journal of Education and Learning*, *6*(2), 239–242. https://doi.org/10.11591/edulearn.v6i4.168.

Kraleva, R., Sabani, M., & Kralev, V., (2019). An analysis of some learning management system. *International Journal on Advanced Science, Engineering, and Information Technology*, *9*(4), 1190. https://doi.org/10.18517/ijaseit.9.4.9437.

Lim, K., Nam, Y. O., Eom, S. S., Jang, Y., Kim, D., & Kim Mi, H.,(2020). structural gender differences in LMS use patterns among college students. *Sustainability*, *12*(4465), 1–9. https://doi.org/10.3390/su12114465.

Sharma, M., & Srivastav, G., (2020). Study and review of learning management systems software. In: Saini, H. S., et al., (eds.), *Innovations in Computer Science and Engineering*. Springer. https://doi.org/10.1007/978-981-15-2043-3_42.

Thadathil, G., Chambi, W., Prasad, Y., & Silva, L. E. G. R.,*(2020)*.The Salesian College of India and Salesian University of Bolivia in the context of the pandemic. *Estudios Pedagogicos.*, *46*(3), 287–301.https://doi.org/10.4067/s0718-07052020000300287.

Tinmaz, H., & Lee, J. H., (2020). An analysis of users' preferences on learning management systems: A case on German versus Spanish students. *Smart Learn. Environ.*, *7*(30), 1–17. https://doi.org/10.1186/s40561-020-00141-8.

## CHAPTER 10

# Predicting Switching Intention to a K12 Online International Program during the COVID Pandemic in Vietnam Using a Neural Network Model

HA NGUYEN THI THU,[1] TON QUANG CUONG,[2] TRAN KHAI THIEN,[3] LINH BUI KHANH,[4] and ANH NGUYEN QUYNH[4]

[1]*Department of E-Commerce, Electric Power University, Hanoi, Vietnam*

[2]*VNU-University of Education, Vietnam National University, Hanoi, Vietnam*

[3]*Ho Chi Minh City University of Foreign Languages–Information Technology, Vietnam*

[4]*Information Technology Faculty, Electric Power University, Hanoi, Vietnam*

### ABSTRACT

Under the prolonged influence of the COVID pandemic, education systems around the world have switched to an online learning model. Traditional education has been popular in Vietnam up until now. Therefore, when switching to an online training model, most schools in Vietnam have not yet adapted to the digital transformation. The content of the training program is poor and boring, which makes it difficult to attract learners' focus on lectures. The lack of knowledge will impact the long-term development of children. While international programs are attractive to students in terms

Intelligent Learning Paradigms and Student Empowerment: Digital Integration and Transformation.
Souvik Pal, Ton Quang Cuong, & R. S. S. Nehru (Eds.)

of content and the quality of the eLearning system. Therefore, it has made some parents think about switching to online learning programs at high-quality schools with recognized qualifications all over the world, and the transfer procedure is easy to pre-university study in developed countries. This study was conducted through an online survey with parents in two big cities, Hanoi and Ho Chi Minh, to find out the relationship between demographic factors, parental qualifications, and other influencing factors like perceived price, perceived convenience, and perceived trust. This was then combined with a neural network to train and predict the intention to switch to an online international learning program for parents in Vietnam today. After analyzing 282 samples, it shows that 87% of families with high income and parents working in foreign companies intend to send their children to study in the international baccalaureate program, while only 24% of families with parents working in state companies have the intention for their children to study in an international program. A neural network model is used for training and testing with the error SME = 0.429. The results have shown the remaining problems of Vietnamese education during the COVID time, and the government needs to focus on developing more digital education content and building a plan to train online pedagogical skills in teachers and reassure parents when choosing an education program in Vietnam.

## 10.1 INTRODUCTION

The COVID-19 pandemic that broke out in the past two years has disrupted the education of over 1.7 billion students in at least 192 countries and territories. A year after the pandemic, nearly 50% of students globally are still affected by school closures in whole or in part. Studies by UNESCO and UNICEF show that the longer schools are closed, the greater the risk that children and young people will lose their future (Conto, Akseer, & Dreesen, 2020). More than 100 million children will not reach the minimum reading proficiency level due to the impact of school closures. About 24 million children and young people are at risk of dropping out of school (UNESCO, 2021). School closures also reduce access to vital protection, nutrition, and health services, especially in underdeveloped countries. In addition to the situation of "lack of knowledge," the prolonged closure of schools also significantly affects the mental health of children. There are still nearly 30 countries with complete school closures, affecting more than 100 million teachers and school staff. The world is witnessing a very serious "educational emergency" because the pandemic has negatively affected the right to study and enjoy social benefits at school, which means that the future and happiness of children are also affected (UNESCO, 2021).

To deal with the situation of the COVID epidemic while ensuring stability in education, online training is the form that all countries in the world are choosing. Schools cannot be closed for the long term and children cannot stay out of school, so there must be a distance learning solution. Therefore, distance learning systems such as LMS, LCMS, and online meeting solutions such as Zoom, Google Meet, Teams, Quikcom, etc., are developed to support online teaching and interact more than LMS systems. Video and online teaching solutions are also integrated on LMS and LCMS systems to support both online teaching and course management (Ahmed & Opoku, 2021; Ikeda & Yamaguchi, 2021; Shirish, Chandra, & Srivastava, 2021).

In every country, in addition to developing online training systems, they have built repositories of free video lectures on online education platforms. The US has provided free access to distance courses on the Khan Academy and TED Ed platforms. Another model that has been successfully deployed is the Learn Everywhere platform, where parents can share useful resources to accompany their children. The Ministry of Education of China has launched a nationwide cloud computing program to provide complete teaching materials for all core subjects as well as courses for elementary and middle school students. In addition, TV channels have also increased the live broadcast of teaching programs, providing knowledge to more than 120 million pupils and students across the country. Malaysia also launched a special DidikTV KPM TV channel with a daily broadcast from 7:00 am to midnight dedicated to online education in this Southeast Asian country (Angrist et al., 2021).

The Government of India provided an Indo-Bhutan digital library system that allows free downloading of video lectures and provides e-books for school students to solve major problems: students (book burden), publishers (logistics, book publishing, distribution, etc.) and related educational agencies (edit/change content cycle). Students will benefit from exposure through learning resources and can access richer multimedia content, real-life examples via real-life videos. For their teaching methods, providing content, books, etc., assisting schools with fewer instructional resources, let teachers contribute content or create more relevant documents, nationwide visibility, etc. Initially, electronic contents provided by the National Council for Education Research and Training (NCERT), Ministry of Human Resource Development (MHRD), Government of India are uploaded to the K-12 education portal (Singh et al., 2021). The electronic content provided in this E-Library project are textbooks in EPUB 3.0 version of all 1st to 12th grade for all subjects, audio resources, videos, and interactions documentaries, biographies, novels, etc., and video lessons for grade 12 upper middle years subjects (11 and 12) and Math and Science for high school grades (9 and 10) (http://www.elibrarybhutan.com/aboutus). Meanwhile, In Italy, teachers can access video conferencing tools and lesson plans. Iran allows all children to access the Internet for free.

In Vietnam, since 2020 due to the impact of COVID, online teaching has been used for K12 students, although before that, Vietnam still used the traditional teaching method, it means that only teaching in class and face-to-face communication in the classroom. From 2020, online training systems such as LMS, LCMS have blossomed to support teaching and learning management at all levels (Van & Thi, 2021). However, the problem of Vietnamese education today is not the development of online teaching systems such as Zoom or Google Meet because the learning content is the important problem. Digital content is the one key to accelerate the process of digital transformation in the education industry. Since 2020, Vietnam's Ministry of Education and Training (MOET) has rushed to build the iGiaoduc portal to upload digitized learning materials in the general curriculum into this portal. It has helped support students to access centralized learning resources. In August 2021, the Vietnam Ministry of Education also uploaded Vietnamese textbooks in PDF format on the iGiaoduc system to support students. Students do not have textbooks while the COVID epidemic is breaking out very sharply in many provinces and cities in Vietnam, and social distancing is performed for a long time. However, most of the learning materials on Vietnam's iGiaoduc repository are now hastily collected from television channels of many localities in the country from 2020 up to now, so the lectures are isolated and lack interaction. There are no lectures for practical subjects, lack of reference materials, and only content that encapsulates the high school program. There are many links that are broken, many learning materials point to other links without viewing directly on the system (Maheshwari, 2021; Vu et al., 2020).

From the new school year 2021, most K12 students in Vietnam continue to study online due to the impact of COVID-19 delta mutation. Classroom lectures are boring because of the lack of interaction, network infrastructure is overloaded making it difficult for students to access, and the data warehouse is incomplete making students not want to study (Yu et al., 2021). Many parents are willing to let their children take a year off from school because they hope that will end soon and their children can come back to school. Other parents find a better solution for their children's education because they don't think that the COVID pandemic will end for a short time. COVID created a physical distance, but COVID also creates a closer of global education in a virtual environment, Top K12 schools in the world promote their training programs to learners outside of their country. Therefore, families with good economic conditions intend to enroll their children into the online international training programs. They aim for the best schools in the world that have globally recognized qualifications as a form because they have a perfect learning management system (LMS), complete digital content, and teachers with online pedagogical skills are better.

The purpose of this study is to accomplish the following:

- Surveying the current status of digital content resources for K-12 curriculum in Vietnam.
- Survey on psychology and needs of parents when their children are studying online during COVID time.
- Using a neural network model to predict the intention to study the international K12 program of parents in Vietnam.

Firstly, the study surveyed parents of children studying from middle school and high school in big cities such as Hanoi and Ho Chi Minh City. Secondly, by an analysis of demographic information and an analysis of parents' responses, the study selected factors that impact the changing intention. Finally, this data is trained by a neural network consisting of 17 inputs separated into five measures such as demographic, price, quality, convenience, and trust to predict the intention to learn online international program.

The rest of this chapter is structured as follows: Section 10.2 introduces e-learning and the development of e-learning in Vietnam today; Section 10.3

presents the neural network model used in prediction; Section 10.4 is a description of survey data and analysis; Section 10.5 is the experimental results and evaluation, and finally the conclusion.

## 10.2 LITERATURE REVIEW

### *10.2.1 ONLINE TEACHING*

The continuous development of information technology and the internet has brought significant changes to the lives of humans. The Internet is really an information environment that connects people all over the world, helping them easily share social issues. Based on the internet environment, the software applications are built to be highly shareable, not dependent on geographical location or operating system, creating favorable conditions for everyone. People can communicate, search, and learn very easily and conveniently. The technology has accelerated the development of education technology (Ahmed & Opoku, 2021; Fitzgerald, Scott, & Ryan, 2021). Learning using devices that are connected to the internet and pre-built learning resources would be seen as a fairly complete education ecosystem. Online learning can be called a method that can make students the center in the teaching-learning process, it is more innovative, and even more flexible. Online learning is defined as "experiential learning in a synchronous or asynchronous environment using different devices (e.g., mobile phones, phones, laptops, etc.) with internet access. In these environments, students can learn anywhere (independently) and interact with their teachers and other students" (Singh et al., 2021). In fact, many organizations and companies in the field of e-Learning were born. Many training models by e-Learning have been formed such as technology-based training, computer-based training, web-based training; online training, distance training (Baber, 2021; Kim & Park, 2021; Mali & Lim, 2021).

The effectiveness of online learning can be influenced by many factors such as technological aspects, user-friendly online platforms, classroom activities, and assessments (Goldenson, Avery, Gill, & Durfee, 2021). It is important for schools to know how learners like their online courses and how to understand what factors can affect student satisfaction and their intention to join online courses in the future (Mouratidis & Papagiannakis, 2021; Mukuka, Shumba, & Mulenga, 2021).

### *10.2.2 THE QUALITY OF ONLINE EDUCATION IN COVID TIME PROBLEM*

The online learning environment can provide IT tools to enhance student learning capacity and learning creativity. Under the impact of the global pandemic COVID-19, most schools in the world have had to transform online learning as a good solution (Qazi et al., 2021; Schmitz et al., 2021). Schools and teachers choose flexible technology and pedagogical methods to be able to transmit knowledge to students (Zuo, Ma, Hu, & Luo, 2021). For schools that already have a pre-built infrastructure system, the implementation will be very easy. However, there are still many schools and teachers who are confused with online training, which leads to online teaching passively. Improving the quality of online training becomes very important during this period (Shirish, Chandra, & Srivastava, 2021). Despite the purported positives of online learning, in the COVID-19 scenario, the report of student surveying with many different results. While some students were able to adapt to the "new normal," others struggled with the transformed IT-enabled learning.

There are a lot of studies focusing on the quality of online learning in the COVID-19 time (Angrist et al., 2021; Ardington, Wills, & Kotze, 2021; Bansak & Starr, 2021; Dong, Cao, & Li, 2020; Maheshwari, 2021). In the research of Andrew et al. (2021), online education helps to close the gap between rural and urban students with the same learning resources. In addition, weaker students also benefit from online education; they become more interactive and more confident when learning online. For parents of young children, beliefs and attitudes towards online learning are quite negative according to research by Dong et al. (2020). They surveyed on a large scale 3,275 Chinese parents and found that the majority of them tended to oppose and even reject online learning for three main reasons: unfavorable online learning, children difficult to adapt, parents lacking time as well as expertise to support children's online learning. Most studies have shown that untrained parents are not supportive of their children's online learning. Another study showed that the average academic performance of students was 66% lower than the traditional one. This is due to a lack of home learning support as well as a lack of learning resources. From these studies, it is proved that learning materials and online learning support tools are extremely important in online education. During the COVID-19 time, it will affect the training quality of the following years (Sabates,

Carter, & Stern, 2021). For children in the first grades from South African free schools, research has shown that the rate of decreasing the quality of under-resourced schools is as high as 62% compared to previous years. This means that the education system must change to increase resources and appropriately balance teaching methods to optimize online learning (Ardington, Wills, & Kotze, 2021), A child's short-term learning loss in 3rd grade can accumulate to the equivalent of 2.8 years of learning loss in 10th grade (Angrist et al., 2021) this Prompts education policies to focus on improving resources because it has lasting effects on succeeding generations. Learning content and experiences on learning media other than computers such as mobile phones also affect students' learning efficiency, bad experiences make students refuse online learning, in addition, a good online pedagogical skills teachers will help children learn better (Yuan et al., 2021). For subjects that need to be highly interactive like math, the quality of education needs to be even more focused. In a survey of high school students with remote math learning during school closures due to COVID-19 in Zambia, more than 56% of respondents did not have adequate access to information technology services, information and communication, electricity, and the internet. This also suggests that the government should establish a more adequate infrastructure for online learning.

Most studies proved that the lack of learning resources and inadequate infrastructure are the main reasons decreasing training quality of K12's level, because the young children do not have self-study method and searching online materials, many parents are unable to tutor their students (Bansak & Starr, 2021; Dong, Cao, & Li, 2020). In addition, the pedagogy method should be changed to suit online training method, weak technology skills also affect seriously when transmitting knowledge to students (Ahmed & Opoku, 2021; Shambour & Abu-Hashem, 2021). This is even more evident in schools with low and weak infrastructure, rural areas, high mountain areas. This is the main reason why parents do not want their children to study online, the gap in training quality is becoming more and more serious in low- and middle-income countries in the world (Jordan et al., 2021).

### *10.2.3 ONLINE TRAINING PROBLEM IN VIETNAM*

The first outbreak of the COVID pandemic in Vietnam was at the end of January 2020. From this, the Vietnamese Government decided to close all schools (Maheshwari, 2021). Since March 2020, almost all schools in Vietnam have switched to online teaching. This situation is not easy for teachers or students. For many students and teachers, this is the first time they have encountered online learning. Three main platforms have been used in Vietnam: Zoom, Microsoft Teams, and Google Meet. However, the Zoom platform has not been encouraged by Vietnam MOET due to security problems. Before the COVID-19 era, Vietnamese students used e-learning platforms for English courses or soft skill courses. The e-learning model has been accepted and developed in Vietnam since the last decade but has not been applied to secondary and high school programs. For universities, e-learning methods are also not of interest. They prefer physical classrooms and do not want to switch to virtual or online classrooms (Vu et al., 2020). Since 2020, the IT ability of teachers and students has significantly increased with online learning platforms such as Zoom Meeting, Google Meet, and Microsoft Teams. The majority of schools use the Microsoft Teams platform with Microsoft support for education departments (68%), Zoom (9%), as well as Google Meet (23%), indicating readiness to use technology systems to improve the quality of education and training in Vietnam (Figure 10.1).

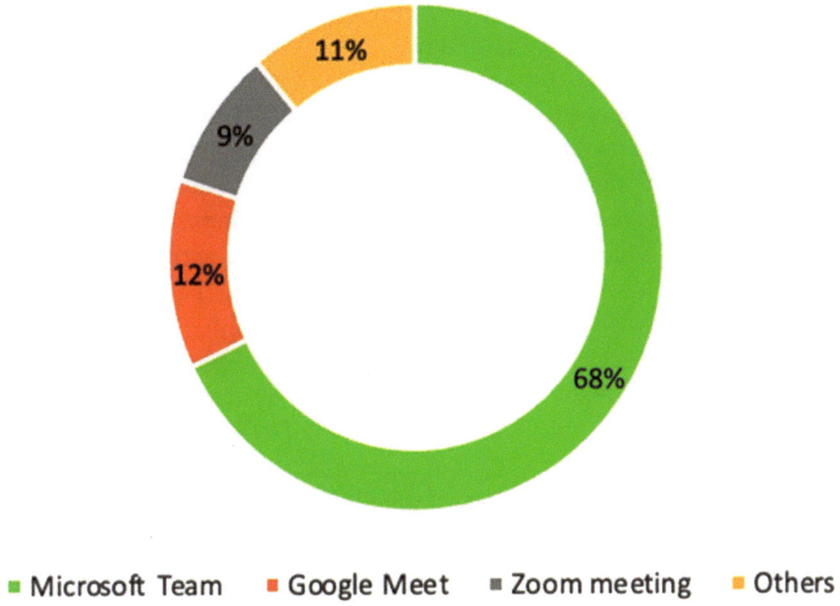


**FIGURE 10.1** Popular online learning platforms chosen by general training schools in Vietnam.

A lot of online learning platforms are provided by international big companies such as Google, Zoom, or Microsoft. For learning content, based on a survey by Edtech Agency, the main types of learning content in Vietnam are English courses, K12 content, and skill courses. Most of the courses are recorded and uploaded on the learning system. Lessons lack interactivity and learning resources are not rich (Table 10.1).

**TABLE 10.1** K12 Courses Classification

| Types of Courses | Ratio |
|---|---|
| Courses for K12 | 23.4% |
| Skills courses | 35.8% |
| English courses | 40.8% |

K-12 education is still important in Vietnam. The ratio of public schools is as high as 82%, but investment in technology infrastructure at public schools is low. According to Circular No. 18/2018/TT-BGDĐT dated 28/2018 of the MOET, which promulgates regulations on education accreditation and recognition of national standards for secondary and high schools in Vietnam, the school assessment standards are requirements for schools to ensure the quality of operations. Each condition corresponds to an area of school performance; there are criteria in each measurement. The secondary school assessment standard includes four levels (Levels 1-4) with increasing requirements. Level 4 is the highest. For the schools to meet national standards at Levels 3 and 4, there are classrooms and subject rooms have enough teaching equipment as prescribed. Laboratory or practice areas have sufficient equipment to ensure regular and efficient operation, teaching equipment, self-made teaching equipment, digital library, and high-speed Internet.

According to statistics from the Vietnam Edtech Agency (https://edtechagency.net), in Hanoi, there are over 20 schools that meet the standard of Level 3 under Circular No. 18/2018/TT-BGDĐT, accounting for more than 3%. In Ho Chi Minh City, that number accounts for 4%. On average, less than 4% of the total number of schools meet the national standards of Levels 3 and 4, due to the lack of technological equipment, well-configured computer labs, and high-speed Internet systems, digital library of lectures, and multimedia textbooks. Therefore, the development of online training in Vietnamese high schools is still limited. The majority of courses are provided by educational technology companies and are offered as short courses because, at the K12 level, the Vietnamese government prioritizes direct training according to the program approved by the government. There are a number of technology tools available for online education, but the skills of both teachers and students are not met. Students find online teaching boring and uninteresting. Sometimes, online content is just theory and doesn't allow students to practice and learn effectively. Boring course content is also a major problem. The currently iGiaoduc portal, which is a website developed by the Vietnam Government, has many broken links, and the content is poor and unattractive compared to other systems that provide learning materials. Pedagogical skills when teaching online are also major barriers.

Therefore, the remaining problems when implementing online training in the time of COVID in K-12 schools are as follows:

- Lack of centralized governance platform;
- Low-tech infrastructure;
- Digital transformation is not comprehensive;
- Poor learning content and resources;
- The quality of training is still low due to not being able to adapt;
- Online pedagogical skills have not met with digital transformation.

Due to the complicated development of the COVID-19 epidemic, more than 20 million pupils and students and nearly 2 million teachers at all levels have not been able to continue with the direct teaching method. Switching to online teaching is an appropriate adaptation in the current context. Online teaching has many advantages, but it also poses many challenges that the Education and Training industry has overcome to avoid the long-term training effects as stated in the studies (Angrist et al., 2021; Sabates, Carter, & Stern, 2021). This study examines the intention of joining in international baccalaureate programs through a number of factors, thereby analyzing and making recommendations to Vietnamese education. From that, it can supplement inappropriate points in order to improve the quality of K12 education.

## 10.3 NEURAL NETWORK

Neural network is an algorithm that is designed to find the basic relationships of dataset based on mimicking the way the human brain works. In which, a feed-forward neural network (FFNN) consists of an input layer, one or more hidden layers, and an output layer. The number of features of the data set will correspond to the number of neurons in the input layer. All of these neurons are connected to each neuron in the hidden layer through connections called "synapses." Each "synapse" is assigned a weight. These weights will be adjusted during the learning process of the artificial neural network to model the relationship between the input and output layers (Figure 10.2).

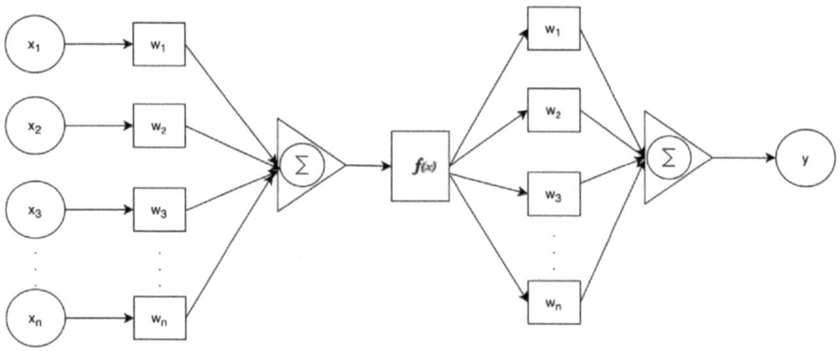


**FIGURE 10.2** An artificial neural network.

The output value of the neural network is calculated by the following equation:

$$y_i^q = g_i^q\left(u_i^q\right) = g_i^q\left(\sum_{j=1}^{n^{q-1}} w_{ij}^q y_j^{q-1} + b_i^q\right) \tag{1}$$

In which; $y_i^q$ is the output of neuron $i^{th}$ in layer with $q^{th} i = 1,2.n^q$ and a $q = 1,2.Q$; $n^q$ is the number of neurons in layer $q^{th}$; $Q$ is the number of layer; $b_i^q$ is the bias of neuron $i^{th}$ in layer $q^{th}$; and $w_{ij}^q$ is the weighted between output $j^{th}$ of layer $q{-}1^{th}$ to neuron $i^{th}$ of layer $q^{th}$ with $i = 1,2.n^{q-1}$.

The error of the network can be calculated by the expression:

$$E(w) = \frac{1}{2}\sum_{j=1}^{n^Q}(d_i - y_i^Q)^2 \tag{2}$$

In which; $d_i$ is the desired output of neuron $i^{th}$ of output layer.

The back propagation method uses a values of input set and output set to find a suitable network model for this dataset. A set of inputs is entered into the presumptive system and creates an output value. And then compared with the real value. Update the weights of the network to set up a new network.

$$y^{q+1} = g^{q+1}(W^{q+1}y^q + b^{q+1} \text{ with } q = 1,2.Q\text{–}1$$

The first Input neurons of network:

$$y^0 = p$$

The last of output neuron:

$$y = y^Q$$

The weights and thresholds are updated according to the descending approximation.

$$W^q\left(k+1\right) = W^q\left(k\right) - \alpha s^q (y^{q-1})^T \quad (3)$$

$$b^q\left(k+1\right) = b^q\left(k\right) - \alpha s^q \quad (4)$$

## 10.4 DATA COLLECTION AND ANALYSIS

The survey was conducted from May to early June 2021 when Vietnam is dealing with COVID for the 3rd time. The total number of survey respondents is 348. The survey respondents are on different levels of the population, but we only keep survey samples of parents with children learning in K12 level. So, after filtering incomplete information, we obtained 282 complete survey forms for further analysis. The variables used for measurement include demographic information, perceived price, perceived trust, and perceived convenience. Table 10.2 is a statistical analysis of demographic information.

In the next step, the study creates a questionnaire and selects input variables for measurement. The input variables partially encode demographics with monthly income, working environment, education, and profession; perceived quality; perceived price; perceived convenience; and perceived trust. Table 10.3 shows the measures and coded variables.

## 10.5 EXPERIMENTAL RESULTS

### *10.5.1 FORECASTING MODELS*

Neural network is a model that has been applied in many studies and has practical applications because the results are highly accurate. In economics and finance, neural network models are used in forecasting economic

**TABLE 10.2** Demographic Characteristics of the Sample

| Variable | Category | Number | Percentage (%) | Variable | Category | Number | Percentage (%) |
|---|---|---|---|---|---|---|---|
| Marital status | Married | 276 | 97.87% | Gender | Female | 231 | 81.91% |
| | Single | 6 | 2.13% | | Male | 51 | 18.09% |
| | Total | 282 | 100.00% | | Total | 282 | 100.00% |
| Age | <20 | 1 | 0.35% | Education | High school | 0 | 0.00% |
| | 20–29 | 116 | 41.13% | | Bachelor | 243 | 86.17% |
| | 30–39 | 107 | 37.94% | | Master | 36 | 12.77% |
| | 40–50 | 58 | 20.57% | | Doctoral | 3 | 1.06% |
| | >50 | 0 | 0.00% | | Total | 282 | 100.00% |
| | Total | 282 | 100.00% | Income monthly | <10 mil | 57 | 20.21% |
| Professional | Officer | 226 | 80.14% | | 10 mil–30 mil | 93 | 32.98% |
| | Retired | 0 | 0.00% | | 30 mil–50 mil | 45 | 15.96% |
| | Housewife | 56 | 19.86% | | >50 mil | 87 | 30.85% |
| | | | | | Total | 282 | 100.00% |
| | Total | 282 | 100.00% | Which grade children are studying | Primary | 2 | 0.71% |
| Number of children | 0 | 0 | 0.00% | | Secondary | 148 | 52.48% |
| | 1 | 19 | 6.74% | | High school | 132 | 46.81% |
| | 2 | 214 | 75.89% | | Total | 282 | 100.00% |
| | >=3 | 49 | 17.38% | | | | |
| Living are | Total | 282 | 100.00% | Type of organization you are working in | Public | 68 | 24.11% |
| | Hanoi | 128 | 45.39% | | Private | 174 | 61.70% |
| | HoChiMinh | 154 | 54.61% | | International | 40 | 14.18% |
| | Total | 282 | 100.00% | | Total | 282 | 100.00% |

growth, GDP, inflation, etc. In the past, learning models often had few hidden layers because of CPUs with low configurations. However, now with the development of technology and high-speed processing systems, the network model shows its power with many hidden layers and more neurons per hidden layer. This will increase the accuracy of calculations. With this type of model, it is called a deep learning model.

**TABLE 10.3** Coding of Question Variables and Input Variables

| Measurement | Variables | CODE |
|---|---|---|
| Demographic | Income monthly | DEMO1 |
| | Working environment | DEMO2 |
| | Education level | DEMO3 |
| | Professional | DEMO4 |
| Perceived quality | learning content is good? | QUAL1 |
| | learning platform is good? | QUAL2 |
| | pedagogy skill is good? | QUAL3 |
| | Make children feel passion? | QUAL4 |
| Perceived price | Tuition fee match with income? | PRICE1 |
| | Willing to pay high costs | PRICE2 |
| Perceived convenience | Attractive advertisement, good service | CONVEN1 |
| | Easy registration | CONVEN2 |
| | Convenient support on many different media | CONVEN3 |
| Perceived trust | The degree is recognized by many countries on the world | TRUST1 |
| | Representative offices are allowed to operate in Vietnam | TRUST2 |
| | Flexibility to switch to other education programs | TRUST3 |
| Intention | Intend to study or not? | INTEN |

This study uses an artificial neural network model to predict the intention of parents in Vietnam to give their children the opportunity to study in prestigious international programs. The combined input factors based on surveys include demographic factors, perceived quality, perceived price, perceived convenience, and perceived reliability. After coding the questions, the number of neurons in the input layer is 17 neurons. Through experimentation, we chose the number of hidden layers to be 2, as it provided suitable network processing time and low error (Figure 10.3).

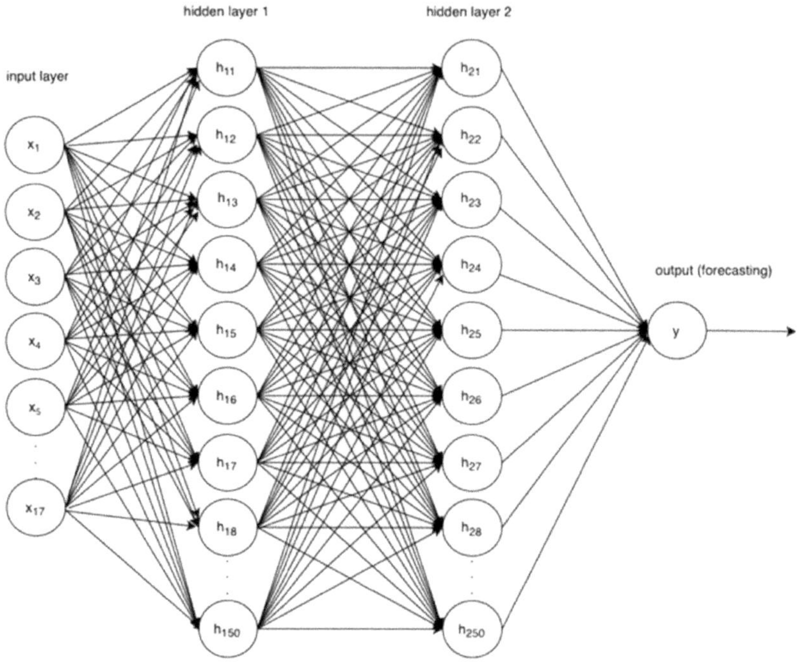


**FIGURE 10.3** Neural network model for forecasting.

We divided data for training and testing. Training data accounts for 80% and 20% for testing. Research using Rapid Miner as a tool for performing and evaluating the model, parameters of this neural network model are as follows:

- Number of input neurons: 17.
- Number of hidden layer neurons 1: 50.
- Number of hidden layer neurons 2: 50.
  Output: 1

The errors after running the model as Table 10.4.

With the above measurement errors, the model is reliable for predicting parents' intention to transition to an international program for their children.

### 10.5.2 FORECAST RESULTS

The study predicts the intention of parents to switch to international baccalaureate programs during COVID when all K12 programs are online. The number of samples used for testing is 56 samples (~20% of 282), in which, there are 21 parents who intend to transfer to the international program for their children, the rest are considering or do not intend to switch (Table 10.5).

**TABLE 10.4** Evaluating NN Model

| Measurement | Value |
|---|---|
| MSE | 0.46572267 |
| RMSE | 0.67224682 |
| $R^2$ (R squares) | 0.72353752 |
| Mean residual deviance | 0.41251257 |
| Mean absolute error | 0.52352683 |
| Root mean squared log error | 0.21354768 |

**TABLE 10.5** Forecast Results

| Total of Samples | 282 |
|---|---|
| Number of samples for training. | 226 |
| Number of samples for testing. | 56 |
| Number of parents have transforming intention. | 21 |
| Switching intention ratio. | 37.5% |

## 10.6 DISCUSSION AND CONCLUSION

International experience in designing E-learning teaching programs, firstly, should update and improve the digital capacity for teachers, from that, teachers to have the capacity to deepen their knowledge (UNESCO, 2021). Such an approach can help teachers to transform from basic knowledge about e-learning to use digital technology for solving complex problems. They also can move from basic IT tools to more complex tools and turn their standard classroom into a collaborative team that they manage and teach online. Furthermore, "teaching by technology requires teachers to extend their knowledge of pedagogical practice over many different aspects." In order to do that, we need to design a training program to improve teachers' capacity in the following aspects: (i) knowledge of E-learning content; (ii) online pedagogical knowledge, methods, and practice; (iii) resources, technology, or new instrument documentation. It also requires changing teachers' beliefs, attitudes, and pedagogical ideas regarding E-learning approaches.

Vietnamese education should focus more deeply on developing digital content and digital learning resources and continue to provide online pedagogical skills training for teachers who are still weak in technology skills. At the same time, the Government of Vietnam needs to have appropriate strategies and policies to further accelerate the digital transformation in education in Vietnam. This includes learning platforms, processes, and the development of MOOCs to help students learn, practice, and improve their student experience.

## KEYWORDS

- **COVID**
- **deep neural network**
- **digital content**
- **education**
- **E-learning**
- **learning content management system**
- **online education**
- **online learning system**

## REFERENCES


Ahmed, V., & Opoku, A., (2021). Technology supported learning and pedagogy in times of crisis: The case of COVID-19 pandemic. In: *Education and Information Technologies* (No. 0123456789). Springer US. https://doi.org/10.1007/s10639-021-10706-w.

Angrist, N., De Barros, A., Bhula, R., Chakera, S., Cummiskey, C., DeStefano, J., Floretta, J., et al., (2021). Building back better to avert a learning catastrophe: Estimating learning loss from COVID-19 school shutdowns in Africa and facilitating short-term and long-term learning recovery. *International Journal of Educational Development, 84*, 102397. https://doi.org/10.1016/j.ijedudev.2021.102397.

Ardington, C., Wills, G., & Kotze, J., (2021). COVID-19 learning losses: Early grade reading in South Africa. *International Journal of Educational Development, 86*, 102480. https://doi.org/10.1016/j.ijedudev.2021.102480.

Baber, H., (2021). Modelling the acceptance of e-learning during the pandemic of COVID-19-A study of South Korea. *International Journal of Management Education, 19*(2), 100503. https://doi.org/10.1016/j.ijme.2021.100503.

Bansak, C., & Starr, M., (2021). COVID-19 shocks to education supply: How 200,000 U.S. households dealt with the sudden shift to distance learning. *Review of Economics of the Household, 19*(1), 63–90. https://doi.org/10.1007/s11150-020-09540-9.

Chang, G. C., Eck, M., McOmish, E., Sass, J., Vargas, T. C., Wallet, P., & Heckmann, C., (2021). What's next? Lessons on education recovery: Findings from a survey of ministries of education amid the COVID-19 pandemic. *UNICEF*.

Clark, A. E., Nong, H., Zhu, H., & Zhu, R., (2021). Compensating for academic loss: Online learning and student performance during the COVID-19 pandemic. *China Economic Review, 68*, 101629. https://doi.org/10.1016/j.chieco.2021.101629.

Conto, C. A., Akseer, S., & Dreesen, T., (2020). *COVID-19: Effects of School Closures on Foundational Skills and Promising Practices for Monitoring and Mitigating Learning Loss* (pp. 1–30). UNICEF – Innocenti Working Paper, WP 2020-13.

Dong, C., Cao, S., & Li, H., (2020). Young children's online learning during COVID-19 pandemic: Chinese parents' beliefs and attitudes. *Children and Youth Services Review, 118*, 105440. https://doi.org/10.1016/j.childyouth.2020.105440.

Fitzgerald, D. A., Scott, K. M., & Ryan, M. S., (2021). Blended and e-learning in pediatric education: Harnessing lessons learned from the COVID-19 pandemic. *European Journal of Pediatrics*. https://doi.org/10.1007/s00431-021-04149-1.

Goldenson, R. P., Avery, L. L., Gill, R. R., & Durfee, S. M., (2022). The virtual homeroom: Utility and benefits of small group online learning in the COVID-19 era. *Current Problems in Diagnostic Radiology, 51*(2), 152–154.

Ikeda, M., & Yamaguchi, S., (2021). Online learning during school closure due to COVID-19. In: *Japanese Economic Review* (Vol. 72, No. 3). Springer Singapore. https://doi.org/10.1007/s42973-021-00079-7.

Jordan, K., David, R., Phillips, T., & Pellini, A., (2021). Education during the COVID-19 crisis: Opportunities and constraints of using EdTech in low-income countries. *Revista de Educacion a Distancia, 21*(65), 1–15. https://doi.org/10.6018/RED.453621.

Kim, S. H., & Park, S., (2021). Influence of learning flow and distance e-learning satisfaction on learning outcomes and the moderated mediation effect of social-evaluative anxiety in nursing college students during the COVID-19 pandemic: A cross-sectional study. *Nurse Education in Practice, 56*, 103197. https://doi.org/10.1016/j.nepr.2021.103197.

Maheshwari, G., (2021). Factors affecting students' intentions to undertake online learning: An empirical study in Vietnam. *Education and Information Technologies*. https://doi.org/10.1007/s10639-021-10465-8.

Mali, D., & Lim, H., (2021). How do students perceive face-to-face/blended learning as a result of the COVID-19 pandemic? *The International Journal of Management Education, 19*(3), 100552. https://doi.org/10.1016/j.ijme.2021.100552.

Maqableh, M., & Alia, M., (2021). Evaluation online learning of undergraduate students under lockdown amidst COVID-19 pandemic: The online learning experience and students' satisfaction. *Children and Youth Services Review, 128*(2020). https://doi.org/10.1016/j.childyouth.2021.106160.

Mouratidis, K., &Papagiannakis, A., (2021). COVID-19, internet, and mobility: The rise of telework, telehealth, e-learning, and e-shopping. *Sustainable Cities and Society, 74*, 103182. https://doi.org/10.1016/j.scs.2021.103182.

Mukuka, A., Shumba, O., & Mulenga, H. M., (2021). Students' experiences with remote learning during the COVID-19 school closure: Implications for mathematics education. *Heliyon, 7*(7), e07523. https://doi.org/10.1016/j.heliyon.2021.e07523.

Qazi, A., Qazi, J., Naseer, K., Zeeshan, M., Qazi, S., Abayomi-Alli, O., Said, A. I., et al., (2021). Adaption of distance learning to continue the academic year amid COVID-19 lockdown. *Children and Youth Services Review, 126*, 106038. https://doi.org/10.1016/j.childyouth.2021.106038.

Sabates, R., Carter, E., & Stern, J. M. B., (2021). Using educational transitions to estimate learning loss due to COVID-19 school closures: The case of complementary basic education in Ghana. *International Journal of Educational Development, 82*. https://doi.org/10.1016/j.ijedudev.2021.102377.

Schmitz, S. M., Schipper, S., Lemos, M., Alizai, P. H., Kokott, E., Brozat, J. F., Neumann, U. P., & Ulmer, T. F., (2021). Development of a tailor-made surgical online learning platform, ensuring surgical education in times of the COVID19 pandemic. *BMC Surgery, 21*(1), 1–6. https://doi.org/10.1186/s12893-021-01203-5.

Shambour, M. K. Y., & Abu-Hashem, M. A., (2021). Analyzing lecturers' perceptions on traditional vs. distance learning: A conceptual study of emergency transferring to distance learning during COVID-19 pandemic. *Education and Information Technologies*, 0123456789. https://doi.org/10.1007/s10639-021-10719-5.

Shirish, A., Chandra, S., & Srivastava, S. C., (2021). Switching to online learning during COVID-19: Theorizing the role of IT mindfulness and techno eustress for facilitating productivity and creativity in student learning. *International Journal of Information Management, 61*, 102394. https://doi.org/10.1016/j.ijinfomgt.2021.102394.

Singh, M., Adebayo, S. O., Saini, M., & Singh, J., (2021). Indian government e-learning initiatives in response to COVID-19 crisis: A case study on online learning in Indian higher education system. In: *Education and Information Technologies* (No. 0123456789). Springer US. https://doi.org/10.1007/s10639-021-10585-1.

UNICEF, (2020). *Are Children Able to Continue Learning during School Closures?* New York, NY.

Van, D. T. H., &Thi, H. H. Q., (2021). Student barriers to prospects of online learning in Vietnam in the context of COVID-19 pandemic. *Turkish Online Journal of Distance Education, 22*(3), 1–16. https://doi.org/10.17718/tojde.961824.

Vu, C. T., Hoang, A. D., Than, V. Q., Nguyen, M. T., Dinh, V. H., Le, Q. A. T., Le, T. T. T., et al., (2020). Dataset of Vietnamese teachers' perspectives and perceived support during the COVID-19 pandemic. *Data in Brief, 31*, 105788. https://doi.org/10.1016/j.dib.2020.105788.

Yu, Z., Abdel-Salam, A. S. G., Sohail, A., & Alam, F., (2021). Forecasting the impact of environmental stresses on the frequent waves of COVID19. *Nonlinear Dynamics*. https://doi.org/10.1007/s11071-021-06777-6.

Yuan, Y. P., Wei-Han, T. G., Ooi, K. B., & Lim, W. L., (2021). Can COVID-19 pandemic influence experience response in mobile learning? *Telematics and Informatics, 64*, 101676. https://doi.org/10.1016/j.tele.2021.101676.

Zuo, M., Ma, Y., Hu, Y., & Luo, H., (2021). K-12 students' online learning experiences during COVID-19: Lessons from China. *Frontiers of Education in China, 16*(1), 1–30. https://doi.org/10.1007/s11516-021-0001-8.

CHAPTER 11

# The Impact of Digital Technology on Indian Education

P. SUBBURAJ[1] and R. LENIN[2]

[1]*Agurchand Manmull Jain College, Chennai, Tamil Nadu, India*

[2]*Department of Management Studies, Guru Shree Shantivijay Jain Arts and Science College, Chennai, Tamil Nadu, India*

## ABSTRACT

Education through the Internet is the Government initiative to ensure the smooth operation of e-learning. E-PG Pathshala is a Ministry of Human Resource Development (MHRD) initiative that provides teachers with instructional e-content. Swayam is an integrated online education platform into artificial intelligence (AI) that has been used to personalize and tailor learning to the unique needs of each learner. NPTEL, NKN, and NAD are just a few of the federal government's current efforts to improve education. The MHRD has released Pragya (Digital Education), a collection of digital education guidelines (MHRD) guidelines. It can take many courses at a fraction of what they cost in a traditional university setting. A technological Savior is a national program for technology-enhanced learning (NTEL) that has been developing. A convenient learning environment for students has been critical to maintaining a safe learning environment and there is a contradiction between the right to education and the lack of access to modern technology. Eye problems – restored health enhancing online education's effectiveness through an integrated approach concentrating on various facets of knowledge. Online education is gaining popularity in India. Research is

Intelligent Learning Paradigms and Student Empowerment: Digital Integration and Transformation.
Souvik Pal, Ton Quang Cuong, & R. S. S. Nehru (Eds.)

now conducted to evaluate the effect of COVID-19 on children's education and the concerns surrounding digital education in India. Currently, the school system is in turmoil due to the Corona virus pandemic and its rising number of COVID-19 cases. Educational institutions have been closed for almost two years. In this situation, online education intervened to avert the destruction of the academic cause. On the other hand, online teaching brings several problems to overcome in education.

## 11.1 INTRODUCTION

E-learning has indeed taken hold in many universities throughout the globe, but this has not always been the case, and there are still certain institutions where this has not been the case. Students at a university where the usage of an e-learning platform to augment the classroom's instructional delivery is not necessary were surveyed in this chapter to see how they felt about utilizing a Moodle platform. However, in the wake of the COVID-19 pandemic, many children have been forced out of school and postponed examinations. Several institutions have switched to an online format to prevent pupils from falling behind in their studies. The pandemic has rocked the school system, necessitating a shift to online learning. Clinging to their phones and computers has become less common among youngsters. As a result, only 15% of rural families in India have Internet access, compared to 42% of urban homes. There has been a dispute about whether or not this change to an e-learning system has hindered the students' growth.

E-learning is a primarily online service. It changes how and when a person learns and incorporates a learning culture into the workplace. It's not only about training and teaching but also personalized learning. E-learning combines web-based training, technology-driven education, and online training. Tablets, PCs, and intelligent phones increase e-learning. Employer-employee relationships are built during work. Here, the business provides resources like e-learning, but workers must develop their skills and employability and maintain their worth to the organization. E-learning encourages people to learn more at work. The idea is that technology's alternative and flexible learning environments help reduce the difficulties of coordinating learning activities with work schedules.

E-learning offers economic and societal benefits over classroom learning. E-visuals, learning feedback, and learning time are further benefits. E-learning has a long-term return on investment—in the digital age. In recent decades, technology has changed everything. Different age groups are obliged to accept new technologies, either voluntarily or unwillingly, to keep up with the technological transformation race. Everything from academia to medical to lifestyle to communication to entertainment to diet to retail to business is influenced by technological advancements. Technological advancements in contact and information have simplified creating, disseminating, and gaining access to information. Learning and technological uptake have been shown to vary with age. As a result, online education significantly impacts society and the nation's development. E-Learning is the creative platform used in the classroom. Educators may use digital technology to provide compelling learning experiences in their courses. These initiatives can be in the shape of blended or online courses and programs, and their goal is to guarantee that e-learning runs smoothly. The Ministry of Human Resource Development (MHRD) Program E-PG Pathshala supplies teachers with e-content. There have been many steps done to make online learning possible in India, including:

1. **E-PG:** Human resource development ministry project to make educational materials available on the Internet, called Pathshala.
2. **SWAYAM:** It's an all-in-one system for taking online classes.
3. **NEAT:** It tries to employ artificial intelligence to personalize and tailor learning to the learner's needs.
4. **National Project on Technology-Enhanced Learning (NPTEL):** It was established in 2003 as a cooperative effort between the Indian Institutes of Technology and the Indian Institutes of Science with funding from the Government of India's Ministry of Education.
5. **National Knowledge Network (NKN):** The National Education and Research Network (NREN) of the country is the NKN, a countrywide, multi-gigabit network. Over 1,700 institutions and five crore students, researchers, and faculty members have now linked together thanks to NKN.
6. **National Academic Depository (NAD):** The Ministry of Human Resource Development's digital education guidelines are PRAGYATA. The PRAGYATA guidelines recommend a daily screen time limit of 30 minutes for children in preschool. A total of one and a half hours per day is allotted to students in Grades 1 through 8, and three hours are allotted to those in Stages 9 through 12.

## 11.2 LIVE ONLINE CLASSES

### *11.2.1 LEARNING*

The term "learning" may be described as "the technique of acquiring new, or altering current, information, behaviors, abilities, attitudes, or preferences." All living things, including humans, animals, plants, and even technology, are hardwired to learn from their prior experiences. Humans' capacity to learn begins at conception and lasts until death. Learners might divide their time between formal, non-formal (or informal), and informal learning.

#### *11.2.1.1 TYPES OF LEARNING*

When it comes to education, the term 'formal learning' refers to "structured, channeled by a formal curriculum" that leads to an official credential such as a high school diploma or a college degree and is often directed and acknowledged by government authority levels where professionally trained teachers take the helm of instruction. "Arranged (or roughly organized), where it may or may not have a formal channel of the curriculum" is what "non-formal learning" refers to as teaching is done by a skilled or experienced teacher or leader in this case. Non-formal learning outcomes like these don't lead to a certificate or degree but significantly increase a person's skills and abilities. There is no predetermined curriculum, and no credits earned is known as 'informal learning.' If you're looking for someone to perform the role of a parent or a friend with more excellent life experience, your teacher can fulfill both roles. 'Social learning is also part of it. Individuals learn from others in their community via observation, social engagement, and relationship-building as part of the phrase "social learning.

#### *11.2.1.2 E-EDUCATION*

It's also known as e-learning or electronic learning, which refers to learning that takes place using computers and the Internet. In this approach, students are taught systematically but with computerized tools. The Internet and a computer are the essential components of online learning, whether inside or outside a classroom. With the help of electronic networks, it is also possible to instruct many students at the same or various periods. In some instances, online learning may enhance or even replace conventional education. Advances in technology and learning methods have broadened their appeal to a broad audience. It may do all of the methods mentioned above learning online. Formal online classes with a predetermined curriculum and a teacher are available. 'Non-formal learning,' such as online courses provided by MOOC, Moodle, and the like, in which lecture notes or videos linked to a given area or domain or subject issue are placed on web portals, are examples of online courses. Instead, 'Informal learning' happens due to browsing online portals and exchanging knowledge through social media. Technology's role in education has evolved as people use smartphones, tablets, and other portable electronic devices. Electronic instructional resources, such as optical discs and pen drives, are progressively taking the role of books. It is also possible to communicate information over the Internet, which is available 24 hours a day, seven days a week, from any location. Modules and chapters are the most common divisions seen in online courses. Readings, PowerPoint, and lectures are often used to provide the material needed to accomplish the activities in each module. Modules require students to complete various assignments, including discussions, scenarios, simulations, projects, and papers. Online learning has a significant benefit in that it may do it at any time and location. Furthermore, since the instructor has remote access to the data, the student is free to move about the classroom as needed. If you're taking a typical course with Canvas, your instructor may access all of the course content at any time, and you and your classmates will always be able to communicate.

#### *11.2.1.2.1 The National Technology Enhanced Learning Program (NTELP)*

Indian Institutes of Technology and the Indian Institute of Science Bangalore (IISB) collaborated with the MHRD to create the NPTEL. In 2003, it was established as a platform for offering distance learning. Web-based and video-based instruction in various sectors was a boon for engineers, scientists, and businesspeople.

## 11.3 THE INNOVATION OF THE MEDIA

- The teacher and student can choose how fast or slow they want to learn and how long they want to do it. A better work-study balance is the result.
- A wide range of courses: The Internet has many resources for teaching and learning across various disciplines. Many universities and higher education institutions (HEIs) offer online programs for different levels and fields.
- As a result, it is more cost-effective than conventional learning. Online classes can save a lot of money on textbooks and travel expenses.
- As a result, online education allows students to work in the environment that best suits their needs.

Other direction:

- There isn't enough positive learning atmosphere for students to thrive in learning. Education is more than just sitting in a classroom all day. Participating in challenging group projects allows students to benefit from one another's knowledge and experience. A massive amount of knowledge is lost due to the shift to online education. They can't use their minds and act as remote receptors because they are staring at a screen.
- Not all students who can afford school can afford phones, computers, or even an internet connection to attend classes online. Lack of technology access–students are experiencing mental stress as a result of this.
- Technology is not accessible to everyone, contrary to the right to education. The shift to online education is tantamount to denying the Right to Education to people who lack the requisite technological means. In addition, the National Education Policy's references to the digitalization of education are in direct conflict with the constitutional guarantee of the right to education.
- Younger pupils, particularly those in Grades 1 to 3, were the most likely to have eye health difficulties due to prolonged use of computers or mobile devices. Due to poor posture and inactivity, older pupils are more likely to suffer from ailments such as neck and back discomfort.

### *11.3.1 ADVANCING EDUCATION PROGRAM*

- Flexible rescheduling of the academic calendar and investigating solutions with schools, instructors, and parents to give education access to a more significant portion of the student population. Physical encounters between teachers and students should be staggered such that not more than 50% of the overall strength attends schools on alternate days and prioritizes the less advantaged pupils who lack access to e-learning. Every kid should have access to a high-quality, fair education as a fundamental right.
- Increasing the Effectiveness of Online Education: Shorter but better dialogues should precede extended, repetitive sessions of one-way communication and inactivity. The teacher's job description should include more than just maintaining order in the classroom; it should also serve as a conduit for transmitting new information.
- Education isn't about competency but about a person's desire to learn. There is a greater emphasis on discovery than memorization. The system should not force students and professors to complete a course regardless of whether or not they have learned anything. Not as much emphasis should be placed on cramming as on learning valuable content well.

## 11.4 INDIA'S EDUCATION TECHNOLOGY

On September 3, 2020, the Indian Express published a story titled "Digital India is not equipped for digital education." This editorial analysis is based on that article. While COVID-19's influence on India's educational system is examined, so is the subject of digital education.

The education sector seems to have no problem because of the corona virus epidemic. The number of COVID-19 cases is growing, and educational institutions are expected to stay closed until at least 2020. Even in 2021, they might be in effect. As a result, online education has come to the aid of the educational cause. However, many issues need to be addressed regarding online education.

## 11.5 CHALLENGES OF DIGITAL EDUCATION

1. **Lack of Proper Study Room:** According to data from the 2011 Census, 71% of families with three or more members live in homes with two bedrooms or less (74% in rural and 64% in urban areas). The topic of how the kids will go to school peacefully is enormous.
2. **Inadequate Internet Penetration:** Data from the 2017-2018 National Sample Survey show that just 42% of families in urban areas and 15% in rural areas have access to the Internet. These numbers show that two-thirds of children will be left out of the online education process; as usual, the hardest impacted will be the marginalized, rural, and impoverished groups. Only 34% of urban and 11% of rural residents reported using the Internet during the prior 30 days.
3. **Slow Internet Speed:** Video conferencing with instructors or viewing recorded lectures are two of the most common forms of online instruction, and both need a fast and reliable data connection. The plan will fall through if Internet speeds aren't fast enough. A similar thing happens in the UT of Jammu and Kashmir, where students often hold demonstrations because they lack access to reliable Internet and cannot study.
4. **No Standard Policy:** Online video of professors lecturing at blackboards is not digital education; instead, it is about using the right platforms, technologies, tools, interaction, curation, content, etc. We don't have a solid plan for digital education that accounts for infrastructure, content, engagement, and translation.
5. **Lack of Social Cohesion:** Once it comes to promoting social cohesion and a sense of fairness for everyone, public schools are likewise a model institution. A place where individuals of different sexes, socioeconomic backgrounds, and cultural traditions may freely interact without having to defer to the superiority of any other group. It is essential knowledge for everyday living that may not be adequately covered by online learning.
6. **Teacher Training:** Educators are responsible for their students' psychological and social well-being. In contrast to social isolation, children's educational experiences promote positive psychological, interpersonal, and behavioral development. Teachers are not given insufficient preparation to convey these concepts via digital means.

7. **Parenting Issue:** Another challenge is to keep thousands of children out of school when their parents return to workplaces post lockdown. Who will assume responsibility for a child's safety and learning at home remains a huge problem.

## 11.6 TECHNOLOGY PROGRESS IN EDUCATION

1. **Bharat Network:** Formerly known as the National Optical Fiber Network (NOFN), plans to link 2,50,000 panchayats at approximately Rs 40,000 crore cost. Each Gram Panchayat in India will have access to at least 100 Mbps of bandwidth thanks to the government's BharatNet program, ensuring that even individuals living in rural areas will have the opportunity to use internet resources. This category includes e-health, e-commerce, e-government, e-education, and e-banking. With universal access, the infrastructure will revolutionize service provision once it is finished and becomes a national asset. Therefore, we need to move quickly.
2. **National Knowledge Network (NKN):** The goal of the NKN, a multi-gigabit national research and education network in India, is to provide all of India's universities and colleges access to the same reliable, high-speed Internet connection. IITs, IIMs, universities, research laboratories, and other e-governance institutions up to the district level are all linked together through the NKN, which was set up as a high bandwidth network. It fosters teamwork in the creation process and creates a database of information applicable to any area. Despite the network's maturity, only a select few institutions make full use of it due to inadequate education, infrastructure, resources, and personnel. Expansion of NKN is planned, which is good news. However, it must also be a central part of the Digital India program and be used to bring e-services to the base of the economic pyramid.
3. **Increased Financing:** Governments should provide more budgetary consideration to support school technical education. The recent rollout of the New National Education Policy (2020), which includes a budget increase to 6% of GDP, is encouraging.
4. **Parents and Teachers Training:** Most educators and parents are not technically savvy. Their knowledge will only benefit pupils if they put in the time to train.

5. **Increase Accessibility:** The epidemic greatly honed our ability to adapt to new circumstances in novel and resourceful ways. Nonetheless, it is also crucial to bring the less vital parts along. As a result, students from low-income backgrounds or who are living with a handicap must have access to remote learning programs. The government should provide such platforms and materials free of charge to encourage digitalization among educators and students. They must ensure that tools like cell phones and computers are available for online education.

## 11.7 ONLINE EDUCATION AND HOMESCHOOLING IN INDIA

Since Prime Minister Modi launched the "Digital India" project, the number of Indian students enrolling in online courses has increased dramatically. The goal of the effort is to use the robustness and adaptability of digital technology to address problems in many different sectors. These have prompted educational institutions to expand their reach by providing online course options. Is India benefiting from online education? Is it money well-spent for a family considering homeschooling? The market for online education in India is expected to increase at a CAGR of 52.2% from 2016 to 2021, from $247 million to $1.96 billion. With a projected 9.6 million online course enrollees by 2021's end, it is safe to conclude that online education in India is flourishing. However, due to the global spread of the COVID-19 virus, parents who want to educate their children from the comfort of their homes must now resort to online education and homeschooling. These parents have numerous concerns and doubts about the viability of online education for their children. So, let's examine the benefits and drawbacks of homeschooling children using the Internet.

### *11.7.1 MAIN* ADVANTAGES OF *ONLINE EDUCATION*

1. **Cost-Effective:** Online college education is considerably more cost-effective than a traditional university, yet it offers students the same quality of instruction. Many useful learning tools are freely available on the web as well. Harvard is only one of several prestigious universities that have made many educational materials and courses accessible online.

2. **Changeable Schedules:** Because of the adaptability of online learning, homeschoolers may take breaks or focus on other activities without missing out on their education. Having more leeway with one's schedule also enables one to study more broadly and include a variety of topics that may pique one's interest. In addition, students may go at their speed, rather than being rushed and under excessive pressure to do well, as is the case in conventional education.
3. **Accredited by the Government:** Many reputable online schools also guarantee you'll get a degree recognized in the real world. Nevertheless, ensure that the Distance Education Council has approved these courses in India.
4. **Extremely Participatory:** Conventional education has relied on inert learning tools like books and black/whiteboards, and it has actively discouraged pupils from adopting mobile devices like computers and cell phones. Students who choose an online learning environment have easy access to many educational resources, including videos and games, which may help make the learning process more engaging and enjoyable.
5. **Self-Reliance is Fostered in the Classroom:** In a regular classroom, students are constantly reminded of due dates and are motivated to stay up with their schoolwork by the pressure of their peers. Youngsters may become more sedentary if they attend school online. Negative consequences for missing deadlines might motivate kids to become more self-disciplined and structured. Furthermore, students who want to pursue their education online are frequently left to fend for themselves rather than relying on their lecturers or classmates when locating informational resources.

### *11.7.2 DISADVANTAGES OF ONLINE EDUCATION*

1. **Distractions:** Since they are not constantly observed, kids who do their schoolwork online are more likely to give in to distractions. Students need to have self-control, focus, and initiative to succeed. Planning study sessions efficiently and allowing for enough breaks can help the student maintain motivation and energy.
2. **Fraudulent Online Courses:** Phishing websites seem legitimate on the surface, but their true goal is to steal your personal information.

Make sure the website's address begins with "HTTP" or "HTTPS," and if possible, use a reputable search engine or the official government website to get the information you need.

3. **No Hands-On Experience:** Courses like chemistry, which benefit significantly from lab work, are not well served by virtual learning.
4. **Lack of Social Development:** Students' capacity to comfortably connect with others in the real world is hindered if they cannot practice their social skills in a structured environment like a classroom. Students may feel safe enough to open up about their issues online.
5. **Harmful Exposure to Screens:** Many hours spent staring at a computer screen may be detrimental to your eyes over time, making online education a risky option for students who want to get their education. It's essential to give your eyes a rest and blink every once in a while. Glasses designed to filter out the blue light from screens may help reduce the risk.
6. **Online Education:** Although homeschooling offers many advantages over conventional education, it is not a good match for subjects that need laboratory work or hands-on experience. However, online education with parental oversight may mitigate many of the problems that have been raised about it. Want more information about homeschooling or distance learning? Talk with one of our counselors.

## 11.8 REASONS FOR ONLINE LEARNING IS THE FUTURE OF EDUCATION

Changes in conventional schooling have occurred rapidly during the last several years. Because of the proliferation of the Internet and other forms of modern technology, traditional classroom instruction is no longer the exclusive means of acquiring knowledge. As long as you have a way to connect to the Internet, you can obtain a good education whenever and wherever you want it. This new period marks the beginning of the revolution in online education. Don't disregard skepticism about online learning just because it exists. It's difficult to fathom the idea of abandoning the safety and structure of a traditional classroom in favor of the vast unknown that is the Internet. However, this option's validity should not be discounted because of such. And it's helpful for a lot of kids. According to a new

Babson Survey Research Group poll, over 30% of U.S. college students take at least one online course. Both young adults and working adults may benefit from online education. This strategy may be helpful if you're a student trying to grasp a challenging topic better or pick up a new ability. Read on for five more arguments in favor of distance learning:

1. **It's Flexible:** Online learning provides both the instructor and the student with the autonomy to choose the speed of the course and the timing of assignments and assessments. Therefore, no sacrifice is necessary while utilizing an online educational platform to achieve a better work-study balance. Learning how to combine job and school effectively is one of the many abilities you'll acquire when taking classes online. Student and teacher collaboration on the same goal may also increase student and teacher autonomy.
2. **It Offers a Wide Selection of Programs:** In a medium as wide as the Internet, there is a limitless number of opportunities to share knowledge and acquire new abilities. Numerous colleges and universities now offer online versions of their courses and degree programs. From quantum physics to music creation, there are courses for every student. You may get a certificate, diploma, or degree from an accredited institution even if you never set foot on campus by studying your program entirely online.
3. **Accessibility:** The flexibility of online education means that you can teach or learn from any location. There is also no requirement for a set work schedule or travel from one place to another. In addition to the time and effort you save, you also avoid wasting money that may be better spent elsewhere. A fantastic way to use the virtual classroom is to go anywhere, as long as you have an internet connection. For instance, online courses might be a great option if you're a student studying overseas and looking for work. While traveling the world, there is no need to stop working or going to school.
4. **It Allows for a Customized Learning Experience:** We have discussed how having options might allow you to learn at your own speed. Yet another benefit of online learning is that it can tailor to each student's unique needs and skill set. The average size of an online class is far lower than that of a traditional one. It may significantly enhance the one-on-one attention you get from your instructor by using an online learning platform that limits

enrollment to a single student at a time. Videos, photographs, and eBooks are just a few examples of the wide variety of online resources, and instructors may further enhance their lectures by including forum discussions and other presentation types. And this additional information is accessible anytime from any place, which will provide you with a more dynamic and tailor-made education.

5. **It's More Cost-Effective Than Conventional Schooling:** Education that takes place online and in a classroom often has a lower overall cost. As an added convenience, many institutions offer a variety of payment plans that allow you to pay in installments or by the course. It facilitates more precise financial planning. Many also qualify for financial aid or reductions, so the total cost is often not too prohibitive. You may also save money from the commute and class materials, which are frequently accessible for free. The financial outlay is less, but the potential returns are higher than competing strategies.

In conclusion, these are only a few of the many advantages of online education, which is why 90% of today's students prefer it over conventional classroom settings. Each kid has their circumstances, so they must make the right choices. While this alternative to traditional schooling is not for everyone, it's still a practical choice with nearly unlimited options for international students worldwide.

## 11.9 MAIN BENEFITS OF DIGITAL EDUCATION

Digital schooling has been developed in the education system and has several advantages over other educational methods worldwide. Furthermore, digital education contributes to the digital 21$^{st}$ century by providing diverse teaching and learning techniques and equipping learners with the necessary abilities. Read on to learn why incorporating technology into the classroom may benefit your children's performance and the primary benefits of digital education. Teachers working in digital education must master new abilities they may not have had the opportunity to gain in their prior positions. Especially when it comes to teaching, the advantages of digital education for students and teachers serve as a tremendous drive for all parties. Instructional and learning approaches that are appropriate for the digital 21$^{st}$ century A variety of instructional and learning methods provide learners with the skills they need to function in the digital 21st-century Skills for the 21st-century. Take a peek at the info graphic for more information. Digital education, according to educators in Sub-Saharan Africa, has the potential to have a substantial impact on classroom instruction and student achievement.

Teachers who have already included technological resources in their lessons will be acquainted with many of the advantages of digital education discussed in this essay. We realize the benefits of online learning. Understanding the value of digital education requires considering how technology has changed how we educate and how important it is to equip today's students with the skills they'll need to succeed in the increasingly digital 21st-century workforce.

### 11.9.1 DIFFERENT TEACHING AND LEARNING METHODS

Regarding teaching and learning methods, digital education can accommodate a wide range of options. Given that digital education may alter students' class participation levels, the following are some observable effects of this trend. Teaching students the knowledge and abilities they'll need to thrive in today's technologically advanced world calls for rethinking both the learning process and the conventional connections between pedagogy and content/skills. The industrial revolution is being pushed forward because of computerization and other digital advancements, as is a change in how we live and work. The Second Machine Age, written by Erik Brynjolfsson and Andrew McAfee, investigates the impact of digital technology on modern culture. They draw parallels between the technical advancements and problems presented by these breakthroughs and those offered by the Industrial Revolution. As educators, we aim to prepare students to operate well in the 21st-century, a century in which digitalization will enrich and control life and work and provide opportunities for both.

### 11.9.2 COMPETENCIES FOR THE 21ST CENTURY

In the past decade, digitization has transformed the way we live, work, and communicate with one another. This trend will continue. As a result, the talents are deemed the most important for the 21st-century. There are all concerned with how to live and work in a digital world. Look at the drawings that summarize these abilities in the section below. Then consider the cognitive abilities depicted in Bloom's taxonomy required to learn and interact successfully in complicated situations.

The learning and innovation skills and the information, media, and technological skills required for studying, working, and living in the 21st-century may divide into cognitive abilities and practical abilities (Figure 11.1).

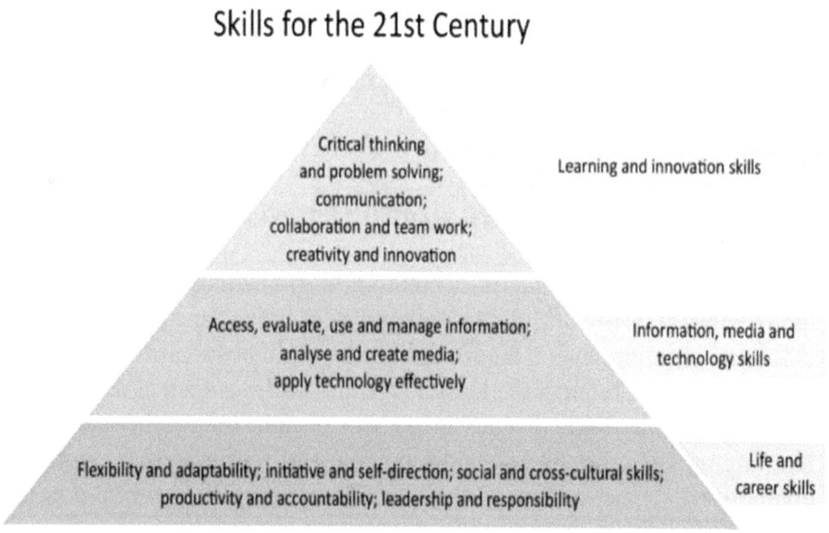


**FIGURE 11.1** Skills for the 21st century.

### *11.9.3 INTELLIGENCE*

As you may have seen, a non-digital curriculum covers cognitive abilities like critical thinking, problem-solving, and creativity. You will know from experience that these talents can be taught and learned without digital tools or surroundings. In developing these abilities, how can digital education help?

### *11.9.4 EDU-TRAINING*

They progress at their own rate. The issue of offline/non-digital learning is keeping up with (or slowing down) the class. With digital education, teachers may adapt learning to individual requirements. In this way, it promotes the development of cognitive skills at the level of each student, allowing some to practice more and others to advance when ready.

### 11.9.5 MORE EDUCATION

Expanded learning refers to learning options outside of the traditional classroom. Learners of all abilities may use digital education to broaden their knowledge and skills or consolidate and develop them by undertaking support activities and similar assignments.

### 11.9.6 ENGAGEMENT BOOST

Engagement and learning require incentives. Teachers may use digital education methods like game-based learning to promote student engagement and improve student performance. Online access to diverse and current resources helps learners expand their knowledge and develop critical thinking skills. Collaborative learning is more straightforward than digital schooling. These are because of digital platforms: Teachers may assign group assignments; students can work together to finish them, and teachers can track their progress. Furthermore, collaborative learning scenarios allow students to critically analyze one another's work and interact to solve difficulties together.

### 11.9.7 LEARNING ASSESSMENT

Digital education improves teachers' ability to diagnose and assess students' cognitive skills. Thus, digital assessment solutions help teachers to provide excellent tailored learning possibilities. Since students using game-based learning tools see each assignment as a new challenge in a competitive environment, these programs also evaluate them in unseen ways. "Digital India" is not yet ready for online learning. It will require diverse approaches to facilitate the shift from traditional classroom instruction to online learning. Those in charge of raising children, educating them, and running the schools all need money and facilities to function well. Learning changes people and gives them agency. Millions of young Indians hoped education would help them escape poverty and gain economic independence. I was born into extreme poverty in a remote Odisha village, yet with just 10 dollars in my pocket, I could attend college and get a master's degree in physics in 1964. In what other places is it possible? I became a new caste—an engineer—and provided for my seven siblings (five sisters and three brothers) by studying physics in India and electrical engineering in the United States. It is a goal of many young Indian people. We were optimistic when the government announced the New Education Policy for 2020. India's children and their parents are becoming more aspirational, leading to an education crisis. The National Knowledge Commission (NKC) worked from 2004-to 2009 to expand, improve, and ensure that all students had access to a quality education that would prepare them for the challenges of the 21st century. Many of the Commission's suggestions, such as creating almost 900 new institutions and a large number of new IITs and IIMs, as well as increased education funding in the 11th five-year plan and the right to education bill, was enacted by the UPA administration. The NEP 2020 vision is an inspiring statement of intent. It's all in the particulars and in maintaining promises if you want to succeed. An investment of 6% of GDP in education, for instance, would be a wise and necessary move. When though? Reduced from 4.1% of GDP in 2014-2015, education spending was 3.2% of GDP in 2020-2021. That is, the same government that slashed education spending by 25% in good times will increase spending by four in bad. In other words, show me what you've got before you give me the moon.

## 11.10 ONLINE EDUCATION SHOULD NOT REPLACE TRADITIONAL CLASSROOMS

Hope does not help in the COVID crisis. Expect the worst and plan for the best—for example, the migrant labor crisis. Education is in trouble now. Increasing COVID cases will likely shutter schools and institutions till 2020. It may stretch through 2021. Can we assure student, teacher, and staff safety? Student Discipline How can we safeguard senior educators? If so, will every school and institution provide it? How do we rethink schools? Can you tell me whether we have enough of everything to return to school? Do instructors get paid if there are no students? Can families afford the cost of education? There are still a lot of mysteries to be uncovered. We addressed the need for continued education throughout the epidemic by making online courses available. Concerns include access, gadgets, material, and curation; teachers; testing; examinations; grades; financing; facilities; wages; parents; and fees. Only approximately 25% of Indian homes have internet access. Rural families have a 15% rate. The disadvantaged, rural, and underprivileged will be hit the hardest. Digital education is not about professors posting recordings of their lessons online. It's about platforms, tools, interactivity, curation, content, etc. We are woefully unprepared. They lack the resources to deliver digital instruction. Private and public schools are alike. But they all expect total costs to pay personnel and maintain facilities. During this epidemic, the financial model for education is crumbling. India's condition has been exacerbated by a lack of digital education policy, infrastructure, and multilingualism.

## 11.11 CONCLUSION

Equal opportunity is a cornerstone of the Indian constitution. The idea of this statement is ruined if we adopt a system that only benefits a portion of the population and ignores the most vulnerable. India is yet to achieve success in digital education if students' rights are being violated or significant academic curriculum options are not being provided and there is much work to be done. The novel audio-video component of digital education enhances the cognitive elements in a child's brain, making it a particularly effective learning method. A blend of information and entertainment in digital education makes it more practical, relevant, and engaging. Students choose this option because it gives them the freedom to study at their own pace and schedule. Teachers, too, like the ease with which they may design their lessons with the aid of technology. With customized packages that combine animations, gamification, and intricate audio-visual elements, teaching becomes a more enjoyable experience. That is to say, we should give the utmost praise to online teaching and learning techniques, but only when they are utilized to supplement and improve traditional classroom settings. The transition from traditional classroom teaching to online learning will need a concerted effort on many fronts.

Digital education has been shown to improve teaching and student engagement, according to many studies. It has been found that teachers who use technology in their classrooms report increased socio-emotional benefits and greater efficiency in their teaching and classroom management. There are many secondary benefits to using digital tools in education, including increased student attention and improved parent-teacher relations. "For students and teachers in India's diverse educational systems, technology-enhanced learning offers numerous advantages and the opportunity for innovative adaptation. We can clearly see this from the large amount of data and information we collected for this study," Rajah Augustinraj, Director, BCG, and lead author of this chapter, stated. For many years, the emphasis has been on making technology more widely available, both within and outside the classroom. After the nationwide lockdown, teachers began to use various digital tools. We learned that the solution was just as critical as permitting access for digital learning to be effective as we had previously thought.

## KEYWORDS

- **digital education**
- **e-learning**
- **homeschooling**
- **India's education technology**
- **Ministry of Human Resource Development**
- **online education**

## REFERENCES

Anuradha, M., (2019). Examining the impact of e-learning on resolving work place issues in manufacturing industries at Chennai City. *The Online Journal of Distance Education and e-Learning*, *7*(2), 81.

Edumadze, J., (2019). Assessing business students' experiences with E-learning in a Ghanian University. *The Online Journal of Distance Education and e-Learning*, *7*(2), 70–80. https://ir.ucc.edu.gh/xmlui/handle/123456789/4178 (accessed on 6 May 2024).

*Gemma Josep is the Content Manager for Classgap, an Online Platform that Aims to Facilitate Communication Between Teachers and Students*. She writes about the importance of online learning, education, and technology and works with Classgap to bring education closer and create a perfect online learning environment.

https://hbr.org/2020/05/digital-transformation-comes-down-to-talent-in-4-key-areas (accessed on 13 December 2023).

https://timesofindia.indiatimes.com/readersblog/pracin-jain-academy/digital-initiatives-in-india-contributing-to-the-functioning-of-the-education-system-29770/ (accessed on 13 December 2023).

https://whatis.techtarget.com/definition/digitization (accessed on 13 December 2023).

https://wirally.com/advantages-of-digital-india/ (accessed on 13 December 2023).

https://www.educations.com/articles-and-advice/5-reasons-online-learning-is-future-of-education-17146 (accessed on 13 December 2023).

https://www.educations.com/articles-and-advice/8-myths-about-language-learning-online-17909 (accessed on 13 December 2023).

https://www.niallmcnulty.com/2017/05/what-are-the-benefits-of-digital-education/ (accessed on 13 December 2023).

https://www.theclassofone.com/blog/advantages-and-disadvantages-of-online-education-and-homeschooling-in-india (accessed on 13 December 2023).

https://www.thehindu.com/education/how-online-learning-can-revolutionise-and-reform-indian-higher-education/article35647848.ece (accessed on 13 December 2023).

https://www.thehindubusinessline.com/info-tech/ (accessed on 13 December 2023).

https://www.thehindubusinessline.com/opinion/how-digitisation-and-technology-are-shaping-education-in-india/article34090642.ece (accessed on 13 December 2023).

## CHAPTER 12

# Designing Course Modules on Competency-Based Teaching Methods in the Context of Digital Transformation: A Case Study for Teacher Education Programs in Vietnam

NGUYEN THI VIET NGA and AN BIEN THUY

*Hanoi Pedagogical University 2, Vinh Phuc, Vietnam*

### ABSTRACT

Currently, in teacher training schools in Vietnam, the effectiveness of digital transformation in organizing teaching activities on vocational skills is still low. The use of digital technology in universities is often limited by the faculty's online teaching methods, the multimedia content of the lectures, and the ability to access educational platforms from across the country, remotely deployed on the Internet. This study aims to determine the range of appropriate learning activities when organizing online teaching for the teaching methods modules in bachelor of pedagogy training and how to manage these learning activities. The study is based on a questionnaire survey about the online learning process with 26 Biology students and 30 Early Childhood Education students, Hanoi Pedagogical University 2. Based on the survey results, the factors affecting the effectiveness of learning activities include subject information, learning organization, teaching technology, student support activities, primary conditions, facilities of learners and lecturers. This research is the basis for exporting the online teaching process

Intelligent Learning Paradigms and Student Empowerment: Digital Integration and Transformation.
Souvik Pal, Ton Quang Cuong, & R. S. S. Nehru (Eds.)

to improve the effectiveness of teaching activities in teacher training. With the same approach, other bachelors of pedagogy training courses can apply digital transformation from this example as a reference.

## 12.1 INTRODUCTION

With the rapid development of information technology, the digital revolution has appeared in all fields. The number of people accessing the Internet on both smart devices has increased significantly. Therefore, it is not surprising that these digital transformation trends also have a strong impact on the education sector. There are many trends in digital transformation in education, such as improving the accessibility of students; how to personalize the learning experience; virtual reality (VR); opportunities to learn on the cloud platform; integrating "internet of things" technology into the school environment; enhanced security on many digital devices; teaching students about "digital citizenship;" digital data. As such, online teaching and learning are just aspects that digital technology brings to the future teaching trend. Digital transformation has turned traditional classes into combined in-person classes or online classes. This process happens even more quickly when the COVID-19 pandemic appears. As the epidemic unfolded, both the school and society worked hard to get learners to continue to go to school using technology to bridge the geographical gap.

Pedagogical students have adult learning characteristics (Malcolm, 1968), including:

1. **Having a Self-Concept:** They can orient themselves and control their learning process, deciding whether to be trained or trained.
2. **Having Past Learning Experience:** Students who have gone through the stages of study in high school and the world experiences derived from academic and social experiences.
3. **Having a Clear Direction and Purpose of Learning:** They learn because they feel it is necessary and relevant to their work in the future, not an obligation to perform.
4. **Ready for Training:** When starting to participate in training, students will learn with a willing and eager attitude. Besides, students are aware of the importance of training and the value brought in the big picture. Students look to training to solve their difficulties and wish to overcome barriers at work.

5. **Motivated by Internal Motivation:** Students develop according to their motivational methods. They choose to train in solving their problems.

Teaching method subjects in pedagogical schools are challenging when lecturers have to balance the practicality of the topic with the conditions of online teaching and the learning characteristics of students. Therefore, lecturers need to prepare well the learning content and how the organization works for teaching students effectively. That is, lecturers need to know how to design science that applies to real-world careers, integrate new concepts and knowledge along with the amount of knowledge available, skillfully integrate teaching knowledge into the learner's life experience to become a positive part of the student's learning process.

This study focused on analyzing trends in the digital transformation of teaching method modules. By identifying the factors that affect online teaching, the content of appropriate learning activities when organizing online teaching lessons teaching methods will improve the quality of training, thereby serving as the basis for building the online teaching process at Hanoi Pedagogical University 2. So, what are the trends in teaching that use digital technology? What modules can integrate digital technology? What responsibility do teachers and learners have in online education? What factors influence the online teaching process?

## 12.2 RESEARCH CONTENT

### *12.2.1 LITERATURE REVIEW*

#### *12.2.1.1 USE OF DIGITAL TECHNOLOGY IN TEACHING*

Digital technology (digital technology) is the subsequent development of information technology with the emergence of some breakthrough technologies of the Industrial Revolution 4.0 (Robert, 2001; Daniel, 2020).

The digital transformation uses digital technologies to change business models, creating new opportunities, revenues, and values (Vial, 2021; Gartner, Inc.) or digital transformation is rethinking how organizations bring together people, data, and processes to create new Microsoft values. Digital transformation is not just digital technology but a transformation step that helps people solve traditional problems; people often prioritize digital solutions over traditional ones (Tabrizi, 2019). Digital transformation is the restructuring of all production and sales processes to become more efficient. However, this does not result in the automatic modification of existing new services and products or the automatic creation of new processes. Digital transformation involves many stages, not simply implementing new IT technologies (cloud computing, the internet of things (IoT), big data, blockchain, AI, and ML).

Digital transformation in education is the application of advanced technologies to enhance the learner's experience, improve teaching methods, and create the environment for the most convenient learning (Bilyalova, 2019). Digital transformation in education focuses on the leading technologies: Applying technology to teaching with new methods and teaching support tools; Applying technology to the operation and management of education. Accordingly, many smart education models are being developed on its application platform in which:

- Firstly, the technology applied in management includes digitizing management information, creating large database systems, deploying online public services, applying Technologies 4.0 (AI, block chain, data analysis) to manage, operate, forecast, support decision-making in the education industry quickly and accurately.
- Secondly, digital transformation is applied in teaching and technology in the classroom, including Smart Classroom, Gamification programming, application when testing, evaluating including digitized materials (electronic textbooks, electronic lectures, e-learning lecture warehouses, multiple-choice question banks), digital libraries, virtual laboratories, implementing online training systems, building virtual universities.

Accordingly, the factors driving the transition in a school are: (1) the state budget is decreasing; (2) the increasing expectations of learners; and (3) technology is evolving. The three basic components of the digital transformation process are – (i) humans; (ii) strategy; and (iii) technology (Fermín Navaridas-Nalda, 2020). Four expected efficiencies when implementing digital transformation: (a) improving the quality of training; (b) improving research efficiency; (c) emerging new training methods/models; and (d) increasing financial resources. Digital transformation in education needs to create an ecosystem smooth with a new approach, not merely teaching through a webcam.

In the field of education, digital transformation has gradually changed the method of teaching-learning from traditional to active teaching methods, helping teachers and learners to promote their thinking, creativity, initiative, and effectiveness (Ifenthaler, 2021; Katyeudo, 2021). The focused classroom model has gradually shifted to online teaching models, using information and communication technologies to support teaching and learning activities. Thereby, learners can access knowledge anywhere, anytime, can be proactive in learning and applying practical aspects to practice. The explosion in educational technology has created non-traditional modes of education, strongly promoting the development of deeply transformative education for people.

In Vietnam, the government has issued many documents guiding digital transformation in education (Decision No. 117/QD-TTg dated January 25, 2017, Resolution 52-NQ/TW dated September 27, 2019, Decision No. 749/QD-TTg dated June 3, 2020) which states that IT application is one of the nine key task groups to effectively implement Resolution No. 29 of the Party Central Committee on comprehensive fundamental innovation in education and training. The national digital transformation program to 2025, oriented to 2030 has been approved. Education and training are one of the top eight priority areas in implementing the National Digital Transformation Program to 2025, oriented to 2030. In practice, from 2018 to now for universities and colleges, the information of nearly 400 schools with 2.5 million students and more than 120,000 teachers has been digitized. At the same time, making connections with educational platforms and the national reporting system, announcing the opening of the identity code system, when the data of the digital knowledge system of Vietnam has also been developed with a huge database. Education and training are key areas that need to promote digital transformation. The goal is to become one of the leading countries in digital transformation in education and training. Higher education plays an important role in the training of advanced and integrated Vietnamese citizens. Both are knowledgeable, skilled, and ready to integrate with the world. The education and training sector has identified digital transformation as an important solution to fundamental and comprehensive innovation in education and training in Vietnam.

The prolonged COVID-19 epidemic causes many difficulties for the education and higher education sector. However, on the positive side, these difficulties are the leverage to promote digital transformation in higher education. Remote training activities and online learning interact directly over the internet and are applied by many universities.

Higher education institutions (HEIs) have been implementing online learning activities. Going through a difficult period, many educational institutions have changed the perception of digital transformation. Digital transformation in higher education is a common trend in the region and the world (Bilyalova, 2019). The trend of digital transformation at the university level is very diverse (Voronin, 2019; Neborsky, 2020; Mikheev, 2021).

One is to expand the audience of learners, increase enrollment quotas by combining online and in-person training; Reduce costs but increase the quality of training.

The second is to collect and analyze big data of learners to find out the factors affecting learning results, thereby adjusting policies, teaching methods, and assessment methods to improve the quality of training and meet the increasing requirements of learners and society.

The third is to use a direct/online network with businesses/employers to train the necessary skills and knowledge so that learners can work immediately after graduation.

The first is the application of augmented reality (AR) to create an interactive learning environment, improving the learning experience for learners.

The second is the application of artificial intelligence (AI) to personalize the learning process and support to improve the efficiency of teaching, management, ministry...

However, digital transformation in education today still faces many challenges (Rodrigues, 2017; Nam, 2020; Marks, 2021), and these need to continue to be overcome, specifically perfected as follows:

- Network infrastructure, IT equipment (such as computers, cameras, printers, machines), transmission lines, Internet services for schools, teachers, students–especially in remote areas, disadvantaged areas–are lacking, outdated, synchronous, many places do not meet the requirements for digital transformation (both in terms of education management and teaching-learning) creating inequalities in education.
- Digitizing, building, updating digital learning, appraising, and sharing digital learning requires a large investment in human resources (including management and human resources) as well as finance to ensure adequate, quality digital learning, meeting learning requirements, research, and reference of students at all levels of study, disciplines, subjects.

- Collecting, sharing, and exploiting educational management data and digital learning requires a common legal corridor in accordance with regulations on copyright, intellectual property, information security, electronic transactions, and information sharing laws, specifically such as: stipulating the list of information subject to mandatory declaration, data entry–distinguished from private personal information under personal rights; copyright provisions for electronic lectures (in which cases are used, what conditions, use in whole or in part); regulations on exploitation of databases, digital data warehouses (who are entitled to exploit, what exploitation, level, what conditions, who appraises, who allows); stipulating the legality of electronic records in general and transcripts and e-books in particular (especially in the case of transfer of schools nationwide).
- The prescribed documents and guidelines on online teaching should be timely such as: Regulations on online learning programs, duration of study, online assessment examination, online learning quality accreditation, recognition of online learning results (different from traditional learning); stipulate conditions for organizing classes and schools on the network environment (both short-term and long-term).

#### *12.2.1.2 TEACHING METHOD MODULES FOR VOCATIONAL SKILLS IN PEDAGOGICAL SCHOOLS*

Due to different education policies in other countries, Vietnam's teacher training program is different from other countries in the world. The teacher training system in Vietnam under the serial model has a training period of three years for college level, four years for university level (Nguyen Thanh Hoan, 2008; Nguyen Van Hien, 2020) (Table 12.1).

Personal pedagogical training schools in Vietnam focus on educational sciences (Nguyen Chi Thanh, 2003; Ministry of Education and Training (MOET), 2010; Nguyen Van Hien, 2020) in which: pedagogical students have about 10 weeks of pedagogical practice during training. Internships can be divided into two semesters: practicing the first five weeks in the third year and practicing the second five weeks in the final year of the course. This is the time to practice teaching in high school and micro-practice in pedagogical universities. Subjects in educational universities have three main parts: General knowledge block, professional education

**TABLE 12.1** Teacher Training System in Vietnam

| Teacher Training Systems by Level of Education | | | |
|---|---|---|---|
| **Level** | **Under Standard** | **Standard** | **Above Standard** |
| Preprimary | – | 12 + 2 and 9 + 3 | 12 + 3 and 12 + 4 |
| Primary | 12 + 2 and 9 + 3 (for difficult areas) | 12 + 3 (college education) | 12 + 4 (higher education) |
| Lower secondary | – | 12 + 3 (college education) | 12 + 3 + 1 (higher education) |
| Upper secondary | – | 12 + 4 (higher education) | 12 + 4 + 2 (post-graduate education) |

*Source:* According to Nguyen Thanh Hoan (2006).

knowledge block, pedagogical professional knowledge block. The general knowledge block includes subjects such as philosophy, foreign languages, educational psychology, and the practice of Vietnamese. The pedagogical professional knowledge focuses on theoretical learning associated with applying to the method of teaching the subject. This section also focuses on training a team of promising teachers to teach to develop the capacity of students according to the subject program in the national general education program. Pedagogical training accounts for 25% of the total teacher training program and includes students practicing teaching inside and outside pedagogical universities. The training process consists of from 120 to 140 credits, with 15% of general knowledge, 60% of professional education knowledge, and 25% of pedagogical professional knowledge. The teacher's professional education knowledge ranges from one program to another, depending on the choice of the student when they enroll in the university. For example, if they want to become a Physics teacher, they must study physics science primarily in specialized learning units. There are two types of science teacher training in Vietnam: the simultaneous, more popular education model and the continuous education model. Each model has its own advantages in terms of the career development of the teacher. In the simultaneous education model, students take classes in professional education knowledge units and pedagogical professional knowledge blocks at the same time. In the continuous education model, students complete the scientific learning unit in the first three years before studying subjects of pedagogical professional knowledge. After completing all the requirements, the teacher candidate will receive a diploma from the college of education. In Vietnam, teacher candidates do not have to take the national teaching exam to be granted a teaching license. Graduates of teacher education programs in Vietnam will become nationally certified teachers if they are admitted to public or private schools. There is no difference in requirements for teacher qualifications between high schools and private schools. Private schools compete by offering high salaries to recruit good teachers. On the other hand, public schools often offer stable job placements and pension plans for workers. In Vietnam today, high-quality public schools in urban areas are still attractive places for good pedagogical students to register to work. However, the recruitment quota for teachers depends on the education development planning of each province. Teacher overcapacity often occurs due to pedagogical institutions training teachers according to their competence without considering the actual needs of local teachers.

The teacher training program in Vietnam has differences, the proportion of pedagogical training courses varies (Hanoi Pedagogical University 2, 2017; Le Thi Phuong, 2018) (Table 12.2).

In addition to the goal, the content of the teacher training program also has differences in the content and duration of teaching pedagogical practice subjects (Hanoi Pedagogical University 2, 2020, 2021) (Tables 12.3 and 12.4).

Thus, between the two training programs, there are quite a lot of differences: (i) about the training objectives: The bachelor of early childhood education of Hanoi Pedagogical University 2 aims to train early childhood teachers with "solid professional capacity," participate in professional work at early childhood education institutions or participate in the work of early childhood education institutions or participate in the work of early childhood education. Professional management at organizations, educational institutions, or educational management agencies; (ii) in terms of training time: quite similar; (iii) in terms of credit number: the number of credits for the bachelor's program in early childhood education taught in English (Draft, 2021) of Hanoi University of Education 2 is 148 credits. This credit number fully meets learners' knowledge, updated with educational innovation in general, and early childhood education. The number of credits for the bachelor's early childhood education program of Unitec University and Artevecle University is 360 and 180, respectively. With this credit, learners could study more intensively about early childhood education; and (iv) the structure of the training program: the design of the bachelor's program in early childhood education taught in English (Draft, 2021) consists of 148 credits, allocated overtime/training plan, creating an overall view,

**TABLE 12.2** Comparing Pedagogical Training Programs in Teacher Training between Finland and Vietnam

| Match Content | Finland | Vietnam | Judge |
|---|---|---|---|
| Training time | Five years | Four years | Vietnam's training time is shorter. |
| Training program | • The theory of educational science;<br>• Professional knowledge;<br>• Reasoning and practice teaching subjects. | • Specialized science;<br>• Educational science;<br>• Pedagogical profession. | Same |
| Percentage of business subjects. | 30% | From 20 to 30%. | – |
| Duration of practice in general. | About a third of the program learning (Pari Sahlberg, 016). | About 1/6 of the program. | Less time spent practicing in Vietnam. |
| Practice time, internship. | • Year 1: Pedagogically oriented internship (2 weeks).<br>• Year 2: Internship in psychology, education, professional training (4 weeks).<br>• Year 3: Internship in subject teaching (monophyletic or multi-subject) (6 weeks).<br>• Year 4: General internship (8 weeks).<br>• Year 5: Career integration, direct training at high school | • Year 3: 1st internship in classroom management (5 weeks).<br>• Year 4: Teaching career internship (7 weeks). | Fewer internships and internships. |

**TABLE 12.3** Comparison Program of the Bachelor of Biological Pedagogy Program of Hanoi Pedagogical University 2 (Vietnam) – Bachelor of Biological Pedagogy of Maryland (USA)

| | | |
|---|---|---|
| | **Same** | |
| **Criteria Content** | **Content** | |
| Goal | All determine the level of training: Bachelor.<br>All identify the job positions of students after graduation:<br>• Teaching teacher;<br>• Technical classes in addition to secondary education. | |
| Content structure | All provide industry-based knowledge, industry base: Cell base, molecular genetics, cell biology, animal physiology, and organic chemistry.<br>All provide professional pedagogical knowledge: Educational psychology, education, pedagogical internships. | |
| | **Different** | |
| **Training Programs Content** | **Bachelor of Biology Pedagogy from Hanoi Pedagogical University 2 (Vietnam)** | **Bachelor of Educational Sciences Specializing in Biological Education from Salem University (USA)** |
| Goal | Training Bachelor of Biology pedagogy with good moral qualities, solid professional capacity to effectively perform the tasks of education, study biology, natural sciences and other tasks of high school assignors and participate in professional management at organizations, educational, and training institutions, research institutes, and other institutions related to the field of biology. | The primary Bachelor of Biological Education (BIOE) program combines the subjects required to obtain a master's degree in conventional biology with the additional courses needed and is recommended for certification to teach biology at the secondary level. Students who complete this program of study will have a solid background in biological sciences and will be able to work in a variety of engineering positions in addition to secondary education. |
| Output standard | There is an output standard. | Do not publish public output standards on the school's web page. |

**TABLE 12.3** *(Continued)*

| | Different | |
|---|---|---|
| **Training Programs Content** | **Bachelor of Biology Pedagogy from Hanoi Pedagogical University 2 (Vietnam)** | **Bachelor of Educational Sciences Specializing in Biological Education from Salem University (USA)** |
| Structure of part content | Total credits: 135<br>• General education: 22 credits.<br>• Industry base knowledge: 15 credits.<br>• Specialized background knowledge: 26 credits.<br>• In-depth knowledge: 28 credits.<br>• Pedagogical profession: 33 credits.<br>• Graduation course: 7 credits. | A total of 102 credits, focusing heavily on basic subjects, teaching segregation, and teaching according to STEM models, in which:<br>• Existing lecture courses in Biology Focus are now considered an academic sequence in the following way: BIOL 141/BIOL 142 → BIOL 302/BIOL 303.<br>• Core biology: 18 credits.<br>• Elective course: choose one of biol 411, BIOL 414, or BIOL 434.<br>• STEM courses.<br>• Education: 32 credits.<br>• Subjects of the National Association of Science Teachers (NSTA) proposed (13 credits). |

**TABLE 12.4** Comparison the Programs Training of Early Childhood Teachers

| STT | Draft of GDMN E-Commerce to Teach ta Degrees (HPU 2, 2021) | Unitec University (New Zealand) | University of Artevecle (Belgium) |
|---|---|---|---|
| Training objectives | **Common Goal**<br>Training bachelor's in early childhood education taught in English with good foreign language ability, solid career capacity; perform the tasks of the preschool teacher well; participate in professional management at educational and training organizations, institutions, or educational management agencies. | **Training Objectives**<br>The bachelor's training in early childhood education (level 7, 360 credits) is capable of in-depth care, early childhood education and in-depth research in the field of early childhood education. Candidates who wish to apply in addition to the general conditions stipulated, must achieve good results in international examinations in English reaching Level 4 in other specialties. | **Training Objectives**<br>Train early childhood education professionals to work for different subjects: children, families with children, educational professionals, external partners, and society with a connection to children. |
| Training time | Four years | Minimum of three years.<br>Up to six years. | Three years |
| Total credits | 148 | 360 | 180 |
| Structure | • General knowledge: 33 credits.<br>• Professional education knowledge: 57 credits.<br>• Knowledge of industry group: 16 credits.<br>• Specialized knowledge: 41 credits.<br>*Compulsory:* 49 credits<br>*Elective:* 02 credits<br>• Pedagogical knowledge: 51 credits.<br>*Required*: 49credits.<br>*Elective*: 02 credits.<br>• Graduation course or alternative courses: 7 credits. | The blocks of knowledge focus on:<br>• Understanding preschoolers and issues related to preschoolers.<br>• Context and education policy.<br>• Teaching and working.<br>• Scientific research. | The knowledge blocks focus on the following contents:<br>• Children and the developing environment.<br>• Education and society.<br>• The combination in the care and education of preschool children.<br>• Work.<br>• Scientific research |

from general to private, meeting the objectives and output standards. The program structure has a coherent and coherent system: general knowledge → the industry group's knowledge → the specialized knowledge → the professional knowledge → the essay, the alternative part.

The system of Unitec University and Artevelde University is different. Because the requirements of learners before applying for admission are pretty high, the e-commerce of the two universities has one thing in common: building in-depth modules on children and social relationships, teamwork, interaction, sociological research, generalized modules are not available because they have accumulated in previous stages.

The teaching method modules belong to the pedagogical knowledge department. It is divided into groups of compulsory modules and electives. At Hanoi Pedagogical University 2, during the COVID-19 pandemic, 100% of teaching methods were conducted online based on the LMS learning platform and Google Meet application (Table 12.5).

However, there are still some shortcomings and limitations of the current education training program in the educational training institutions that need to be overcome (Pham Thi Kim Anh, 2015):

- First, the percentage of training time spent on knowledge blocks is not reasonable. The total time spent on pedagogical knowledge is only 33–36 units of learning (wildlife), accounting for 16–18%. Pedagogical practice only accounts for 10 athletes/210 athletes. General knowledge accounts for 38% of the time.
- Secondly, all training majors in pedagogical schools share the same mass of general education knowledge is unreasonable.
- Third, the program is not suitable for each school. For the duration of the internship, the students is also very little. There are only 8-10 weeks of internships and are also limited to certain classes in high school.

### 12.2.1.3 ACTIVITIES IN ONLINE TEACHING

In online teaching to be successful, there needs to be coordination between school and family, between school, family, and students. Activities in online teaching include teacher activities and student activities.

In order to organize online teaching, teachers need to be prepared for teaching (Downing & Dyment, 2013; Phan, 2017). Online teaching activities follow lessons or topics in the general education program, ensuring the

**TABLE 12.5** Pedagogical Professional Courses of the Bachelor's Degree in Biology and Early Childhood Education at Hanoi Pedagogical University 2

| Pedagogical Professional Knowledge in the Bachelor's Training Program in Biology | Credit Number | Pedagogical Professional Knowledge in the Bachelor's Training Program in Early Childhood Education | Credit Number |
|---|---|---|---|
| Professional knowledge | 37 | Professional knowledge | 47 |
| Mandatory, in which: | 33 | Mandatory, in which: | 45 |
| Psychology 1 | 2 | Early childhood psychology. | 2 |
| Psychology 2 | 2 | Early childhood education. | 2 |
| Education 1 | 2 | Methods of language development for preschoolers. | 3 |
| Education 2 | 2 | Organizing methods for preschoolers to familiarize themselves with literary works. | 3 |
| Pedagogical practice 1 | 2 | Method of forming math symbols for preschoolers. | 3 |
| Biology teaching reasoning. | 2 | Scientific education methods for preschoolers. | 3 |
| Practice designing a plan to teach biology. | 2 | Music education methods for preschoolers. | 3 |
| Teaching natural sciences in high school. | 2 | Methods of organizing visual activities for preschoolers. | 2 |
| Teaching biology 10 in high school. | 2 | Physical education methods for preschoolers. | 3 |
| Teaching biology 11 in high school. | 2 | Methods of staging art programs in preschool. | 3 |
| Teaching biology 12 in high school. | 2 | Scientific research methods specialized in preschool. | 2 |
| Specialized scientific research methods and specialized education. | 2 | Pedagogical practice 1 | 1 |
| Pedagogical practice 2 | 2 | Pedagogical practice 2 | 1 |
| – | – | Pedagogical practice 3 | 1 |
| – | – | Pedagogical practice 4 | 2 |
| Pedagogical practice 1 | 3 | Pedagogical practice 1 | 3 |
| Pedagogical practice 2 | 4 | Pedagogical practice 2 | 4 |
| Elective 1 (choose 1 of 8 courses) | 2 | Electives (choose 1 of 5 courses) | 2 |
| Elective 1 (choose 1 of 8 courses) | 2 | – | – |

interaction between teachers and students in the teaching process (MOET, 2021). In online teaching activities, teachers and learners perform the main activities as follows:

- **On the Teacher's Side:** Organize online lessons to give lectures and guide students to study; assigning the task of learning and examination; assessment of students' academic performance; monitoring and supporting students to exploit learning content from online teaching materials; advising, supporting, answering questions, and answering questions of students.
- **On the Student Side:** Attending online lessons organized by teachers; carrying out learning activities and examinations and assessments as required by teachers; exploiting learning content from online teaching materials, asking questions and answering questions for teachers and other students.

To implement teaching activities, it requires teachers to integrate many skills to prepare well for lesson preparation, organize lessons, check learners' results (MOET, 2021). When performing these activities, teachers should pay attention as follows:

- Firstly, when preparing lessons, teachers need to pay attention to identifying the core content of the lesson, ensuring feasibility, increasing the active working duration of students, reducing the duration of real-time online connections.
- Secondly, when developing a lesson plan, it should be noted: (i) Based on the requirements of the program to determine the lesson objectives; (ii) In the process of designing each activity, we need to consider choosing the appropriate teaching and learning equipment for each corresponding activity; (iii) With the same objectives, there may be many operational design options depending on the conditions of teaching equipment, learning, and the object of the student; (iv) The application of different positive teaching methods and techniques also gives us different options to meet the objectives of each activity; and (v) take four steps to organize the implementation of a learning activity to ensure the interaction between teachers and students (transfer of learning tasks, performance of tasks, reports, and discussions, conclusions-comments).
- Thirdly, when organizing online teaching, depending on the content of the lesson, teachers can flexibly use the lesson plan in many ways

when performing. However, with the goal of reducing the duration of real-time online connections, while increasing the autonomous working duration of students. Therefore, the teaching process can be flexibly transformed: Phase 1 (Before direct connection): Assign tasks on LMS or alternative tools; Phase 2 (Direct Connections): Report, discuss the results of the task in phase 1 and form knowledge and skills (Zoom, Google Meet, Microsoft Teams, …); Phase 3 (After a direct connection): Apply directly in the classroom or through the connected platforms of the class.

On the other hand, teachers need to prepare thoughtful learning materials to be ready to teach online (Moore-Adams, 2016), equipped with foundational skills in information technology (Bennett & Lockyer, 2004; Caena & Redecker, 2019), student assessment skills in online learning (Robles & Braathen, 2002; Seifert & Feliks, 2019) includes: designing assessment tools, selecting application software that matches the assessment tool, earning, and responding to information from learners to tailor teaching.

In addition, for teachers to organize online learning effectively, teachers need some of the following considerations (According to UNICEF Vietnam):

- Know the main features of the online platform you are using. Learning platforms offer a wide range of features such as grouping, screen sharing, and learning material management, as well as communication support. It is important for teachers to understand the advantages and limitations of the foundation to plan lectures effectively. To make sure the session goes well, teachers need to check the features before entering the lesson.
- Apply appropriate technology and teaching methods. Unlike teaching and interacting directly with students in the classroom, online lectures seem to confine teachers to a small screen, leaving students away from the content of their studies. Prolonged, one-way online sessions tend to cause students to become distracted after 10–15 minutes. Therefore, teachers may consider organizing or breaking down the session into short lectures, which come with a variety of activities to engage students.
- Monitor the student's academic initiative and progress through each lesson. To monitor the student's academic initiative and progress

over time, the following ways can be done: Assess the student's learning by giving out assignments, quizzes, polls, and summaries of the basic knowledge imparted in the classroom to monitor the student's progress; Build a personalized learning experience by dividing the class into small groups to encourage students to exchange and discuss; Reward the positive behaviors of students by creating badges (certifications) online and giving them to students as a reward so they can save them on file. Looking at and displaying badges can help them be more motivated to learn.

- Encourage parental participation in facilitating students' online learning. Creating a home environment that supports learning is extremely important.
- Design interactive learning activities. Apply activities such as debate, teamwork, project implementation, case studies, role-playing, and presentations to help students acquire skills other than classroom knowledge and make lectures more enjoyable. You can use a variety of online collaboration tools to support group activities.

#### *12.2.1.4 FACTORS AFFECTING ONLINE TEACHING ACTIVITIES*

In an experimental study based on Bayesian discovery factor analysis (Thi Tinh Thuong Pham and CS), it was shown that students' online learning outcomes were influenced by six factors in descending order, respectively: learner characteristics, usefulness of lessons, course content, course design, ease of use, and faculty competence (Thi, Hoang, & Doan, 2021). The factors affecting differences in different areas such as: Technology level has the greatest influence, affecting 47.8% on the effectiveness of online teaching, followed by the factors of action of learners affecting 35.2%, the actions of lecturers affecting 32%, and course characteristics affecting 27.9% on the effectiveness of online teaching (Nguyen Minh Minh) Lobes and cs, 2021; Nguyen et al., 2021). In another study, using online survey methods, discovery factor analysis methods, multivariate regression, and qualitative analysis methods were used to analyze the answers. The results of the discovery factor analysis show that there are five main factors affecting students' online learning, including faculty quality and course design, favorable conditions, time management, student satisfaction levels, and other factors. Multivariate regression analysis confirms that all five factors have had an important influence on predicting the effectiveness of students' online learning (Nguyen et al., 2021); and Gronlund (2009) has conducted an overview study of the challenges in implementing online learning in developed and developing countries. The results of the study grouped the challenges into four aspects: learners, technology, courses, and context. The results of the study also show that technology will be less of a challenge for developed countries, as the technology platforms in those countries have developed highly, meeting the technological requirements of implementing online learning.

The study by Ali and his team (2018) looked at 259 works that were involved in factors that hindered the success of online learning, which were published in prestigious journals between 1990 and 2016. Using a mixed analysis method, the study identified factors that could hinder the success of online learning, including pedagogy, technology, and learners.

In an experimental study, Puri (2012) conducted a survey of 214 learners at both undergraduate and graduate levels, identifying six of the factors that influence the success of online learning (in order of importance), namely: pedagogy, institutions, technology, reviews, support, and interfaces.

Musa & Othman's (2012) study of 850 undergraduate students also found technology to be the most important factor, in addition to three other factors: learner engagement, the role of teachers in promoting interaction, discussion, and the timely provision of learning materials on the system.

Xaymoungkhoun and the coauthors (2012) using the technology adoption model framework and AHP hierarchical analysis methodology on experimental interview data have shown the importance of organizational, technological, and pedagogical factors in addition to factors that belong to learner motivations and attitudes in contributing to the success of online learning.

Also based on the technology adoption model, which also has an expansion that includes cultural, supporting, and teacher elements, Ahmed (2013) looked at the problem from a narrower perspective, which is the willingness of teachers to participate in the use of online learning. Using the multiple regression method to analyze an investigative sample consisting of 281 observations, the author found the cultural factor had the strongest impact. As such, the role of cultural factors has an indirect impact on the success of online learning through the impact of encouraging the participation and use of online learning by teachers.

### 12.2.2 RESEARCH METHODS

In Vietnam, there are many pedagogical universities, but there are seven schools considered as key pedagogical universities, including Hanoi Pedagogical University 2. Pedagogical universities all train pedagogical bachelors to become teachers of preschool, primary, secondary, and high school. Our research aims to impact Vietnam's bachelor of pedagogical training during the digital transformation period. So, in this study, we selected the study sample as early childhood education students and biology pedagogical students, because they represent those who will become early childhood and general education teachers. We randomly took 26 students in biology and 30 students in early childhood education who were studying subjects related to teaching methods skills to survey with questionnaires and interviews.

#### 12.2.2.1 OVERVIEW OF SURVEY RESEARCH METHODS

Survey research is a method that involves using questionnaires or pre-standardized interviews to systematically collect data about people, interests, thoughts, and behaviors. It was established as an official method of scientific research that began only in the 1930s to 1940s, and the pioneer was the sociologist Paul Lazarsfeld as he examined the effects of radio stations on the formation of political views in the United States. From there, this method became a very popular technique for quantitative studies in the social sciences.

Survey research has inherent strengths compared to other research methods. First, surveys are a great means of evaluating a wide range of unobserved data such as preferences, characteristics, attitudes, beliefs, behaviors. Second, survey research is also ideal for collecting remote data about a research object that is too large to directly observe. With a large area, such as a country, data can be obtained using mail, email, or telephone from a small sample but is carefully selected to ensure that the object of study is fully represented in that sample. Third, due to its discreet nature and ability to meet requests conveniently for respondents, survey questionnaires are preferred by many. Fourth, interviews may be the only way to reach some groups of study subjects without the available sample selection direction. Fifth, some survey studies allow for the detection of minor problems even in large-scale surveys with multiple variables and may also allow for comparative analysis of study object groups (e.g., comparisons within a group and between groups). Sixth, survey research will be more time-, effort, and cost-effective than most other methods such as experimental research and case studies.

Depending on the method of data collection, survey research can be divided into two large categories: questionnaire surveys (be it by mail, group conduct, or online surveys), interview surveys (be it personal, telephone, or small group discussions). Questionnaires are tools completed by respondents in written language, while interviews are completed by interview participants based on verbal responses.

#### *12.2.2.2 QUESTIONNAIRE SURVEY*

The questionnaire, invented by Sir Francis Galton (1822–1911), is a standardized research tool, consisting of a set of questions aimed at capturing feedback from respondents:

1. **Survey Purpose:** The research team collects students' opinions on the program, form, content, and digital transformation during the learning process at the school, especially in the division of teaching methods. This helps the research team review and evaluate the status of digital transformation and implement action plans to improve and improve quality.
2. **Survey Subjects:** 26 students in Biology Pedagogy and 30 students in early childhood education.
3. **Survey Content:** We investigate through questionnaires related to:
    - The provision of information on subjects in online teaching;
    - Organizing learning in online teaching;
    - Teaching technology is being used by lecturers in online teaching;
    - Activities to support learners to be able to study online;
    - The suitability of learners' personal conditions with the implementation of online teaching;
    - Activities of the teaching staff in online teaching sessions.
4. **Survey Forms and Tools:** The collection of feedback from students on digital transformation in the pedagogical bachelor's training courses, especially the teaching method modules conducted in the form of surveys by questionnaires, questionnaires include specific variables according to the survey content. Each variable is measured

by the survey subject's level of consent to the corresponding question. The degree of consent is expressed by one of the integer scores from 1 to 5 with the meaning: (i) disagree; (ii) slightly agree; (iii) relatively agree; (iv) quite agree; and (v) very agree.

The questionnaires were designed by the research team, then sent to five random students who were not subject to the survey for their answers. This allowed the team to pre-examine the question to detect questions that were vague, lacked clarity, or contained biased words. After the questionnaire was edited and standardized, the team sent it to the students involved in the investigation by email and received the students' reply by email.

5. **Survey Time:** We conduct surveys at the time when students are in semester 6 of the training course. At that time, students were participating in courses related to theory and general teaching methods and sections related to the method of teaching the specific contents of the trained major.
6. **Data Processing:** After receiving the answers of the students who were investigated, the team conducted rough processing to obtain the data of statistical value. The set of data of statistical value is analyzed by specialized statistical data analysis software to give the evaluation results according to each criterion and indicators. The average score of the assessment of variables, the evaluation of factors is converted into the evaluation level according to the rule in Table 12.6.

**TABLE 12.6** Conversion Table between Score and Rating Level

| TT | Tb Point Range | Rating Level | Proposed Action |
|---|---|---|---|
| 1 | 4.21–5.00 | Good | Solutions are needed to maintain and enhance. |
| 2 | 3.41–4.20 | Fairly | We need a solution to improve. |
| 3 | 2.61–3.40 | Average | A solution is needed to fix it. |
| 4 | 1.81–2.60 | Weak | A solution is needed to fix it now. |
| 5 | 1.00–1.80 | Less | A solution is needed to fix it now. |

#### *12.2.2.3 INTERVIEW INVESTIGATION METHOD*

Interviews are a more personal form of data collection than questionnaires and are conducted by skilled interviewers with the same form of information collection as in table surveys. However, unlike a questionnaire, the interview scenario may contain special instructions for the interviewer that the respondent is not privy to. The interview will also provide an opportunity for the interviewer to record personal comments and opinions. In addition, unlike mail-in surveys, interview investigations can further clarify the issues raised by the respondent or the questioner who gives additional probing or suggestive questions.

1. **Interview Purpose:** This gathers more information and opinions of students on the factors that affect the effectiveness of learning and teaching method sections when the school organizes online classes. This helps the research team to make adjustment measures to improve and improve the quality of teaching.
2. **Interview Subjects:** 10 students in biology pedagogy and 10 students in early childhood education.
3. **Interview Content:** We interview questions related to the content:
   - What parts of the teaching method do you learn in person, what parts of which lessons do you learn online? What part of the study do you learn in person in conjunction with online?
   - Do you indicate the advantages and limitations when you learn to use the online form in the past?
   - What factors need to change, and how to change so that the learning process uses online form more effectively?
   - Do the activities related to digital transformation organized by lecturers improve the quality of teaching lessons? Why?
   - What activities do you think in teaching lessons need to be changed?
4. **Interview Form:** The team used the form of group interviews: a group of 10 bachelor's students in Biology pedagogy and a group of 10 undergraduate students in early childhood education. The two groups were interviewed separately in two different rooms. During the interview process, the interviewer records and can assist, lead, and ensure each interview participant can answer.
5. **Interview Time:** The interviews are conducted after the students have been studying teaching method modules that use the technologies of digital transformation.
6. **Data Processing:** After the interview, the team analyzed the qualitative data in the recording or interview minutes.

### 12.2.3 RESULTS AND DISCUSSIONS

#### 12.2.3.1 ONLINE TEACHING PROCESS

Hanoi Pedagogical University 2 builds a learning management system (LMS), which is an information system built on an open-source environment. The goal of the system is to provide support for learners (students, students, ...) to access the rich and diverse resources of the University, so that learners can learn on their own, self-foster on the spot on a regular and continuous basis https://lms.hpu2.edu.vn. Each faculty and student participating in teaching and learning will be granted an account and password to access the LMS system. The information of the course will be put on the LMS system by the school, learning activities, assignments will also be posted here by lecturers and students. In Vietnam, not only at Hanoi Pedagogical University 2, but other universities are also using their LMS systems to manage learners' learning activities.

As the COVID pandemic gets complicated, most schools must organize online teaching, which promotes digital transformation activities in teaching. To date, the use of the LMS system of pedagogical universities and online teaching takes place at the following levels:

- **Level 1:** 100% of traditional classrooms, which means that even though online classes take place, the format is that the faculty meets students in person through online meeting room tools such as Zoom, Google Meet...
- **Level 2:** The LMS system is a platform that stores and shares several learning resources.
- **Level 3:** LMS is used in conjunction with e-learning. E-learning is now incorporated into educational modalities and philosophies and has become an important component of the classroom organization process with philosophies such as flipped classrooms.
- **Level 4:** Courses that are truly digitally transformative, E-learning is a complete learning platform that changes the entire activity from learning, teaching, quality management.

In our study, the learning content of the teaching method modules was designed by us at level 3, namely the offline method combined with the online of the reverse classroom model. Here, students learn theory on the LMS system. Offline sessions with lecturers are devoted to mastering skills and discussions.

In order to design an online teaching plan for students, Phan Thi Bich Loi has come up with a process of five stages: (i) planning; (ii) teaching design; (iii) organizing the implementation; (iv) post-assessment of teaching implementation; and (v) improvement. Our research used this process in the design of our teaching activities. The stages specified by the research team into requirements are as follows (Figure 12.1):

- **Phase 1: Planning:** This is the first stage of the process of organizing online teaching. It is necessary to identify issues of the teaching organization, the objectives of the course, the learning activities, and ways to best support the student's learning, the tasks the student needs to complete as well as the opportunity to help students to prove their academic achievements.
- **Phase 2: Teaching Design:** I In teaching design, it is necessary to focus on: identifying learning objectives, determining learning content and resources, selecting teaching methods, selecting technology, selecting methods, forms of assessment tests, designing types of assessments.
- **Phase 3: Implementation Organization:** The role of teachers when organizing the course includes organizing online and in-person learning activities, managing students, supporting, and maintaining student learning activities, motivating, and engaging students, checking the assessment of students' academic performance...

  As mentioned above, during this period we designed learning activities at Level 3 of online teaching using the reverse classroom model. Specifically, this stage consists of the following steps:

  - **Step 1: Study First on LMS:** At this step, students visit the LMS system to perform activities such as watching lecture clips, reading materials, doing assignments, discussing on forums, asking interactive questions with lecturers or other students...
  - **Step 2: Study Directly in Class:** At this step, students perform activities such as: asking questions, clarifying the contents, listening to the lecturer lecture, practicing skills, discussing situations, debating situations, giving personal presentations, and group presentations...
  - **Step 3: Complete the Lesson on LMS:** At this step, students perform activities such as: continuing to watch clips, Q&A through the forum, online with lecturers when needed, maintaining the continuous learning process after the class step.

- **Phase 4: Post-Implementation Assessment of Teaching:** Assessment for online teaching and learning is based on the following three main areas:
  - **i. Pedagogy:** learning activities that underpin lessons.
  - **ii. Resources:** Content and information provided to learners.
  - **iii. Distribution Strategies:** Issues related to the way in which the course distributes content to learners.
  - **Stage 5: Improvement:** At the improvement stage, the design process, the teaching organization is restarted from scratch to incorporate all the changes made to improve the course/lesson for the next course/lesson.

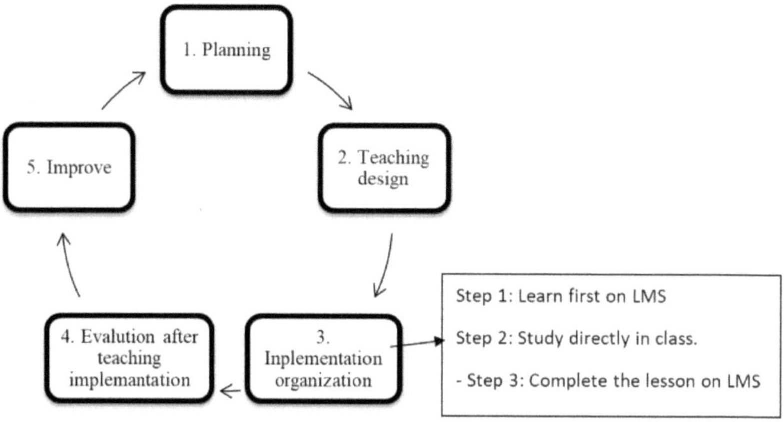


**FIGURE 12.1** On-duty teaching process.

We found this process to be very suitable for the practical conditions at Vietnam's pedagogical universities, so we used this process to carry out our teaching process.

### *12.2.3.2 DEVELOP A TEACHING PLAN AND ORGANIZE TEACHING ACTIVITIES*

Based on the process in Section 12.2.3.1, we have developed plans and organized online teaching in a number of sections for the Bachelor of Biology pedagogy and the Bachelor of Early Childhood Education. We would like to introduce an illustration here of one of these modules, which is the section "Active teaching methods and techniques in Biology." This is one of the basic parts of the bachelor's degree in biology pedagogy. We take this as a case in point for other bachelors of pedagogy:

➢ **Phase 1: Planning:** From the detailed outline of the section, this step we determine: Each chapter of the module has theoretical contents in class, seminar, practice so it is necessary to determine the objectives, content, materials of each session. Each chapter should envisage learning activities and ways to best support the student's learning; It is expected that the tasks students need to complete and how to evaluate their academic performance.

For example, in the section "Active teaching methods and techniques in Biology" there is Chapter 2 "Positive teaching methods" there are:

- **Objectives:** After the student completes this chapter, he/she will:
  - Distinguishing teaching perspectives, teaching methods.
  - Present the nature, advantages, limitations, processes, and conditions of application of some positive teaching methods.
  - Designed by the curriculum using active teaching methods.
  - Organize the implementation of the lecture according to the designed curriculum.
- **Content:**
  - **Theoretical Content:** Some active teaching methods in biology include Hands-on teaching methods; Method of teaching by angle; Method of teaching project; Methods of scientific research; Method of using practical situational exercises.
  - **Practical Content:** Design the curriculum and organize the teaching of topics/lessons using the teaching technique "tablecloth."
- **Learning Materials:** It is the syllabus, lectures of lecturers provided on the LMS system.
- **Expected Learning Activities:**
  - **Theoretical Part:** Students read the material themselves on the LMS system and complete learning tasks. The content will be reviewed and discussed by the lecturer at the in-person lesson.
  - **Practical Part:** Students are engaged with each other and with lecturers at face-to-face sessions.

- **Phase 2: Plan Design:** At this step, the information on the LMS system about the subject should be presented specifically. The lecturer will be the designer of this content on LMS. The contents required on the LMS are: Detailed outline of the course; About lecturers is an online class link; Plan to teach each lesson.

  At each session, students will follow the schedule, access on the LMS system, the instructor's instructions to receive learning materials, questions, tasks assigned to the individual or assigned to the group. In addition to the teaching plans in each chapter are also specified. Each chapter will design the student's learning activities (what is that learning activity? Where does it take place? Working with whom? How does it work? How are the resources and supporting materials?), stating what activities students perform on the LMS system, what activities are carried out in the live class.

  For example, the design of the teaching plan in Chapter 1, on the LMS lecturers put up learning materials and tasks. About Chapter 1 document there is a document for students to read and learn the theory, one document is a test slip for students to experience. After that, students will read the instructor's instructions, here there are both instructions for studying Chapter 1, as well as the task students must perform before going to class in person.

  In addition, in the design of the teaching plan in Chapter 1 for the in-person session, the lecturer also designed activities: personal presentations on the tasks students have performed before class, discussion of the content of Chapter 1 and lecturers closing knowledge of Chapter 1.

- **Phase 3: Implementation Organization:** Students follow the learning process in three steps in the process of the reverse classroom model. Specific examples when studying Chapter 1 of the section "Methods and techniques of active teaching in biology."

  - **Step 1: Study First on LMS:** At this step, students visit the LMS system and read two documents provided by the teacher. The first document is about "the process of processing information of the brain" and the second document is a quiz about personal learning style. After reading the documents, students complete the quiz in Document 2. They also find a document on the perspective of teaching, which includes teaching methods and techniques that were discussed in the previous section. Additionally, they collect an existing curriculum and examine what it presents about active teaching methods and techniques. These tasks are performed individually by students and in groups. The final product of this activity is submitted by students to the LMS system.

- **Step 2: Study Directly in Class:** At this step, students go to the class directly with the lecturer. Students will give a personal presentation on completing the quiz and state their learning style. Then, faculty for student groups present the products they have worked with in teams at home. Finally, debate and lecturers' close knowledge Chapter 1.
- **Step 3: Complete the Lesson on LMS:** Lecturers assign assignments on LMS for students to perform at home.

➢ **Phase 4: Post-Assessment of Teaching Implementation:** At the end of teaching each chapter or each subject, the lecturer can assign tasks or tests to evaluate the student's learning process. All the exercises submitted by students will be saved, including the time of submission and the content of the work. Grading and feedback for students will be provided through the LMS system.

➢ **Phase 5: Improvements:** In this step, the design process, the teaching organization is started all over again to incorporate all the changes made to improve the course/lesson for the next course/ lesson.

### *12.2.3.3 FACTORS AFFECTING ONLINE TEACHING*

#### ***12.2.3.3.1 Survey Results***

As the COVID pandemic deepens, universities have shifted their form of in-person teaching to online. At that time, with the school's LMS and online teaching tools such as Zoom, Google Meet... Online teaching only stops at Levels 1 or 2. That is, lecturers meet students in person through online meeting room tools such as Zoom, Google Meet... and the LMS system is a platform that stores and shares a number of learning resources. When students participated in the teaching method in this form, the research team sent questionnaires to 26 students of the Faculty of Biology and 30 students of the Department of Early Childhood Education of Hanoi University of Education 2. The results have been processed and obtained as in Table 12.7.

According to the results in Table 12.1, the factors related to online teaching are being evaluated well, which are information about the subject, Teaching Technology, and Faculty Activities. This is also easy to understand because the information about the subject, such as goals, learning programs, part content, study plan, necessary materials in the learning process, and the method of examination of the assessment of the module, is clearly shown in the detailed outline of the module. This outline is published on the school's website. In terms of teaching technology, pedagogical universities build LMS and use easy-to-use teaching software. Before conducting online teaching, the school trains in the tools and software used in the teaching process. The activities of lecturers are also well evaluated because in the universities, they are all lecturers trained from pedagogical schools. They have very solid professional and professional knowledge. They are also trained to be able to teach in person and online to achieve high efficiency.

**TABLE 12.7** Assessment of Each Factor Affecting On-Call Teaching

| STT | Factor | Smallest | The Biggest Point | Average Score | Standard Deviation | Rating Level |
|---|---|---|---|---|---|---|
| 1. | Subject information. | 3.00 | 5.00 | 4.6058 | 0.61714 | Good |
| 2. | Learning organization. | 2.67 | 4.67 | 3.7866 | 0.76147 | Fairly |
| 3. | Teaching technology. | 1.83 | 5.00 | 4.2885 | 0.83474 | Good |
| 4. | Student support activities. | 2.00 | 4.33 | 3.7333 | 0.77183 | Fairly |
| 5. | Conditions of the learner's facilities. | 1.33 | 5.00 | 4.1282 | 1.03313 | Fairly |
| 6. | Activities of members. | 3.00 | 5.00 | 4.6538 | 0.60810 | Good |

However, according to Table 12.1, there are three factors that are evaluated at a decent level, which need to be improved, which are: learning organization, learner support activities, and the facilities for learners. For the two factors of organizing learning and supporting activities, learners mainly face issues related to the organization of learning activities in an effective way. Especially activities related to group discussions and practice. As for the factor of the material condition of the learner, it is mainly due to the unstable internet connection of the learner during the learning process or because the learner's learning device is not a laptop but a phone, leading to limited interaction and the use of specialized software. From the general results of the factors affecting the quality of online teaching and the causal conjectures, the team analyzed the survey results on each question in the questionnaire to find out the specific reasons for the ineffective online learning (Table 12.8). The results are shown in Group 2.

According to the results in Table 12.8, we noticed that three factors are evaluated at a decent level in Table 12.7, the results in each question are also quite good.

As for the Learning Organization factor–according to the survey, it is found that students are very hardworking and attend the full range of online study sessions according to the schedule that the school arranges. However, the time learners are surveyed is the time of the COVID pandemic, learners must learn completely online, so they feel very tired of having to sit in front of a computer all day to attend online lessons. Therefore, in this content they rated at a decent level (3.73 points). So here, the team also aims to arrange the time to study online and in person to prevent learners from feeling tired and bored. Or create learning tasks so that learners can discuss groups or practices with nature or society. For the question of whether the activities organized by lecturers during and outside the online sessions motivate learners to actively learn, the rating level only receives an average level (3.13 points). This may explain why the learning organization model uses only online meeting rooms via Zoom, Google Meet. Meanwhile, the LMS system only provides the learning resources of the whole module. Thus, learners are not given specific instructions on learning activities. There is no flexible change in the form of organizing learning activities. This greatly affects the quality of teaching. This directed the team to use the reverse classroom model to improve the effectiveness of online teaching.

For learner support activities: all three questions given are evaluated by students at a good level. Specifically, students are fully guided to participate in online learning with 3.58 points. Here it's probably not that they can't use online teaching tools, but how do they engage in activities, what content, with whom, how to evaluate? I haven't been guided by my teacher. This makes it easy for students to have easy access to the necessary sources of learning materials, each subject is only evaluated at a decent level. They also feel that ongoing online learning makes it difficult for them to receive timely

**TABLE 12.8** Specific Assessment of Each Question Related to Factors Affecting On-Field Teaching

| STT | Question | Point the Smallest | Point the Largest | Point Average | Deviation Standard | Level Assess |
|---|---|---|---|---|---|---|
| | **Factor: Subject Information** | | | | | |
| 1. | Learners are introduced to the objectives, content, and structure of each subject. | 3 | 5 | 4.69 | 0.549 | Good |
| 2. | Learners are well aware of the study plan in each subject learn. | 3 | 5 | 4.54 | 0.647 | Good |
| 3. | The student is introduced to the necessary materials for each subject. | 3 | 5 | 4.65 | 0.629 | Good |
| 4. | Learners are well aware of the methods and criteria for evaluation in each subject. | 2 | 5 | 4.54 | 0.761 | Good |
| | Factor: Learning Organization | | | | | |
| 5. | Learners can attend a full range of online lessons in accordance with the schedule. | 2 | 5 | 4.50 | 0.812 | Good |
| 6. | The length of each online session does not do; students are tired of attending. | 2 | 5 | 3.73 | 1.041 | Fairly |
| 7. | Activities organized by lecturers during, and outside online sessions motivate learners to actively learn. | 2 | 4 | 3.13 | 0.908 | Average |
| | **Factor: Teaching Technology** | | | | | |
| 8. | Online teaching technologies are being used by lecturers to allow learners to easily participate in the session. | 2 | 5 | 4.31 | 0.788 | Good |
| 9. | Online teaching technologies are being used by teachers to allow learners to understand the central issues of each session. | 2 | 5 | 4.31 | 0.884 | Good |
| 10. | Online teaching technologies are being used by faculty to allow learners to easily complete learning requirements. | 2 | 5 | 4.27 | 0.874 | Good |
| 11. | Online teaching technologies are being used by teachers to allow learners to easily interact with teachers during learning. | 1 | 5 | 4.38 | 0.941 | Good |

**TABLE 12.8** *(Continued)*

| STT | Question | Point the Smallest | Point the Largest | Point Average | Deviation Standard | Level Assess |
|---|---|---|---|---|---|---|
| 12. | Online teaching technologies are being used by teachers to allow learners to easily interact with their classmates during learning. | 1 | 5 | 4.23 | 1.032 | Good |
| 13. | Online teaching technologies are being used by faculty to give learners easy access to learning content. | 2 | 5 | 4.23 | 0.951 | Good |
| | **Factor: Student Support Activities** | | | | | |
| 14. | Learners are fully guided to participate in online learning. | 3 | 4 | 3.58 | 0.643 | Fairly |
| 15. | Learners have easy access to learning resources; necessary training for each subject. | 1 | 5 | 4.12 | 1.107 | Fairly |
| 16. | Students receive timely support from teachers when necessary. | 2 | 4 | 3.50 | 0.812 | Fairly |
| | Factor: The Condition of the Learner's Facilities | | | | | |
| 17. | Learners have the necessary technological equipment for participate in study sessions and complete learning requirements. | 1 | 5 | 4.27 | 1.079 | Good |
| 18. | Learners have all the information technology skills they need; necessary to participate in study sessions and complete learning requirements. | 1 | 5 | 4.12 | 1.071 | Fairly |
| 19. | The current residence of learners ensures information technology conditions to participate in study sessions and complete learning requirements. | 1 | 5 | 4.00 | 1.265 | Fairly |
| | Factor: Employee Activities | | | | | |
| 20. | Teachers are well prepared for classes. | 3 | 5 | 4.65 | 0.629 | Good |
| 21. | Teachers make sure they have time to go to class. | 3 | 5 | 4.68 | 0.627 | Good |
| 22. | The teacher fully implements the content of the class. | 3 | 5 | 4.62 | 0.697 | Good |
| 23. | Teachers ensure pedagogical behavior during sessions learn. | 3 | 5 | 4.69 | 0.549 | Good |
| 24. | Enthusiastic lecturers in teaching and guidance learners. | 3 | 5 | 4.65 | 0.629 | Good |

support from faculty (3.5 points). Thus, with the results of the evaluation in this factor, we further affirm that students need to be specifically instructed in each learning activity in each session on the LMS system. Lecturers need to design sessions with materials, learning tasks on their LMS system, and support both online and offline to improve teaching efficiency.

For the condition of the learner's facilities, there are two aspects that are evaluated at a decent level. The first is that the learner does not have the necessary information technology skills to participate in the study sessions and complete the learning requirements. The second is that the student's whereabouts do not meet the conditions of information technology to participate in the sessions, learn, and complete the requirements. In this regard, faculty can help students overcome their lack of information technology skills by selecting instructional videos that utilize the necessary technologies and uploading them to the LMS system as learning materials. This way, students can learn on their own.

As such, the content of the student survey is evaluated at a decent level, the research team makes suggestions for improvements to improve the quality. Particularly, the content evaluated on average is "Activities organized by lecturers during and outside the online session that motivates learners to actively learn" in the "Learning Organization" factor that needs to be changed, and the research team has proposed to use the reverse classroom model in the next modules and has shown in Section 12.2.3.2.

##### *12.2.3.3.2 Results of Interview Survey*

After conducting online teaching with an inverted classroom model in the section "Active teaching methods and techniques in Biology" for students in biology pedagogy and "Childcare and hygiene" for students in early childhood education, the team conducted group interviews with two groups of students in two faculties, each with 10 students. The results are as follows:

1. **With the Question:** "What parts of the teaching method do you learn in person, and what parts of the lessons do you learn online? What part of the study do you learn in person in conjunction with online?" All the students named the sections they learned in person when the COVID pandemic had not yet appeared. They then must learn online entirely, however, they only transition from in-person learning to online learning by meeting faculty via Zoom

or Google Meet, and the LMS system is the place for faculty to put learning resources up. There is a group of students in the Department of Biology who say that they have been taught a part in the form of a combination of online teaching and in-person teaching. This shows that digital transformation in the teaching process in pedagogical universities using the reverse classroom model is quite possible.

2. **With the Question:** "Did you tell us the advantages and limitations of learning to use online in the past?" we found that most students in both groups thought that the use of the inverted classroom model in online teaching made them more satisfied. The learning tasks are clearly stated by the lecturer, so their self-study efficiency is improved. In addition, they also said that when using the reverse classroom model, they received support from both classmates and lecturers through the LMS Forum section. The learning of theoretical knowledge becomes more active.
3. **With the Question:** "What factors need to change, and how to change so that the learning process uses online form more effectively?" Students are eager to use the reverse classroom model to combine online and in-person learning forms. They also want the learning resources on LMS to be expanded further with learning tasks so that they can further expand their knowledge capital.
4. **With the Question:** "Do the activities related to digital transformation organized by the lecturers improve the quality of teaching the teaching method? Why?" 100% of those interviewed agreed with the idea that the activities related to digital transformation that teachers use will improve the quality of teaching. In terms of reasons, there are many different opinions, some people think that they like to study online because they do not have to move to class, study anytime, anywhere. Some people assume that they can learn on their own in accordance with their abilities, in accordance with their free time. Some people think that they can better understand the tasks of the lecturer when talking to other members of the class on the Forum...
5. **With the Question:** "What activities do you think in teaching the teaching methods need to be changed?" Most students want to increase more practical activities and exchange activities in the classroom.

> Theories do not need to be taught in class but just answer the questions of students when they learn on their own without understanding.

Thus, through the results of the interview survey, we found that students are quite satisfied and eager to learn the lessons of teaching methods through digital transformation by the inverted classroom model. Faculty at pedagogical universities can use our online teaching plan design process and refer to the illustrated teaching plan in the "Active Teaching Methods and Techniques in Biology" section to be able to expand in other sections. However, to know more accurately about the effectiveness of this digital transformation, the study needs to continue and there are assessments using quantitative metrics.

## 12.3 CONCLUSION

Thus, through the survey of students, it has been shown that factors affecting the quality of online teaching include information about subjects, learning institutions, teaching technology, learner support activities, the condition of learners' facilities, and the activities of lecturers. A typical case at Hanoi Pedagogical University 2 shows that the factors that need to be improved for the online teaching process to be effective are: learning organization, activities to support learners, and the facilities conditions of learners.

Our research has also launched an online teaching process in the 5-stage digital transformation process, which pays special attention to Phase 3 – the implementation organization consists of three steps of the reverse classroom model, which is – (i) pre-learning on LMS; (ii) study directly in class; and (iii) complete the lesson on LMS. This process has been used and implemented on several sections when teaching students in Biological Pedagogy and students in early childhood education, which is a case in case of teacher training in Vietnam. After testing this process and applying the reverse class model, we received results from interviewing students involved in the process. The interview results initially showed the success of the model in increasing the interest and quality of students' learning. With such results, other lecturers can also apply inverted classroom processes and models in their teaching process in other parts, in other training disciplines, thereby improving the quality of teaching in pedagogical universities.

## KEYWORDS

- **digital conversion**
- **digital technology**
- **interview investigation method**
- **online teaching**
- **pedagogical universities**
- **pedagogy training**
- **teaching methods**

## REFERENCES

Adam, M., (2021). Digital transformation in higher education: Maturity and challenges post COVID-19. *International Conference on Information Technology & Systems* (pp. 53–70). Springer.

Alexey, M., Yana, S., & Alexander, V., (2021). Current trends in the digital transformation of higher education institutions in Russia. *Education and Information Technologies, 26*(4), 4537–4551.

Behnam, T., (2019). *Digital Transformation is Not About Technology* (Vol. 13, pp. 1–6). Harvard business review.

Bilyalova, A. A., Salimova, D. A., & Zelenina, T. I., (2019). Digital transformation in education. *International Conference on Integrated Science* (pp. 265–276). Springer.

Daniel, S. W. T., (2020). Digital technology and COVID-19. *Nature Medicine, 26*(4), 459–461.

Dirk, I., (2021). *Digital Transformation of Learning Organizations*. Springer Nature.

Francesca, C., & Christine, R., (2019). Aligning teacher competence frameworks to 21st century challenges: The case for the European digital competence framework for educators (*digcompedu*). *European Journal of Education, 54*(3), 356–369.

Gregory, V., (2021). Understanding digital transformation: A review and a research agenda. *Managing Digital Transformation*, 13–66.

Hanoi Pedagogical University 2, (2018). *Study of Finnish Experience in Training and Retraining of General Teachers, Managers of General Education Institutions, and Pedagogical Lecturers (Task 8),* 50–60.

Hanoi Pedagogical University 2, (2020). *Self-Assessment Report on the Training Program of Bachelor of Early Childhood Education (Citing the Comparison of the Bachelor's Training Program in Early Childhood Education with Some Other Training Programs).*

Hanoi Pedagogical University 2, (2021). *Self-Assessment Report on the Training Program for Biological Pedagogy (Citing the Comparison of the Bachelor's Program in Biology Pedagogy with Some Other Training Programs).*

Jillian, D., & Janet, E. D., (2013). Teacher educators' readiness, preparation, and perceptions of preparing preservice teachers in a fully online environment: An exploratory study. *The Teacher Educator, 48*(2), 96–109.

Katyeudo, K. De. S. O., & Ricardo, A. C. De. S., (2021). Digital transformation towards education 4.0. *Informatics in Education.*

Le Thi, P., (2018). Finnish teacher training program a reference perspective for training high-quality teachers in grammar pedagogy at Hong Duc University. *Hong Duc University Science Journal, 42*, 86–98.

Luis, S. R., (2017). Challenges of digital transformation in higher education institutions: A brief discussion. *Proceedings of 30$^{th}$IBIMA Conference.*

Marcel, R., & Sandy, B., (2002). Online assessment techniques. *Delta Pi Epsilon Journal, 44*(1), 39–49.

Ministry of Education and Training, (2010). *Circular: Promulgation of the Ministry of Higher Education Framework Program in Pedagogy and University Level (No. 37 /2010/ TT-BGDDT).* https://thuvienphapluat.vn/van-ban/Giao-duc/Thong-tu-37-2010-TT-BGDDT-Bo-Chuong-trinh-khung-giao-duc-dai-hoc-khoi-nganh-116308.aspx (accessed on 6 May 2024).

Ministry of Education and Training, (2021). *Circular on Management and Organization of Online Teaching in General Education Institutions and Continuing Education.* No. 09/2021/TT-BGDDT, https://thuvienphapluat.vn/van-ban/Giao-duc/Thong-tu-09-2021-TT-BGDDT-quan-ly-va-to-chuc-day-hoc-truc-tuyen-trong-co-so-giao-duc-pho-thong-449937.aspx (accessed on 6 May 2024).

Ministry of Education and Training, (2021). *Fostering Materials: Increasing Online Teaching Capacity (for Secondary Teachers)*, 13–16.

Moore-Adams, B. L., Monty, J. W., & Jonathan, C., (2016). Learning to teach online: A systematic review of the literature on K-12 teacher preparation for teaching online. *Distance Education, 37*(3), 333–348.

Nam, H. H., (2020). Digital transformation in the field of education and training: Status and solutions. *Journal of Information and Communication*, 2.

Navaridas-Nalda, F., (2019). The strategic influence of school principal leadership in the digital transformation of schools. *Computers in Human Behavior, 112*, 106481.

Neborsky, E. V., (2020). Digital transformation of higher education: International trends. *International Scientific Conference "Digitalization of Education: History, Trends and Prospects" (DETP 2020)* (pp. 398–403). Atlantis Press.

Nguyen, C. T., (2003). *Training High Qualified Teachers in Vietnam: Challenges and Policy* (No. 2003).

Nguyen, M. T., et al., (2021) Factors affecting the effectiveness of online teaching at universities in Hanoi. *Thai Nguyen University Journal of Science and Technology*, pp. 252–261.

Nguyen, T. H., et al., (2021). Factors affecting the online learning efficiency of students of international faculty, Thai Nguyen University. *Journal of Science and Technology – Thai Nguyen University, 226*(13), 52–61.

Nguyen, T. H., (2006). Teacher training in Vietnam. *Human Rights Education in Asian Schools*, IX.

Pham, T. K. A., (2015). *Teacher Training Program in Vietnam – Some Inadequacies and Development Orientations.* Report at the International Scientific Conference:

"Developing the training program of education – Opportunities and challenges. Thai Nguyen University of Science and Technology.

Phan, T. B. L., (2021). Proposed online teaching design process. *Vietnam Journal of Educational Sciences*, (42), 7–12.

Politburo, (2019). *Resolution 52-NQ/TW Dated September 27, 2019 of the Politburo on a Number of Guidelines and Policies to Actively Participate in the 4th Industrial Revolution.*

*Prime Minister of Vietnam*, (2020). Decision No. 749/QD-TTg dated June 3, 2020 of the Prime Minister on approving the "National Digital Transformation Program to 2025, oriented to 2030.

Robert, A. R., (2001). A history of instructional design and technology: Part I: A history of instructional media. *Educational Technology Research and Development, 49*(1), 53.

Sue, B., & Lori, L., (2004). Becoming an online teacher: Adapting to a changed environment for teaching and learning in higher education. *Educational Media International, 41*(3), 231–248.

Tami, S., & Orna, F., (2019). Online self-assessment and peer-assessment as a tool to enhance student-teachers' assessment skills. *Assessment & Evaluation in Higher Education, 44*(2), 169–185.

Thanhm T, N, P., & Ly Thim T, D., (2017). Teacher readiness for online teaching: A critical review. *International Journal Open Distance E-Learn. IJODeL., 3*(1), 1–16.

The Prime Minister of Vietnam, (2017). Decision No. 117/QD-TTg dated January 25, 2017 approving the project "Strengthening the application of IT in the management and support of teaching-learning activities, NCKH contributes to improving the quality of education and training in the period of 2016–2020, oriented to 2025.

Thi Tinh, T. P., Hoang, A. L., & Doan, T. D., (2021). The factors affecting students' online learning outcomes during the COVID-19 pandemic: A Bayesian exploratory factor analysis. *Education Research International*, 2669098.

Van, H. N., (2020). Vietnamese education system and teacher training: Focusing on science education. *Asia-Pacific Science Education, 6*(1), 179–206.

Voronin, D. M., Saienko, V. G., & Tolchieva, H. V., (2020). Digital transformation of pedagogical education at the university. *Proceedings of the International Scientific Conference "Digitalization of Education: History, Trends and Prospects": (DETP 2020)*, 757–763.

# Index

## B



## C

## R



## S